History of the Chicago Urban League

UNIVERSITY OF MISSOURI PRESS, COLUMBIA AND LONDON

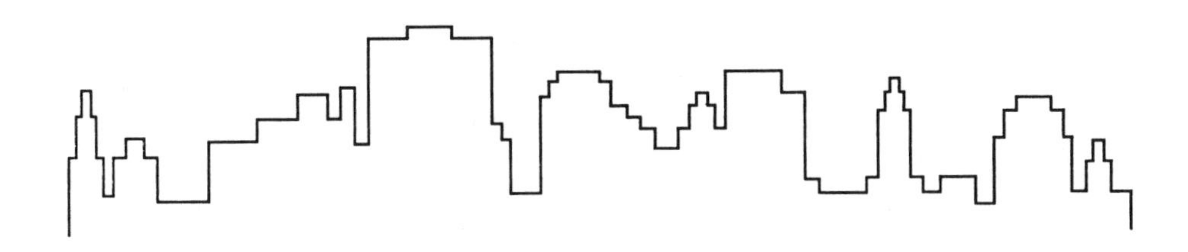

History of the Chicago Urban League

ARVARH E. STRICKLAND
Introduction by Christopher R. Reed

University of Missouri Press, Columbia, Missouri 65201
Printed and bound in the United States of America

5 4 3 2 1 05 04 03 02 01

Cataloging-in-Publication data available from
the Library of Congress

ISBN 0-8262-1347-2

⊗™ This paper meets the requirements of the
American National Standard for Permanence of Paper
for Printed Library Materials, Z39.48, 1984.

Printer and binder: Thomson-Shore, Inc.

To my Mother

Contents

Introduction to the 2001 Edition

Christopher R. Reed

Private communication in 1917 between members of the Urban League's leadership clearly delineated the circumstances under which a newly formed affiliate of the organization would either thrive or fail organizationally in Chicago. National Urban League president L. Hollingsworth Wood, in New York, wrote to philanthropist Julius Rosenwald's Chicago representative, William C. Graves, that "you will realize . . . that the Urban League group in any community is not the most difficult to satisfy . . . , but rather the so-called 'Advancement Group' who are more vociferous and inclined to act on theory than the facts of a situation." African Americans sought both economic and civil rights, the latter so promising theoretically but so elusive in actuality.[1] Whites purportedly acting in behalf of blacks based their actions on the necessity to relieve the privations blacks faced by providing for their essential needs. Their needs, in this instance, would be determined by factual data rather than speculation, wish-fulfillment, or theorizing. Furnishing social welfare services, helping to raise educational standards, assisting in self-improvement efforts, and securing basic employment opportunities sufficed to convince the white members of the Chicago Urban League that they were effectively helping blacks adjust to their new, northern, urban environment. Just as important, this set of services also satisfied the civic agenda of prominent whites in the various spheres of the city's Establishment—corporate, civic, charitable, and political.

Throughout its first forty years, the Board of Directors of the Chicago Urban League, primarily composed of conservatives, moved in

[1] L. Hollingsworth Wood to William C. Graves, September 27, 1917, Chicago Urban League File, Julius Rosenwald Papers, Regenstein Library, the University of Chicago. Recently, Professors Dona Cooper Hamilton and Charles V. Hamilton have collaborated on *The Dual Agenda: Race and Social Welfare Policies of Civil Rights Organizations* (New York: Columbia University Press, 1997), which argues persuasively that it was possible to combine a social welfare approach with protest activism to advance the status of African Americans. More importantly, they documented the torturous path this overlooked dual agenda took over the last seventy years. Had they the will and advantageous conditions, the Chicago Urban League could possibly have achieved success through two approaches merged into one well-coordinated agenda.

a cautious manner, "in that they opposed abrupt or radical change, especially in race relations" (110). For their part, they favored the image of the League as innocuous and primarily concerned with social work. Their opposites, characterized by Arvarh Strickland as progressives, operated primarily at the staff level and continually earned the displeasure and sometimes the full wrath of the board whenever they promoted programs that seemed relevant to the times but in contradistinction to the League's image.

In programs and policies, this created a dualism in ideology between aggressive protest and social work. It represented, however, only part of a *double* dualism besetting the Chicago Urban League pioneers as they sought total organizational efficacy. Another struggle over governance between members of the biracial Board of Directors and the all-black secretariat accounted for the other important, contentious binary concern. These African Americans, comprising some of the best that the "New Negro" mentality produced, preferred a more activist stance consistent with a relevant program that by necessity had to be somewhat confrontational, or militant. Evidence of this tension appeared throughout the annals of the Chicago Urban League, 1916–1956, and provided the gist of Strickland's thesis undergirding the writing of *History of the Chicago Urban League.*

Originating from a doctoral dissertation dealing with the adjustment of African American migrants as they encountered the forces of urbanization, especially during the Great Migration of 1916–1919, Professor Arvarh E. Strickland's work evolved "from a general interest in the orientation of the urban Negro" to become the "history of one significant organization in this field." In this study of how these countervailing, dualistic struggles manifested themselves historically, Strickland focused on the nexus between labor, capital, and race relations during the first half of the twentieth century. As essential scholarship on the dynamics of life in Chicago, it further closed a gap of nearly two decades of scholarly deficiency on black Chicago generally, along with specifics on workplace demands and their linkage to race relations. Although Gunnar Myrdal's *An American Dilemma* (1944) viewed race relations comprehensively and as a matter of national importance, not since the publication of St. Clair Drake and Horace R. Cayton's *Black Metropolis* in 1945 had African Americans and an organization attempting to espouse their cause received such treatment.

Yet as part of a genre (local-level narrative) that has most recently yielded to postmodern, theoretically based, general studies, *History of the Chicago Urban League* has most recently received short shrift. Its reintroduction to scholarship is welcomed, as was the case of *Black Metropolis,* reissued by the University of Chicago Press (1999), since these works contribute significantly to a better understanding of institutional life, organizational governance, interracial linkage, and divergent class interests. Moreover, as an organizational study treating the local-level contribution to a national organization's efforts,[2] it further represents a foundation from which sound theory can emanate. In his methodology, Professor Strickland used all of the available primary resources at hand, skillfully utilizing oral sources to complement the written ones. The former consisted of personal interviews and therein tapped into the trove of memory of persons who had been participant-observers in and of the Chicago Urban League's growth and pains. One major disadvantage of the interviewing technique of that period was in its civility, since it showed great latitude for a respect for privacy. Interviewees were not identified; had they been, we might today be able to make a clearer assessment of what motivated their actions and thinking.[3] Its strength, though, resounded in its ability to interrogate directly three presidents, namely Earl B. Dickerson, Dr. Nathaniel O. Calloway, and Hugo O. Law, and key staff, Albon L. Foster, Howard D. Gould, and Frayser T. Lane. Unfortunately missing, though, was the testimony and memory of Executive Secretary Sidney Williams. The trove of written records consisted of more than official reports and annual reviews, since it included manuscript collections, memoranda, and correspondence.[4] Overall, Strickland's research techniques allowed him to probe into the motivations for policy decisions and actions that unraveled the enduring problems of governance, funding, staffing, and programming.

---

[2] See Nancy J. Weiss, *The National Urban League, 1910–1940* (New York: Oxford University Press, 1974) for a comprehensive view of the national organization with numerous, sometimes expanded, references to the Chicago Urban League.

[3] See James Q. Wilson, *Negro Politics: The Search For Leadership* (Glencoe, Ill.: Free Press, 1960). This political science study from the University of Chicago depended heavily on interviews to develop its analysis of power and powerlessness in interracial relations in Chicago.

[4] The Records of the Chicago Urban League are held in the University of Illinois at Chicago Libraries. Additional written sources are to be found at the Regenstein Library of the University of Chicago, which houses the Papers of Julius Rosenwald and those of Salmon O. Levinson, both members of the Board of Directors of the Chicago Urban League. The Library of Congress also contains materials on the Chicago Urban League in the Papers of the National Urban League. Some misunderstanding might now exist about these written sources, perhaps emanating from Nancy Weiss's *National Urban League.* She indicated that the records were destroyed in a fire (viii). Indeed, there was a fire in 1918, but not all of the records previous to the event were destroyed and many important ones are available.

Governance and programming represented the two areas whence the League's major problems emanated. Throughout the organization's history, the wishes of the white corporate leadership commanded ultimate respect as it supported the League as its favored vehicle for providing for the city's labor market needs along with dealing with what it perceived to be the needs of the burgeoning black community.[5] Financing flowed from its coffers and from the affiliated Chicago Community Fund, Community Trust, Chicago Association of Commerce and Industry, Rosenwald Foundation, and other charitable sources. Deviation from their wishes usually occurred in the area of programming. Whenever League activities appeared too militant and more similar to what was to be expected from a civil rights organization in the form of social activism, the threat of a removal of funding loomed. The first major discord occurred in 1929 when the Rosenwald Foundation removed its financial support; later, in 1955, the Chicago Community Fund effected the closing of the organization for a six-month period to allow for reorganization, removal of a troublesome executive secretary, and institution of a more moderate program.

Staff personnel who challenged the traditional role of the League severely confounded the conservative wing of the leadership on the League's official governing body, the Board of Directors. The latter were black as well as white, with an African American physician as board president constantly urging a slowdown in aggressive activism during the 1950s. The conservatives' remedy resulted in structural changes. Two previous reorganizations took place early in the Chicago Urban League's history because of board displeasure with the actions of the staff. Between 1944 and 1946, internal struggle over the shape of the League's program, which had grown increasingly activist under the leadership of Executive Secretary A. L. Foster, led to his dismissal. To the dismay of the board, his successor, Sidney Williams, amplified the spirit that Foster had started in making the League a relevant organization in the lives of the people of the Black Belt (or the South Side, now popularly called Bronzeville). Williams was even more activist than Foster, speaking, organizing, cooperating, and challenging in the manner of a civil rights militant who wanted the theoretical American Dream to bear fruit in his lifetime. The result was disastrous for the League; funding dropped, and by July 1955 the organization shut down for a prescribed period of six months.

---

[5] See Wilson, *Negro Politics*, 138, 139.

A second reorganization brought in a new executive secretary, Edwin C. "Bill" Berry, who proved no less militant and no easier to control than his three predecessors. There was a major difference, however, and it was found in what he said, how and when he articulated his views, and the reaction they incurred. Berry once described Chicago as "the most segregated city in America" at a National Urban League function in Detroit. When news of his pronouncement reached Chicago, it angered the city's Establishment, along with Mayor Richard J. Daley. His declaration also accomplished something just as telling: He won greater support from the black community than had been seen before. The possibility of increased black funding unfortunately still lacked the power to replace white funding, so the perpetual limitation on what could be said or done in the name of the League still required restraint, even by the charming Berry.

Professor Strickland's narrative traces the evolution of the Chicago Urban League in chronological fashion, an approach essential for basic understanding of history, especially in the absence of a comprehensive history of the lives and accomplishments of the African Americans of Chicago.[6] While lacking a clearly enunciated thesis because there was neither a preface nor an introduction, Strickland's work did firmly establish this dictum: "The problem was to get white acceptance of the Negro's right to live in Chicago" (262). The necessity for the introduction of the African American laborer into the industrial work force en masse to meet wartime production needs showed acceptance under duress. So was the welcome manifested by the corporate world to migrating workers into the 1920s postwar labor market to offset the demands of organized white labor. The difficulty that whites had in general was with recognition of African Americans as full-fledged citizens enjoying their full civil rights—as neighbors, students, consumers, voters, workers, competitors—rights that would only be gained through protest advocacy.

As to the genesis of the Chicago Urban League, without a doubt the organization owed its existence to the urgent need associated with assimilating tens of thousands of southern workers into the Chicago

---

[6] Within a year of the publication of *History of the Chicago Urban League,* Allan H. Spear's *Black Chicago: The Making of a Negro Ghetto, 1890–1920* (Chicago: University of Chicago Press, 1967), appeared, the first scholarly history on turn-of-the-century black Chicago. Other than part 1 of Drake and Cayton's *Black Metropolis* (New York: Harcourt, Brace, 1945), which amounts to a historical sketch of black Chicago presumably written by the late Dr. Lawrence D. Reddick, no comprehensive, nor near comprehensive, history exists.

labor force during the First World War. Their rough social adjustment to urban living represented a concomitant problem with which the Establishment had to deal. As black and white civic, community, and corporate leaders pondered a course of action, they collectively agreed on the League as the proper channel through which to ameliorate any problems encountered. At the heart of the policies and programs that the League endorsed stood the belief that the African American worker could play an essential role in sustaining the well-being of Chicago's economy. Through the years, the League remained true to this mission despite fluxes in the general economy affecting the labor market. Throughout, Strickland clearly illustrated the complexity of the League's course as it attempted to balance the interests of African American labor, white employers, and white-dominated labor unions. The League, then, had the unenviable position of being placed repeatedly between the black worker and his employer (who paid the League's bills) as well as between the black worker and organized labor (which feared black workers more as strikebreakers than saw the need to embrace them as coworkers).

Constantly Strickland showed that the Chicago Urban League was susceptible to the national and regional economies. Between 1919 and 1924, recession dictated that the League become "a distributor of relief" (71). This was a warmup to the Great Depression, which found the League between 1930 and 1934 acting as a conveyer of housing to the homeless, in effect, "lodging house operators" (107). The advent of the New Deal allowed a basically moribund League to once again open its Department of Industrial Relations and help dispense referrals to government-sponsored work.

Beyond its focus on continual internal struggles, *History of the Chicago Urban League* revealed how the League shared in the intellectual tradition of the University of Chicago's renowned Department of Sociology. The League's first president, Professor Robert E. Park, helped develop the "Chicago School" of research, which linked human behavior with physical environment. Park also shared in the mentoring of the budding sociologists Charles S. Johnson and E. Franklin Frazier, both destined to achieve national prominence after their combined stints at the university and the League. For its part, the League's Department of Research, as an arm of that academic institution, succumbed too often to the arrivals and departures of its researchers, such as Johnson and Frazier. Nonetheless, the impressive collection and analysis of data on race relations contributed to the League-linked Chicago Commission on Race Relations, which produced the impressive post-riot study and tome, *The*

Negro in Chicago (1922). As to the membership on the commission, it included Urban Leaguers Julius Rosenwald, Victor Lawson, and Dr. George Cleveland Hall, while Charles S. Johnson wrote the bulk of the study.[7]

As to the structure of *History of the Chicago Urban League,* the author established his own temporal framework revolving around important events in the continuous transformation of the Chicago Urban League. The one exception was Chapter 5, which was devoted to the decade of the thirties with an emphasis on the Great Depression and New Deal. Choosing not to confine himself to more readily identifiable occurrences such as world wars (1914–1918 and 1939–1945) and political changes in Chicago city government (the Thompson years, 1915–1919 and 1927-1931), Strickland was better able to convey the saga of the League as a centerpiece of Chicago reform history.

The dynamics of World War I and the Great Migration are covered in Chapter 2, "The Founding Years, 1915–18." Here, the League's imprint on the landscape of Chicago was forged as it built its program around the relevant needs of industrial relations, research, and coordinated social services. More recent scholarship, such as James Grossman's *Land of Hope: Chicago, Black Southerners, and the Great Migration* (1989), complements this story of the southern migrant as laborer with the motivations for his and her sojourn northward and with the reception they received once in the city.

The violence and turmoil of the Chicago Race Riot of 1919 and the recession that followed the conclusion of World War I were determined to be turning points in the League's history. These are covered in Chapter 3, "Violence and Uncertainty, 1919–24." It is during this period that "actually, the Chicago Urban League had reached the climax of its effectiveness and public appeal" (81). This was brought about by new circumstances surrounding the armistice. With peace, "there was no longer a steady demand for labor, and the migrant was increasingly considered an unwelcome intruder" (56). William M. Tuttle Jr.'s *Race Riot: Chicago in the Red Summer of 1919* (1970) describes and analyzes the multifaceted roots of the riot with an emphasis on the importance of the labor element that Strickland revealed.

Chapter 4 covers the period 1925–1929, during which a new executive secretary, Albon L. Foster, arrived to lead the League during a period

[7] Arthur I. Waskow's *From Race Riot to Sit-In: 1919 and the 1960s* (Garden City, N.Y.: Doubleday, 1966) provides useful background material to the influence of this document over the years on life in Chicago.

of stagnancy. Significantly, the saga of the Chicago branch of the National Association for the Advancement of Colored People paralleled that of the Chicago Urban League in the latter's struggles for organizational vitality. The Chicago NAACP was organized in 1910 and was committed completely to attaining realization of the theoretical equalities promised in the Declaration of Independence and the U.S. Constitution. It suffered through some of the same struggles that plagued the League, but an early transformation in its governance, program, membership, and resources paved the way for its achieving its goal of institutional status in the lives of black Chicagoans by the 1930s.[8] Six years later, the League was organized specifically to meet the needs of migrants seeking wartime employment in Chicago's industries. Through the years, both organizations would sometimes share executive leaderships, and they competed for community funds, cooperated in issues of common interest, and celebrated both separate and collective victories. The Chicago Urban League's community worker, Mrs. Olivia W. Bush Banks, became the Chicago NAACP's interim executive secretary in the early twenties. Attorney Earl B. Dickerson held the League's presidency twice while serving as alderman of the Second Ward, member of the Fair Employment Practices Committee, and NAACP national board member. After the League terminated the services of executive secretary Albon L. Foster, he was welcomed into the ranks of the Chicago NAACP as a fund-raiser and organizer in the 1940s and 1950s.

By 1925, in order to meet the needs of its constituents, the Chicago NAACP not only reorganized but also took a decidedly unified race tone. This spared it from the dilemmas the Chicago Urgan League faced with its double dualism. The leadership of the Chicago NAACP became predominantly African American, fund-raising emanated from the black community, and the agenda reflected what the black community desired at any given time. This racial consciousness was also reflected in the ranks of black labor, the Pullman Porters in particular. The same year, the Brotherhood of Sleeping Car Porters and Maids organized in New York under the leadership of A. Philip Randolph. The stand of the Chicago Urban League, if it had followed the national office dictates of its former executive secretary, T. Arnold Hill, would have been to oppose unionization (73). Chicago, as a national railroad center, indeed had a role in the labor struggle of the Pullman Porters as shown in a relatively recent labor study. As it was, the League concerned

[8] See Christopher Robert Reed, "Politics and Protest in Chicago during the Depression-Decade, 1930–1939" (Ph.D. diss., Kent State University, 1982).

itself with rising unemployment and the need to protect jobs already held by black workers in the stockyards.[9]

The decade of the 1930s opened with the Chicago Urban League lacking a staff, program, and funding. The devastation of the depression was described by Strickland thus: "All sections of the city suffered, but the Negro community was hit hardest" (104). Assisting the homeless to secure housing covered the bulk of League activities. With its conservative leadership, taking this course of action was almost predictable. Once the New Deal was inaugurated, circumstances changed dramatically. Meanwhile, a plethora of radical groups demanded immediate amelioration of conditions, but to their chagrin defenders of the status quo sought out the organizations with whom they felt most comfortable. This meant the League remained an organization that recognized only "conciliatory methods" as acceptable for change (110).

Yet, by 1934, a revitalized League did hire Howard D. Gould to head its Department of Industrial Relations. Its efforts were limited, in that it worked to improve employment opportunities only in government-sponsored work through Emergency Advisory Councils. At the same time, League staffers, but not its board, indulged community activism by helping organize the Chicago Council of Negro Organizations, the Negro Chamber of Commerce, and the Negro Labor Relations League (130). Board pressure ensued after it recognized a drift from its traditional conservative stance, one, in fact, at variance with the national office. So the staff acted surreptitiously in its efforts (122). Then, although the League fought for black workers' inclusion in the Public Works Administration, the League stood on the sideline as the workers in the mass-production industries organized their forces to protect workers' rights through racially inclusive unions.

With the advent of World War II in 1939, and the U.S. entry in December 1941, the League still preoccupied itself with matters that should have been considered extraneous to the needs of the times. This is the subject of Chapter 6, entitled "Internal Dissension, 1941–47." As the city anticipated and then received sixty-five thousand migrants seeking work, the League did not exert itself to take a leadership role in the city. Instead, it helped to find jobs for migrating laborers, proposed a five-year plan for community self-improvement, and added a public

[9] See William H. Harris, *Keeping the Faith: A. Philip Randolph, Milton P. Webster, and the Brotherhood of Sleeping Car Porters, 1925–1937* (Urbana: University of Illinois Press, 1977); see also Rick Halpern, *Down on the Killing Floor: Black and White Workers in Chicago's Packinghouses, 1904–54* (Urbana: University of Illinois Press, 1997).

relations department to improve interracial contact. However, it was not energized enough to raise sufficient funding for its operations and found itself on the sidelines in promoting better race relations when Mayor Edward Kelley formed his Commission of Race Relations in 1943. Also, the League, under A. L. Foster's management, alienated many of its own staff over their desire to unionize. After this fiasco and others, Foster was removed from his post in 1947.

However, peace, order, and vitality did not occur with Foster's departure; instead, the "Time of Troubles" ensued and is discussed in Chapter 7, which covers the years 1947–1955. The hiring of a new executive director, Sidney Williams, brought the League its most activist staff leader in its organizational history. Outspoken, independent, confrontational, and administratively uncontrollable, Williams soon had the board wishing for his dismissal, which occurred in July 1955. During his tenure, Williams allied the League with the aspirations of an activist black community and thereby tarnished the organization's image in the eyes of the city's Establishment, whose immediate expression of disapproval was financial. The debilitating influence of outside funding bodies, especially the Community Fund, was so great that none of the progressives on the Board of Directors would consider assuming the presidency of the League. The League's second reorganization took place beginning in July 1955 as Williams was ousted from office.

A "new" Urban League appeared with the arrival of incoming Executive Secretary Edwin "Bill" Berry in January 1956, hence the title of Chapter 8, "Reorganization and the 'New' Urban League, 1955–59." While the "new" Urban League did not always secure the Establishment's approval of the League's program, Berry won many of the demands of African Americans by using his finesse to make progress within the system. What Strickland discovered in Berry's approach was the executive secretary's ability to attack the causes rather than the effects of racial discrimination, while at the same time the "old handmaiden's approach" of social casework, mass planning, and block organizing proceeded (197).

By the time of the Civil Rights Revolution of the 1960s, which is covered in Chapters 9 and 10, the League still faced the plague of dualism, but it had an effective spokesman in Bill Berry to promote its interests. The League became more relevant than ever in the lives of African Americans and all Chicagoans. As Strickland concluded, "the 'new' Urban League has made significant contributions to the efforts being made to realize [the goal of entering the city's mainstream]; but without the 'old' Urban League, there could have been no 'new' Urban League" (264). As to the contributions of both phases of the League, during the last decade of the past century, the appearances of several publications in Chicago history further serve to set the record straight about its role and accomplishments, all shown in a broader context than presented in *History of the Chicago Urban League.* The real estate magnate, civil rights activist, and past president of the Chicago NAACP, Dempsey J. Travis, has tapped into revived memory and published *An Autobiography of Black Chicago* (Chicago: Urban Research Press, 1981) and *An Autobiography of Black Politics* (Chicago: Urban Research Press, 1987). In each work, new dimensions of the League's activities and the extent of its involvement in mass-level concerns emerge. The most recent scholarship on what was considered to be the League's sister organization, the Chicago NAACP, also devoted attention to the problem of remaining relevant to the increasingly militant demands of Chicago's burgeoning working-class population.[10] In the realms of Chicago history, labor studies, migration history, and institutional studies, *History of the Chicago Urban League* has earned a lasting place in historical scholarship by remaining as relevant over time as the Chicago Urban League itself.

[10] See Christopher Robert Reed, *The Chicago NAACP and the Rise of Professional Black Leadership, 1910–1966* (Bloomington: Indiana University Press, 1997).

Preface to the 2001 Edition

Arvarh E. Strickland

Growing up in Hattiesburg, Mississippi, I was blissfully ignorant that there was such a thing as an Urban League movement. Although from an early age I was painfully aware of the racism and Jim Crow that circumscribed our lives in Hattiesburg, from what I had heard older people in my community say about the quality of life in Chicago, Illinois, I was sure that Chicago was probably the last place on earth I would ever want to call home. Of course, those were famous last words, since I wound up living in Illinois and Chicago for a decade. During my second year at Tougaloo College, I probably ran across a brief reference to the Urban League in August Meier's Negro history course textbook—the first edition of John Hope Franklin's *From Slavery to Freedom.* My generation of African American college students, however, was mainly interested in studying about slavery and the Civil War and Reconstruction periods.

My first visit to Chicago only served to deepen my conviction that the quality of life for African Americans in that city was inferior to that enjoyed by many in my Jim Crowed neighborhood. As a teenager, I was sent to far-away Albion, Michigan, to represent the youth of the segregated Mississippi Conference of the Methodist Episcopal Church at the predominantly white meeting of the National Conference of Methodist Youth. Another African American youth and I returned on the same train, and we had a several-hour layover in Chicago. He asked that I accompany him to Chicago's South Side to search out and visit friends from his hometown of Hazelhurst, Mississippi. Having been warned of the dangers of the big city, I was reluctant to venture too far from the train station, but he finally prevailed upon me to do so.

My fear and apprehension were heightened when we entered the vestibule of a high-rise apartment building and he could not find his friend's name on a mailbox. Being older and more adventurous than I, he rang several bells, and when people yelled out of windows to ask who was ringing their bells, he asked if they knew his friend. The responses were not very friendly. Fortunately, it was the right building, and the friend heard the commotion and came to open the door for us. The family members were young recent migrants, and their first Chicago home was a basement kitchenette, which I later learned to refer to euphemistically as a "garden apartment." There was hardly room for four of us in the cramped space they called home. I was greatly relieved to get back to Twelfth Street Station and to board the train for Mississippi.

Fortunately, I experienced other aspects of Chicago life during subsequent visits. In 1952, I entered the University of Illinois at Urbana-Champaign as a graduate student in the college of education. My bride of one year and I moved into a university apartment and began to participate in graduate student life. We also made contact with relatives in Chicago and spent enjoyable visits with them. Even so, when we returned south the following year, I still had not become urbanized, and I had not had experiences that convinced me that there was a great deal of difference in the racism endured by the great majority of African Americans in Illinois and that which oppressed those in Mississippi.

After completing my military service and after teaching several years in Alabama and Mississippi, I returned to the University of Illinois to pursue a doctorate. This time, I came to study history, the field of my college major, but I was not interested in specializing in the traditional areas of slavery and the Civil War and Reconstruction. Fortuitously, I chose to work with J. Leonard Bates, a Progressive Era scholar, and I became interested in this relatively neglected period in African American history. Nevertheless, choosing a dissertation topic became a major challenge. My professors had drummed into my head the accepted canon of historical scholarship at that time: Written history must be based upon primary sources, and oral history was highly suspect. So, I reasoned, mistakenly, that if any African American organization had good records and an appreciation for preserving its heritage, it would be the Urban League, and there was an active League branch in Chicago. Once the topic was set, the real challenge began.

My small-town southern naïveté was probably evident to everyone but me when I called the office of the Chicago Urban League and announced that I was a graduate student at the University of Illinois and that I was writing a history of their organization. Of course, I had trouble getting past the switchboard operator, and on the occasions when I succeeded, a secretary would inform me that the professional staff members were busy and would have to get back to me. None ever did.

During a visit with the associate minister at the Methodist church I attended on campus in Urbana, I started venting my frustrations about my inability to even talk to anyone on the League staff. To my great surprise, he said that he could help me with that. I am certain that my first thought was that I needed a little more than prayer at that point. But he told me that his brother in Chicago was a supporter of the Urban League and that he knew the executive director personally. He promised to call his brother and to make an appointment for me.

As it turned out, his brother was a corporate lawyer with a La Salle Street firm. We walked from his office to the Chicago Bar Association headquarters, where Edwin C. "Bill" Berry joined us for lunch. I left that lunch with a firm commitment from Berry that I would receive full cooperation from his staff. From the beginning, I had a bias against people associated with the Urban League. I expected them to be elitist and snobbish, and my experiences in trying to reach staff members by telephone heightened this perception. Then, although I was grateful for the results, the fact that I needed the help of a white, suburban lawyer to get an appointment with the head of an African American advancement organization deepened my latent antielitism. Nevertheless, through the years I developed a genuine fondness for Bill Berry and the Urban League people I met while doing research for my study. Moreover, even though in my heart I remained a small-town person, I also developed a love for Chicago, and I came to understand better the dynamics of urban life.

I learned early on that my dream of finding an organized set of papers and records to facilitate my work was largely a fantasy. I was told that the early records had been destroyed in a fire. Existing files that were not in current use were scattered helter-skelter in a storage area, but I was given access to this material. (Later, I was permitted to organize the papers for microfilming, and the originals were deposited at the University of Illinois at Chicago.) Consequently, I was greatly dependent upon the helpful and efficient reference room librarians at the University of Illinois to assist me in searching out and borrowing fugitive reports and other source materials from libraries throughout the country. I also received excellent cooperation from librarians and staff persons in Chicago libraries and public and private agencies.

I found, however, that it was not the documents but the people that I interacted with as I traveled around Chicago by public transportation, lugging an ancient oversized reel-to-reel tape recorder, that contributed most significantly to my education and to my maturation as a person and as a scholar.

During my first visits to the League office, I felt most at ease with the clerical staff, and, fortunately for me, several of them seemed to adopt me as their own southern migrant orientation project. Mrs. Odessa Cave Evans and I hit it off right away. She and Frayser Lane were the longest-serving employees. He epitomized the old-style, social-work-oriented professional staff person. She knew everyone who had been involved in a significant way with the League, and she knew where most of the skeletons were stored. I first did a formal interview with her, but I came back to her time and time again for information and guidance. She helped me to identify the key people to talk to, and she called several of them to make appointments for me. No one she called refused to see me. She also made me aware of questions that I should ask of those who had been involved in certain events or special phases of the League's work.

One of the older men that Mrs. Evans insisted I talk to was supposedly critically ill and not expected to live very long. She and others urged me to get to him immediately or I would miss a valuable informant. I had a wonderful visit with this man and left him hoping that all would be well with him. Later, when I moved to Chicago and began further research to revise and extend my study in preparation for publication, I expressed sorrow that I would not be able to talk to him again and asked when he passed away. This elicited a smile from the person I asked, and I was told that he had gotten married and was ensconced with his new bride in a love nest in Michigan. Mrs. Evans, as well as others, must not have been fully aware of the power of love. Unfortunately, though, I still was not able to talk to him again.

As would be expected, the information I received from the interviewees was of uneven value, but the receptions I received were uniformly cordial and friendly. In some cases, my understanding was broadened as much by what was not said as by what was said. Of course, there were areas in which some current and former staff members were reluctant to venture. Two or three board members were quite reserved in what they would discuss when a microphone was in front of them. In these cases, I often turned the recorder off and even stopped taking notes. But when the interview was over, I made notes as soon as possible. Others, however, were quite open in discussing sensitive areas. At the time I interviewed him, Albon L. Foster was the executive officer with the Cosmopolitan Chamber of Commerce—formerly the Negro Chamber of Commerce—and he met with me several times in his office. Of course, he was proud of the role he played as head of the League and went to great lengths in recounting the major events of his administration and explaining the reasons for his actions.

Dr. Nathaniel O. Calloway and Hugo B. Law, the main actors in the 1955 reorganization of the League, both invited me into their homes. Calloway's office and his home were in the Prairie Shores complex, and Law's home, in the Hyde Park area—with its modern design and atrium—was impressive. Both men provided detailed explanations of their sides of the questions involved in the reorganization and gave frank responses to my questions. It was apparent that neither of these men could have a deep understanding of the lives of the masses of black Chicagoans whom they were committed to serving, but they were both dedicated men.

My journey along Forty-seventh Street and around the corner to a once fashionable area of Kenwood to interview Mrs. Irene McCoy Gaines was a memorable experience. Upon entering the Gaines home I received a polite and genteel welcome from Mrs. Gaines. The atmosphere was like stepping back into Bronzeville of an earlier day. Mrs. Gaines was generous with her time, and, in addition to her own League work, she recalled for me the roles played by a number of other women and women's organizations. Her recollections were assisted and supplemented by those of her husband, Harris B. Gaines, who was confined to bed in an adjacent room. He was a pre–New Deal Republican who represented Chicago's first district in the Illinois General Assembly from 1929 to 1936.

I returned to Forty-seventh Street to find the office of Howard Gould, who served as industrial secretary during the Foster years. I spent many interesting hours with Gould in his office, where he made documents from his files available to me. While working on the revision, I had talked to him several times at his favorite "watering hole," a lounge in the Lake Meadows complex. Gould was one of the activist staff members of the Foster period, and the information he provided on some of the League's clandestine activities was quite helpful.

I was truly excited when I was granted an interview by Earl B. Dickerson in his office at the Supreme Liberty Life Insurance Company. I had never before been in the presence of an African American businessperson with such an elaborate office, presided over by an obviously efficient secretary. Moreover, I had never before been served a cocktail in the middle of the afternoon in a business office or anyplace else. Dickerson, or maybe it was the cocktail, soon put me at ease. It turned out that I knew a number of his relatives in Madison County, Mississippi, and after a bit of informal conversation, he launched into his Urban League experiences.

Looking back, Bill Berry was probably the most unforgettable person I encountered. I did not conduct a formal interview with him, but anytime I could corner him for a few minutes, I questioned him about whatever was on my mind at the time. When I moved to Chicago, I came to know him and his wife Betsy much better. On a number of occasions we were together at workshops or retreats, several in Lake Geneva, Wisconsin. Since I was a smoker at the time, his chain-smoking did not bother me, and I was pleased that when we were meeting in dry locations, Bill and Betsy always had a couple of bottles in their luggage. Bill—I never thought to ask him how a man named Edwin obtained the nickname Bill—was a storehouse of interesting stories, and it was apparent that he was also a polished and skilled politician. Bill was an inveterate talker, and listening to him was an introductory course on urban life and the problems faced by African American organizations.

My greatest disappointment was the failure to get an interview with Sidney Williams. During my early visits to Chicago, I believe that he was out of the country. When he returned, I called a number of times, but I was unable to get an appointment. My recollection is dim on this, but I think that he was ill, and I learned later that his wife was a jealous guardian of both his health and his reputation. So I completed the book without having the opportunity to interview this former executive director whose work and leadership had greatly intrigued me.

Later, I did meet the Williamses, and Sidney and I kept in touch with each other on and off even after I left Chicago. He often chided me for not talking to him before writing my study, and each time, I reminded him that the onus for that was on him. He boasted that if I had talked to him, I would have written a much different book. I seriously doubted that, but I always regretted that we did not meet until after the study was in print.

All in all, the people I met and the experiences I had while researching my dissertation helped to prepare me for life in Chicago. When I moved there at the beginning of the turbulent years of the 1960s to teach at the Chicago Teachers College, South—now Chicago State University—I had already undergone the first stages of my transformation to an urban dweller.

Acknowledgment

The author is indebted to numerous individuals for invaluable assistance in completing the researching and writing of this study. Professor J. Leonard Bates gave guidance, criticism, and encouragement as the project progressed from a general interest in the orientation of the urban Negro migrant to the history of one significant organization in this field. That part of the study treating the history of the Chicago Urban League up to 1956 was submitted as a doctoral dissertation at the University of Illinois. Professor August Meier also read this section of the manuscript and made valuable suggestions.

Edwin C. "Bill" Berry and his staff opened the files of the Chicago Urban League to me and greatly facilitated my work through their cooperation and helpful suggestions. The late Mrs. Odessa Cave Evans was especially generous with her time in making materials available and in making contacts with interviewees. I am deeply grateful for the assistance given in many ways by Alvin Prejean, Deputy Director, Harold Baron, Director of Research, Mrs. Jayne Chandler, and other members of the professional and clerical staff.

Librarians at the University of Illinois, the University of Chicago, Newberry Library, and the Welfare Council of Metropolitan Chicago were exceedingly helpful in locating sources.

Frayser T. Lane, Albon L. Foster, Alexander L. Jackson, and Earl B. Dickerson shared with me many rich insights drawn from their long involvement in the Urban League and other movements for Negro advancement.

Through the interest of A. D. Beittel, former president of Tougaloo College, the Board of Home Missions of the Congregational and Christian Churches provided a grant which made possible an extended stay in Chicago. I am also indebted to Mr. and Mrs. Frank Robinson for opening their home to me for extended periods.

To all of the individuals who consented to be interviewed, I am deeply grateful, especially to Howard D. Gould who also gave me access to files he saved from his career with the Urban League.

For their moral support and sacrifices during the past years while the "book" was the center of our home, I wish to thank my wife, Willie Pearl, and my sons, Duane and Bruce.

History of the Chicago Urban League

1

ORIGINS OF THE URBAN LEAGUE MOVEMENT

In the years between 1896 and World War I, the reforming ferment that pervaded American life had its greatest impact on the race question in the cities of the North. Although at this time the dominant sentiment, both in the North and in the South, favored Negro subordination, there were strong voices in dissent. Chief among these were the northern reformers — social scientists, social workers, and journalists. It was these groups that raised the question of racial adjustment to the level of inquiry given other vital social problems. They fostered a new climate of opinion which gave rise to interracial organizational activities for Negro betterment. The National Urban League — one of the oldest and best established movements working for the improvement of the Negro's social and economic conditions — began under the auspices of these reforming groups. The new social concepts of this period led to the development of three specialized organizations which combined in 1911 to form the National Urban League.

To a number of social theorists, the racial practices prevailing after 1877 posed a threat to democracy. John R. Commons — in his *Races and Immigrants in America,* first published in 1907 — called race relations "the most fundamental of all American social and political problems." He felt that without "equal opportunities before the law and equal ability of classes and races to use those opportunities," American democracy could not survive. The nation's fundamental problem, according to Commons, was not the physical amalgamation of the diverse racial strains comprising its population, but the achievement of a "mental community." In other words, there had to be "mental and moral assimilation."[1] As far as the Negro was concerned, this meant keeping the door of citizenship open, while conducting a definite program to prepare him for full participation in democratic institutions. But, more fundamental to Negro advancement was the development of leadership within Negro ranks. These leaders needed the cooperation of white leaders in situations where they would meet on equal terms. Commons considered the development of such leadership the role of higher education.[2]

Walter E. Weyl issued a similar admonition. To him the question was not one of like or dislike for the Negro but the necessity of dealing with reality. The Negro was inescapably a part of American life and, therefore, a potent determinant in the success or failure of American democracy. While disfranchisement could be used as a temporary expedient, a permanent policy of repression would only lead to dire consequences. Weyl saw possibilities that the plutocracy might use the Negro to its own advantage in resisting the democratization of industry and politics. As Negroes grew in numbers and in "Negro consciousness," there would also be the danger of racial war, resulting in "a backwash of civilization, a recurrence of barbarism," which would reach every section of the nation.[3]

Yet, Weyl and other theorists perceived a more immediate and subtle danger. This opinion was embodied in the concept that held undesirable attributes to be infectious. Weyl gave one of the more dramatic expressions of this view when he warned that "our self-protection, as much as our sense of justice, must impel us toward the increase in the Negro's ability, *morale,* and opportunity. Just as a diphtheritic Negro will infect a white man, just as the tubercle bacillus, oblivious of the color line, will go from the black man's home to the Aryan's, so weakness, immorality, ignorance, and recklessness will spread from one race to the other as a prairie fire from farm to farm. Whether we love the Negro or hate him, we are, and shall continue to be, tied to him."[4] Racial adjustment, therefore, became a question involving the self-interest of all Americans.

Several of the speakers and participants at the National Negro

---

[1] John R. Commons, *Races and Immigrants in America* (New York: The Macmillan Company, 1913), pp. 1-21.
[2] *Ibid.,* pp. 39-52.
[3] Walter E. Weyl, *The New Democracy* (rev. ed.; New York: The Macmillan Company, 1914), pp. 342-345.
[4] *Ibid.,* p. 345.

Conference of 1909, held in New York City, carried this idea even further. Albert E. Pillsbury of Massachusetts considered it unfair to northern and western states to apportion Congressional representation to southern states on the basis of their total populations when these states had disfranchised Negro voters.[5] William English Walling warned of the economic exploitation and repressive measures made possible against "poor whites" by the subordination of Negroes,[6] while Charles Edward Russell appealed to the working man and property owner to beware of attempts to negate sections of the Constitution, for "if they can nullify the Constitution with regard to franchise, they can nullify it with regard to anything else."[7]

However, it was the muckraking magazines and journalists that played the leading role in opening the race question to public inquiry. Though usually more restrained in their approach than when dealing with municipal corruption and corporate abuses, the muckrakers brought their penetrating investigative techniques and literary ability to bear on the race question. The editors of the muckraking organs — especially *The Independent, McClure's,* and *The Arena* — opened their publications to writers who challenged the traditional stereotypes of the Negro and exhorted the public on the evils of discrimination.

The southern protagonist still had his hearing, but he did not go unanswered. For instance, one number of *The Arena* had an article protesting against making the "Negro" Philippine Islands an American territory and another proclaiming the uneducability of the Negro. These were balanced by others condemning lynching and making appeals to the "higher sense of justice" of white Americans. One of the latter was by the fiery Negro crusader, Ida B. Wells-Barnett.[8]

McClure's initiated the analytical treatment of the race question with an article by Carl Schurz.[9] Schurz examined the mistakes of all sides in dealing with the problems facing the nation at the close

[5] Albert E. Pillsbury, "Negro Disfranchisement as It Affects the White Man," National Negro Conference, *Proceedings . . . 1909* (New York: 1909), pp. 180-195.

[6] William English Walling, "The Negro and the South," National Negro Conference, *Proceedings,* pp. 104-106.

[7] Charles Edward Russell, "Address," National Negro Conference, *Proceedings,* pp. 220-221.

[8] "The White Man's Problem," *The Arena,* XXIII (Jan., 1900), 1-30.

[9] Carl Schurz, "Can the South Solve the Negro Problem?" *McClure's Magazine,* XXII (Jan., 1904), 259-275.

of the Civil War. In assessing the course of race relations in the South, he pointed to the illogic and patent danger in trying to subvert democratic institutions in order to suppress the Negro. Schurz felt that the Negro's fate could be left to the South only if that section sought to achieve racial adjustment on the basis of "the fundamental law of the land" and without attempts at circumvention of that law.

Yet, in concluding his "diagnosis," Schurz could give no concrete suggestions for solution of the problem. His dilemma was characteristic of such writings on the race question. This was the one problem that the Progressive mind found insoluble through legislation. Schurz concluded that the race question could "not be quickly and conclusively solved by drastic legislative treatment, which might rather prove apt to irritate than to cure. What is done by legislation can usually be undone by legislation, and is therefore liable to become subject to the chances of party warfare." Under such circumstances, an educative process seemed to hold the greatest promise. "The slow process of propitiating public sentiment," Schurz said, "while trying our patience, promises after all the most durable results."[10]

For its next major project in this area, *McClure's* turned to the subject of lynching. Ray Stannard Baker did two articles covering the southern and northern aspects of this enigma.[11] In this instance, a solution was proposed. For even while reciting the injustices perpetrated against Negroes innocent of any crime, Baker made no judgments on the broader aspects of race relations. Lynching was just a "symptom of lawlessness." Since the white man had "taken all the responsibility of government," he had the obligation to insure justice and to practice reverence for law. The citizen should have no reason to resort to mob law, for there should be no doubt that

[10] *Ibid.*, p. 275. Some historians deny that journalistic treatments of the race question were done in the same spirit as investigations on other subjects. Since a belief in the efficacy of legislation for the correction of social ills was considered a distinguishing characteristic of the muckraking mind, it is contended that writings which prescribed education as a remedy did not follow the muckraking tradition. Thus, they were not reformative in intent. See, for example, John Hope Franklin, *From Slavery to Freedom: A History of American Negroes* (New York: Alfred A. Knopf, Inc., 1947), p. 431. Cf. Louis Filler, *Crusaders for American Liberalism* (new ed.; Yellow Springs, Ohio: The Antioch Press, 1950), pp. 278-280.

[11] Ray Stannard Baker, "What Is a Lynching?" *McClure's Magazine*, XXIV (Jan., 1905), 229-314; XXIV (Feb., 1905), 422-430.

every criminal would be dealt with in court. Therefore, the solution to lynching was simply strict law enforcement.

Three years later, Baker's analysis of racial violence in the North was supplemented by a more impassioned treatment by William English Walling. This article, in *The Independent,* reported the race riot in Springfield, Illinois. Walling warned that when such occurrences became "general in the North every hope of political democracy will be dead." He climaxed his article with the rhetorical challenge: "Who realizes the seriousness of the situation, and what large and powerful body of citizens is ready to come to their aid!"[12]

However, the most thorough muckraking treatment of the Negro's position in American life, "Following the Color Line," was another series by Ray Stannard Baker. These articles, first appearing in *The American Magazine,* were subsequently published in book form.[13] Baker combined the journalistic technique of first-hand observation with the social scientist's penchant for impartiality. He traveled throughout the North and South gathering materials and information. While offering no radical solution to the race problem — Baker's advice was to depend upon education, time, and patience — this work stood in strong contrast to the usual writings of that era. He tried to present conditions as they were, without condemnation on either side.

In any case, the primary significance of the muckraking articles was not the conclusions reached by their authors. These works were valuable for the contemporary picture of race relations they presented and the controversy they aroused. Through them the American people had access to the "inside story" on the Negro, along with those on the trusts and other social problems. The degree of impartiality reached by men like Schurz and Baker was rather remarkable considering the dominant temper of the time in respect to the Negro. Furthermore, the personal biases of the muckrakers were dwarfed by the national picture of exploitation, humiliation, and suffering they disclosed. These men and their magazines helped to bring a gradual change in the climate of opinion on race relations.

In northern cities — such as New York, Chicago, Philadelphia,

---

[12] William English Walling, "The Race War in the North," *The Independent,* LXV (Sept. 3, 1908), 529-534. This article led to the convening of the National Negro Conference of 1909, out of which came the N.A.A.C.P.

[13] Ray Stannard Baker, *Following the Color Line: An Account of Negro Citizenship in the American Democracy* (New York: Doubleday, Page and Company, 1908).

and Boston — there were, in addition, a growing number of social reformers, mainly social workers, who sought ways of alleviating suffering caused by social and economic conditions. Social workers, not yet fully accepted as professionals, were striving to rise above their traditional alms-dispensing functions. They adopted the scientific method for ascertaining the quantitative facts about social conditions and followed a rather pragmatic philosophy in ameliorating the effects of social disorder. Yet, in general, social work retained elements of traditional humanitarianism, characteristic of the early philanthropists and relief givers. In the years 1900 to 1917, social workers were as much dedicated to general reform as to meeting the needs of the indigent.

The reforming activities of the social workers differed from those of the social scientists and the journalists in several respects. In the first place, the social worker rejected the possibility of eliminating all social ills through a sweeping change in either the political or economic system. He sought to deal with the effects of the system, rather than to change it. While neither the social theorists nor the journalists of the Progressive Era envisioned radical alterations in American institutions, they went further than the social workers in advocating basic changes.

Yet, within the narrow limits of their areas of concern, social workers were more revolutionary in their timetable of reform than the other two groups. The social worker was concerned with the immediate elimination of suffering. He was interested in the present, not in evolving institutions that held promise of change. Working conditions in industry, wage levels, health improvement, housing reform, and other social and economic ills could be changed immediately through legislation and other measures directed specifically at the individual evil. This was the aim of the social worker, for he was interested in bettering the conditions of the living generation, removing the suffering that he witnessed daily.

Finally, social work differed in its method of investigation. The most fundamental attribute of social work as an emerging profession was its dedication to the scientific processes. While depending upon such disciplines as sociology, economics, biology, and political science for scientific methodology and modes of thought, social workers used these processes less abstractly and qualitatively than the early practitioners of the other disciplines. The speciality of the social worker was quantitative investigation.

There was a similar deviation from the work of the muckrakers. The journalists depended upon literary skills and used qualitative judgments; the social worker wanted materials that were reducible to statistical terms. Both groups sought to stimulate public awareness, but the work of the journalist was exhortative, that of the social worker aimed at directing individual and group action toward the elimination of a specific social evil.

In spite of these differences, social workers owed a great debt to journalism. The muckrakers exerted a great influence in conditioning the American mind for social criticism. They introduced a new "realism" into American life that removed the customary reticence toward exposing industry, labor, and business, and such evils as poverty and vice to close scrutiny. The muckrakers engaged in realistic, if not scientific, investigations of social conditions. These journalists did more than any other group in bringing that public awareness that precedes reform.[14]

It was, however, the social worker who forged a definite link between investigation and reform. This was particularly true in the area of race relations and the improvement of living conditions among urban Negroes.

The first study of a Negro community using the scientific processes was motivated by social workers. In 1895 Miss Susan P. Wharton of the Philadelphia College Settlement contacted the Provost of the University of Pennsylvania seeking University cooperation for a study of the Negro in Philadelphia. The officials of the University expressed a willingness to participate in an investigation utilizing the methods employed by Charles Booth in London and the investigators at Hull House in Chicago.[15]

William E. B. Du Bois was engaged by the University to conduct the investigation, and Isabel Eaton assisted him by surveying domestic service in Philadelphia under the auspices of the College Settlement. No definite program of reform was expected to result from this project. Its chief purpose was to provide information which would serve as "a safe guide for all efforts toward the solution of the many Negro problems of a great American city."[16]

But, New York, not Philadelphia, became the center for investi-

[14] See Richard Hofstadter, *The Age of Reform: From Bryan to F.D.R.* (New York: Vintage Books, 1960), pp. 186-214.
[15] William E. B. Du Bois, *The Philadelphia Negro: A Social Study* (Philadelphia: University of Pennsylvania, 1899), pp. viii-x.
[16] *Ibid.*, p. 1.

gative activities and movements for Negro advancement. In 1904, Mary White Ovington, a young settlement worker, began her long career in Negro causes by commencing an investigation of Negro life in New York. Miss Ovington's study was not completed and published until 1911,[17] but in the intervening years she was active in betterment movements and in disseminating information on Negro life in New York.[18]

The same year that Miss Ovington began her investigation another New York settlement worker, Frances A. Kellor, published a study of employment agencies in the major cities of the North. Miss Kellor exposed the deplorable conditions and unscrupulous practices to which young women were subjected while seeking work.[19] A few years later, in 1909, George Edmund Haynes began, as a doctoral thesis at Columbia University, a study of the Negro wage-earner and businessman. This investigation was directed through the Bureau of Social Research of the New York School of Philanthropy.[20]

The investigations and writings of social theorists, journalists, and social workers were indicative of a new trend in race relations. In the first place, such activities evidenced a renewed concern for and interest in the welfare of the Negro. They showed the existence of a growing curiosity about the actual conditions under which non-whites lived and worked and the implications their way of life held for the general community.

This renewed interest also was manifested in an impetus toward organizational activities. A new type of organization, interracial in structure, began to emerge during the first decade of the twentieth

---

[17] Mary White Ovington, *Half a Man: The Status of the Negro in New York* (New York: Longmans, Green, and Co., 1911). See also Mary White Ovington, *The Walls Came Tumbling Down* (New York: Harcourt, Brace and Company, 1947), pp. 10-52.

[18] Miss Ovington was a member of the board of the National League for the Protection of Colored Women, did settlement work among Negroes, and was one of the leaders in the founding of the National Association for the Advancement of Colored People. Her articles on Negro life included: "The Negro Home in New York," *Charities,* XV (Oct. 7, 1905), 25-30; "Fresh Air Work Among Colored Children in New York," *Charities,* XVII (Oct. 13, 1906), 115-117; "The Negro in the Trades Unions in New York," *The Annals of the American Academy of Political and Social Science,* XXVII (May, 1906), 551-558.

[19] Frances A. Kellor, *Out of Work: A Study of Employment Agencies: Their Treatment of the Unemployed, and Their Influence upon Homes and Business* (New York: G. P. Putnam's Sons, 1904).

[20] George Edmund Haynes, *The Negro at Work in New York City: A Study in Economic Progress* (New York: Columbia University, 1912).

century. The social investigators and those they drew into the direction and support of their projects formed the white nucleus that cooperated with the so-called "Negro militants" and "conservatives" in forming organizations for Negro betterment.[21]

One of the earliest of the cooperative type organizations was the National League for the Protection of Colored Women. This agency resulted from Miss Kellor's study of employment offices. Although the conditions exposed in the study were not unknown, this book brought them to the attention of sympathetic groups. As early as 1898, the participants at the Hampton Negro Conference heard a recital of the pitfalls, including the activities of employment agents, awaiting the southern Negro girl who went to northern cities in search of a better life.[22] However, no systematic investigation was undertaken until the New York Summer School of Philanthropy sponsored Miss Kellor's study in 1902. The involvement of other groups in supporting this investigation, such as the College Settlement Association and the Woman's Municipal League of New York, added to the possibility of remedial measures being taken.[23]

In March, 1905, Miss Kellor made an appeal for public support of an organization to work among Negro women. An article in *Charities* outlined briefly the immoral, dishonest, and exploitative practices used by many employment agencies. Since the Negro migrant lacked the protection provided by the Traveler's Aid Society and sympathetic friends to immigrants and other groups entering

---

[21] This is not to imply that the trend toward interracial cooperation in Negro betterment organizations supplanted all-Negro organizational efforts. Although there was very little such activity among Negroes immediately following the Civil War, a number of civic and professional type organizations began to appear in the 1880's. However, protest or reform movements such as T. Thomas Fortune's Afro-American Protective League and its successor, the Afro-American Council, were transitory and of little lasting effect. Even the famed Niagara Movement is best remembered for its dramatic meetings and the role of its members in the establishment of the N.A.A.C.P. For a brief survey of organizational activities at this time see B. F. Lee, Jr., "Negro Organizations," *The Annals of the American Academy of Political and Social Science,* XLIX (Sept., 1913), 131-137; Fannie Barrier Williams, "Social Bonds in the 'Black Belt' of Chicago: Negro Organizations and the New Spirit Pervading Them," *Charities,* XV (Oct. 7, 1905), 40-44. Cf. August Meier, *Negro Thought in America, 1880-1915: Racial Ideologies in the Age of Booker T. Washington* (Ann Arbor: The University of Michigan Press, 1963), chap. VII.

[22] Hampton Negro Conference, *Report,* II (Hampton, Virginia: Hampton Institute Press, July, 1898), 62-69.

[23] Kellor, *Out of Work,* pp. v-vii.

cities, these women had little chance of escaping the corrupt employment system. The solution proposed was to provide for Negro women, through an organization formed for this purpose, the type of sympathetic assistance given other newcomers to the city.[24]

Such an organization, the National League for the Protection of Colored Women, was started in the summer of 1905. Through the Inter-Municipal Committee on Household Research, this League started branches in Philadelphia and New York. Both branches had interracial boards — Miss Kellor was an officer in both branches — that brought together Negroes active in civic groups and white social workers and sympathizers for Negro causes. Workers were provided to meet travelers arriving from southern points and to give them protection from unscrupulous employment agents. By securing the cooperation of reputable lodging houses, places to live were provided.[25] Later the organization added the finding of suitable employment as a part of its function. Agents of the League were also maintained at southern transportation centers where many of the migrants began their journeys North or had to transfer from one form of transportation to another. Such agents were stationed in Norfolk, Baltimore, and Memphis.

At about the same time, another organization was coming into being in New York. The Committee for Improving Industrial Conditions of the Negro in New York was organized around 1905, but its inception is more obscure than that of the National League for Protection of Colored Women. There seem to have been fewer social workers among its white supporters. Several of the white members — like the chairman, William Jay Schieffelin — were backers of southern Negro schools, especially Hampton and Tuskegee Institutes. The purpose of the Committee, as stated in the *New York Charities Directory,* was "to secure the facts regarding the industrial conditions of the negroes in New York and to create a public opinion in favor of giving them better opportunities for self support."[26]

Five years later the third group that was to form a part of the National Urban League was organized. During his study of eco-

---

[24] Frances A. Kellor, "Southern Colored Girls in the North," *Charities,* XIII (Mar. 11, 1905), 584-585.

[25] Frances A. Kellor, "Assisted Emigration from the South: The Women," *Charities,* XV (Oct. 7, 1905), 13-14.

[26] *New York Charities Directory,* comp. Mary E. David (17th ed.; New York: Charity Organization Society, 1907), p. 277.

nomic conditions among Negroes, George E. Haynes was convinced that Negro social workers were needed to help the migrant in making an adjustment to urban life. Haynes said of this need: "My research suggested that in a period of less than 30 years one-half the Negro population of the nation would be living in the urban sectors. It was obvious therefore that the Negro educational institutions should begin training social workers and other leaders to serve city newcomers and that general welfare agencies should be encouraged to place and utilize these trained workers to help the newcomers to learn to live in town."[27] He discussed these ideas with Frances A. Kellor and Ruth Standish Baldwin, widow of William H. Baldwin, Jr. — President of the Long Island Railroad and Trustee of Tuskegee Institute. When the Committee for Improving Industrial Condition of Negroes in New York refused to incorporate the training of social workers into its program, a new committee was formed.

In 1910, a group met at the New York School of Philanthropy, called together by Mrs. Baldwin. Haynes presented a report on his researches and offered the conclusion that the situation had "broader aspects than jobs and the protection of colored women from a 'black slave' traffic." The real need was for "broader, basic social action." Out of this meeting came the Committee on Urban Conditions Among Negroes in New York.[28]

This new committee had broader purposes than the two older organizations. It proposed to study social and economic conditions in cities and coordinate "all agencies seeking to better urban conditions among Negroes." Where such agencies did not exist, the committee intended to create them. It also assumed the obligation of training Negro social workers.[29]

Upon completion of his work at Columbia University in 1910,

---

[27] National Urban League, *Fiftieth Anniversary Yearbook,* ed. William R. Simms (New York: National Urban League, 1961), p. 45. The selection by the late George Edmund Haynes in this *Yearbook* is based on an essay he wrote shortly before his death.

[28] *Ibid.* See also George Edmund Haynes, "Interracial Social Work Begins," National Urban League, *Fortieth Anniversary Yearbook* (New York: National Urban League, 1950), p. 7; L. Hollingsworth Wood, "The Urban League Movement," *Journal of Negro History,* IX (Apr., 1924), 117-120.

[29] National League on Urban Conditions Among Negroes [National Urban League], *Bulletin,* III, No. 2 (Nov., 1913), 6-7. During the period covered in this chapter, annual reports, reports of surveys and investigations, special announcements, and publicity materials were all issued as bulletins. Some of these had distinctive titles; others did not. Hereafter all of these publications will be cited as *Bulletin,* differentiated by volume and number.

Haynes accepted an appointment at Fisk University in Nashville, Tennessee, where he was to institute the teaching of "sociology and allied matters."[30] Arrangement was made with Fisk University whereby he was permitted to spend part of his time in New York serving as Director of the Committee on Urban Conditions Among Negroes. To carry on the work of the Committee in his absence, a part-time field secretary was employed. Emanuel W. Houstoun, a graduate of Atlanta University, divided his time between the work of the Committee and graduate study.

In October, 1911, the three organizations — the National League for the Protection of Colored Women, the Committee for Improving Industrial Condition of Negroes in New York, and the Committee on Urban Conditions Among Negroes in New York—combined and adopted the equally unwieldy name of National League on Urban Conditions Among Negroes.[31]

The progress of the work undertaken by the combined organization soon necessitated a full-time person. So, in April, 1911, Eugene Kinckle Jones, a graduate of Virginia Union and Cornell Universities, came to New York from his high school teaching duties in Louisville to begin a long career in the Urban League movement. Jones became Associate Director and later Director, and Haynes devoted full time to his educational work at Fisk and the League's work in the South.[32] Under the direction of Jones and Haynes, within a few years the three separate organizations had been shaped into a new and stronger social agency.

Nevertheless, before World War I, the National Urban League was primarily a New York organization with some national features. The founders envisioned a program applicable to urban centers throughout the country, but a program and an organizational structure had to be developed. A nationally coordinated program using social work as an instrument of racial adjustment was a relatively new idea with few precedents to use as guides.

The new National Urban League had to develop and prove the effectiveness of a program in keeping with its philosophy and purposes. While the combined association incorporated the activities of

---

[30] *Fisk University News,* I (Nov., 1910), 3-4.

[31] By 1919, the shorter form, National Urban League, had come into general use.

[32] *Fiftieth Anniversary Yearbook,* pp. 45, 47; *New York Charities Directory,* comp. S. Eldridge (20th ed.; New York: Charity Organization Society, 1911), p. 594.

its constituent organizations, its purposes were much broader than the sum of those of the component units. In addition to industrial studies and traveler's aid, the League proposed "to promote, encourage, assist and engage in any and all kinds of work for improving the industrial, economic, social and spiritual conditions among Negroes."[33]

The effective implementation of such broad purposes required tested program activities, methods, and techniques. Only the still experimental processes of social work afforded any guidance in these areas. Through necessity, the greater part of the available resources was used in developing the program in New York. This was fortunate in that by 1917 the New York experiences served as the basis for a National Urban League blueprint for social service work among urban Negroes throughout the country. Since the national movement evolved as a rather loose combination of local organizations, this blueprint had to be flexible and adaptable to specific conditions in other cities.[34]

The climate of opinion, as well as the complexity and cosmopolitan character of New York, made it an ideal proving ground for a multiplicity of projects. By 1911, the work of the League's antecedent organizations and that of the social reformers, journalists, and social workers had created the beginnings of a climate of acceptance for interracial cooperation on behalf of the Negro.[35] Also, techniques for fostering coordination and cooperation among existing organizations could be tried. New York had a relatively large number of civic betterment type organizations designated as Negro organizations or Negro branches. The *Charities Directory* for 1907 listed about sixteen such agencies.[36] Of great significance was the fact that New York offered possibilities in financial resources for the support of the fledgling organization. As the financial capital of the nation, the city was the home of many of the leading philanthropists and foundations, as well as of business and industrial groups from which funds were obtained.

A wide range of welfare and social service activities were under-

[33] *Bulletin,* III, No. 2 (Nov., 1913), 7.
[34] *Bulletin,* VII, No. 2 (Dec., 1917).
[35] See Ovington, *The Walls Came Tumbling Down,* chap. II, pp. 100-106; Baker, *Following the Color Line,* pp. 141-142; Oswald Garrison Villard, *Fighting Years: Memoirs of a Liberal Editor* (New York: Harcourt, Brace and Company, 1939), pp. 196-197.
[36] *New York Charities Directory,* 1907, *passim.*

taken. Some of these were inherited from the antecedent organizations; others were unique to the combined agency. The improvement of economic conditions was accepted by the National Urban League as its principal mission, but in the early years more attention was probably given to the immediate social service demands caused by the migration. Nevertheless, economic advancement was and continued to be an important article in the League's profession of faith.

Efficiency was the shibboleth of the League's industrial program. During the Progressive Era, the embattled plutocracy placed great stress on efficiency as justification for industrial and labor policies. Reformers sought to humanize the concept of efficiency to make it compatible with industrial democracy. They talked in terms of the increased production that would result from better working conditions, more consideration for the needs of the worker, and recognition of labor's rights.[37] However, the concept was applied to the Negro's industrial struggle in its more elemental form. It was contended by some northern writers and many Negro leaders that the Negro's work opportunities in northern cities were restricted more by lack of skills and inefficiency in the skills he possessed than by prejudice and discrimination.[38] This contention provided a framework for the application of social work methods to the improvement of industrial conditions. The Urban League undertook the task of raising the worker's level of efficiency in terms of new skills and increased proficiency in old ones.

The League's Industrial Department made a modest start in this field by organizing associations of workers and trying to open employment opportunities. A Colored Public Porter's Association was organized to "guard the traveling public against unscrupulous porters" and to raise "the reliability and efficiency of its members." The cooperation of real-estate men was sought to provide training for elevatormen and hallmen in apartment houses. These workers were also formed into an association to try to screen men entering these

[37] Weyl, *The New Democracy,* pp. 149-152; Herbert Croly, *Progressive Democracy* (New York: The Macmillan Company, 1914), pp. 397-405.
[38] See John Gilmer Speed, "The Negro in New York: A Study of the Social and Industrial Condition of the Colored People in the Metropolis," *Harper's Weekly,* XLIV (Dec. 22, 1900), 1249-50; Baker, *Following the Color Line,* chap. VII; Kellor, "Southern Colored Girls in the North," p. 584. Cf. Kelly Miller, "The Economic Handicap of the Negro in the North," *The Annals of the American Academy of Political and Social Science,* XXVII (May, 1906), 543-548.

jobs and to improve the living conditions of the workers. The Colored Chauffeur's Association presented a different problem. In this instance, the question of discrimination in garage accommodations and licensing by the state had to be faced. The League justified its role in promoting this more militant type organization by pointing out that "the question of increased efficiency of workmen is always paramount in the minds of staff members of the Urban League when workers in various occupations are organized." Carpenters and other craftsmen were placed in jobs through the existing Mechanics Association, and efforts were made to organize the lower East and West Side longshoremen into an efficiency organization.[39] Only in the case of theater orchestras was membership sought for workers in regular labor unions.[40]

Placement work was a natural outgrowth of the League's campaign to open new job opportunities. By 1913, a Vocational Exchange had been opened. This office was not supposed to engage in direct placement. It was to be a "clearing house" from which applicants were sent to commercial or free employment agencies.[41] The organization denied any intention of usurping the placement function of existing agencies, maintaining that its role was "of a larger and more fundamental scope," the opening of new positions.[42] In spite of such pronouncements, the League did not long forgo the advantages in publicity and support to be derived from direct contact with employers and workers. By the end of 1916, announcements were being made of placements in the tobacco fields of Connecticut, pump works in Massachusetts, and industrial plants in New York.[43] In fact, on the eve of World War I, the League, which had earlier expressed opposition to migration, became through its industrial activities an agent of migration.[44]

Two other features, vocational guidance and the training of workers, which were to become important parts of the industrial program had their beginning in the prewar period. At that time such work was conducted on a very limited scale. The main con-

---

[39] *Bulletin,* III, No. 2 (Nov., 1913), 12-13.
[40] *Bulletin,* V, No. 1 (Nov., 1915), 13.
[41] *Bulletin,* III, No. 2 (Nov., 1913), 13.
[42] *Bulletin,* III, No. 7 (Feb., 1914).
[43] *Bulletin,* VI, No. 4 (Nov., 1916), 10, 14-15.
[44] See Francis D. Tyson, "The Negro Migrant," in U.S. Department of Labor, Division of Negro Economics, *Negro Migration in 1916-17* (Washington: Government Printing Office, 1919), p. 121.

tribution of the League was the publicity it gave to opportunities for training in public night schools. In one instance, a financial contribution was made to aid in purchasing supplies for such a school.[45] The widespread unemployment in New York during the winter of 1914 provided an opportunity for more direct work in training workers. The Mayor's Committee on Unemployment provided $8,340, with which the League conducted a workshop for the unemployed.[46] Men prepared bandages and surgical dressings, and a limited number of women were given a course in "household arts" and paid a small wage while in training.[47]

The League gained in several ways through its service to the city. The stature of the organization was raised through demonstrated usefulness. Also, publicity in the form of news articles and editorial endorsements was given that would otherwise have been difficult to obtain. Above all, public funds were available to the League for supporting types of work to which the organization was already committed.

As in other areas, the League's work in housing was conducted along a peculiarly social work line. Rather than attack the great barriers that relegated the Negro to the ghettos of Harlem and other separate communities, the League's program was designed to make living conditions better within the framework of the existing pattern. A policy of selection was advocated whereby "reputable and disreputable persons" would be segregated in different tenement houses and neighborhoods. A list of houses "certified by investigation as being tenanted by respectable people and being physically clean and wholesome" was compiled to aid selected tenants in finding homes. The Negro was urged to develop a "moral consciousness" and insist on good management of housing units. To help the tenant do his share, a program of education was instituted to foster sanitation, proper upkeep, and knowledge of city services and regulations. In some cases, the eviction of families with questionable morals was urged.[48] Of a more far-reaching nature was the effort to get real-estate interests to cooperate in the construction of houses suitable to the economic status of the Negro community. In such projects, the quantitative data in reports on surveys and investiga-

[45] *Bulletin,* III, No. 2 (Nov., 1913), 13.

[46] *New York Evening Post,* Dec. 28, 1915, from reprint in *Bulletin,* V, No. 6 (Apr., 1916).

[47] *Bulletin,* V, No. 1 (Nov., 1915), 16.

[48] *Bulletin,* III, No. 2 (Nov., 1913), 16-17.

tions were used to show evidence of need and the possibility of profits.[49]

Traveler's aid was perhaps the best organized function inherited by the League. The National League for the Protection of Colored Women had maintained workers at various centers to assist the traveling woman. The National Urban League continued this service and extended it to include men. Finally in 1915, the Traveler's Aid Society hired a Negro woman and assumed responsibility for this service in New York.[50]

A large number of activities which can be classed generally under the heading of welfare work were undertaken for the uplift of the New York Negro. Both juvenile and adult delinquency received special attention through corrective and preventive program activities. Up to 1915, probation supervision for offenders before the Court of General Session was furnished.[51] The greatest emphasis was placed on prevention and correction of delinquent behavior among juveniles. Big Brother and Big Sister work, designed to provide wholesome adult supervision for boys and girls who had become involved with the law, was an early feature of this program. Special bulletins were distributed describing these activities and soliciting volunteers to serve as Big Brothers and Big Sisters.[52]

Efforts to provide opportunities for recreation played a leading role in the campaign to prevent juvenile delinquency. As early as 1911, the League was urging the establishment of more play areas in Harlem. In that year, the organization conducted an experimental playground. When in 1915 the city erected two playgrounds in the Negro community, the League felt that its work was achieving some results.[53] Boys' and girls' clubs also furnished opportunities for recreation. In addition to regular social clubs, the boys of Harlem were organized into a Juvenile Park Protective League to spy out infractions of city ordinances, such as building violations. It was hoped that such activity would ease gang tension between Negro and white youth by involving Negro boys in community policing efforts.[54]

Fresh air work was another feature of the League's juvenile pro-

[49] *Bulletin,* V, No. 1 (Nov., 1915), 20; *Bulletin,* VI, No. 4 (Nov., 1916), 12.
[50] *Bulletin,* V, No. 1 (Nov., 1915), 16.
[51] *Bulletin,* III, No. 2 (Nov., 1913), 14; *Bulletin,* V, No. 1 (Nov., 1915), 17.
[52] See *Bulletin,* III, No. 3 (Nov., 1913); *Bulletin,* III, No. 8 (Mar., 1914).
[53] *Bulletin,* V, No. 1 (Nov., 1915), 22.
[54] *Ibid.,* pp. 17-18; *Bulletin,* VI, No. 4 (Nov., 1916), 11.

gram. Each summer about 150 boys between twelve and sixteen years of age were given a two-week outing at a camp in Verona, New Jersey. The site was provided free by two Negro real-estate men and contributions were sought to cover other expenses. League involvement in such a pursuit was explained by pointing to the refusal of other agencies to accept these boys throughout the summer.[55] By 1918, camp operations had been abandoned, but the League still engaged in other types of fresh air work.[56] War conditions brought a de-emphasis on welfare activities of this type and more concern for employment and war-related work.

Health improvement did not become a formal part of the program until around 1915. In March of that year cooperation with the National Negro Business League was started in sponsoring National Negro Health Week. The League workers conducted what was labeled a model campaign. They distributed literature, held mass meetings, and delivered health addresses in churches and Sunday schools.[57] In July of the same year, the League started the experiment of operating a convalescent home. The Burke Foundation, which specialized in such grants, provided the funds, and on July 9, 1915, a home was opened in White Plains, New York, to care for Negro women.[58] The following year a more spacious building was obtained and provisions made for men.[59]

From the great variety of activities carried on in New York, the League staff gained valuable experience in the selection of projects, techniques for their execution, and methods of gaining support. In comparison with New York, the national program during this period seemed rather limited. However, the national work was fully as important as the local activities to the future development of the organization. The League's efforts in the training of social workers and its dedication to the principle of expansion played a leading role in the evolution of the organization from a local agency to a national movement.

Three methods were used to implement the training of social workers. The League cooperated with Fisk University in providing

---

[55] *Bulletin,* V, No. 7 (June, 1916); *Bulletin,* III, No. 2 (Nov., 1913), 17; *Bulletin,* V, No. 1 (Nov., 1915), 22.

[56] *Bulletin,* VI, No. 4 (Nov., 1916), 12; *Bulletin,* VIII, No. 1 (Jan., 1919), 20.

[57] *Bulletin,* V, No. 1 (Nov., 1915), 8, 23-24.

[58] *Bulletin,* V, No. 3 (Dec., 1915).

[59] *Bulletin,* VI, No. 3 (Oct., 1916).

training through its new department of social sciences. In addition, scholarships were offered to undergraduates at selected Negro colleges, and fellowships were awarded for graduate study in New York.

The training course in Nashville started on a modest scale. In 1912-13, this program consisted of "courses in Economics, Sociology, Negro History and Social Investigation and . . . lectures by experts in Social Work from various cities."[60] League funds made possible the "experts in Social Work," and the courses listed were probably the school's regular offering in social sciences.[61]

The following year, 1913-14, provision was made for field work and plans made for a special course in social service training. Seniors in sociology were given field work through a settlement, Bethlehem House, established by the Woman's Missionary Council of the Methodist Episcopal Church, South, in cooperation with the University.[62] By 1915, the training course had been divorced from the regular social science courses and was designed specifically for the training of social and religious workers.[63]

The social service training course was "to give thorough, theoretical and practical training for those who wish to prepare for service as probation officers, settlement workers, kindergarten directors, executive secretaries of civic betterment organizations, institutional church workers, church and charity visiting, home and foreign missionaries."[64] Seven subjects in religion, sociology, statistics, "Negro Problem," domestic science, and manual arts comprised the curriculum. This program was designed principally as a graduate course; however, students who had finished high school could gain admission to some subjects and Fisk students could take the training course concurrently with their college work.[65] Students who received direct financial aid as League "fellows" had to "have completed a course in a college of good standing or its equivalent." In addition, candidates for fellowships were screened by examination.[66]

Through contacts with other Negro colleges, the League supple-

---

[60] *Bulletin,* III, No. 2 (Nov., 1913), 10-11.
[61] *Ibid.,* p. 24.
[62] *Fisk University News,* V (July, 1914), 5-6; *Bulletin,* VI, No. 4 (Nov., 1916), 20-21.
[63] *Bulletin,* V, No. 1 (Nov., 1915), 12.
[64] *Fisk University News,* V (July, 1914), 6.
[65] *Ibid.*
[66] *Bulletin,* VI, No. 2 (Oct., 1916).

mented the efforts being made at Fisk to train social workers in the South. Students in these institutions were encouraged to study sociology and economics and to consider social work as a career.[67] In 1914, the League held a scholarship contest open to students at Howard and Virginia Union Universities and Talladega, Morehouse, and Paine Colleges. Examinations were given to contestants in either economics or sociology. However, entries came from only three of the eligible institutions. This lack of enthusiasm prompted the League to discontinue the contest and use the funds in sponsoring lectures at Negro colleges. It was felt that "an expenditure in this direction promised better results."[68] Summer schools at colleges and meetings of ministers and teachers were used as mediums for lectures on migration and the problems of Negroes in cities.[69] This educational work in the South had immediate value in providing publicity for the organization, but the dividend in trained social workers came in later years. In 1915, only one graduate of Fisk had completed the full course for social workers.[70]

The fellowships offered for study in New York produced more immediate results. Starting in 1911, living expenses were provided for two students a year to study at the New York School of Philanthropy. Candidates for these awards had to satisfy the League that they were definitely committed to careers in social work. These fellows assured the League of having at least two workers to assist the New York staff. The "practical experience" to supplement their academic work was usually received through the League.[71]

After completing their training, many of the League fellows took positions in the national office or were available to staff the local affiliates as they were organized. Others took positions in schools or other agencies throughout the country where they became potential sources of influence and support for the movement. The League could list six fellows in 1915 who had completed their year of study in New York. One of the six was engaged in further study, and five had accepted employment, generally as teachers. However, they all maintained some connection with social work, either on part-time jobs or as volunteers. William N. Colson, a teacher at Virginia Union University, was director of the National Urban League affil-

[67] *Bulletin,* III, No. 2 (Nov., 1913), 10-11.
[68] *Bulletin,* III, No. 6 (Jan., 1914); *Bulletin,* V, No. 1 (Nov., 1915), 10.
[69] *Bulletin,* V, No. 1 (Nov., 1915), 8-9.
[70] *Ibid.,* p. 12.
[71] *Bulletin,* III, No. 6 (Jan., 1914); *Bulletin,* VI, No. 2 (Oct., 1916).

iate in Richmond, Virginia.[72] The first fellowship recipient, James H. Hubert, later entered the Urban League movement and served as Executive Secretary of the New York Urban League.[73]

In later years, the training of League fellows was undertaken by other schools. Eugene Kinckle Jones reported in 1925 that students with League grants were studying at the University of Chicago, the University of Pittsburgh, the Pennsylvania School of Social and Health Work, and Simmons College. The New York School of Social Work (formerly the New York School of Philanthropy) was still taking its quota of appointees.[74] Financial support for this part of the program also increased. Foundations, fraternal organizations, bequests, local League branches, and other agencies provided funds to promote the training of social workers.[75]

The *Fortieth Anniversary Yearbook* boasted of an expenditure of $100,000 on the fellowship program during the preceding forty years. In that period 118 fellows received training. By 1950, fellows occupied positions on all levels in the Urban League movement, and the League could point to a college president and directors of schools of social work as fellows who had made exceptional contributions.[76]

Also of fundamental importance was the League's dedication to national expansion. There were at least three avenues open through which the League could extend its work into other cities. Several branches were inherited from the National League for the Protection of Colored Women. But, in most instances, these consisted of little more than a travel agent working at steamship docks or railroad terminals. Yet, contacts could be made through them for the institution of a broader program. Several cities already had organizations that conformed to the League's social work philosophy. These only needed to be shown the advantages of national affiliation and incorporated as League branches. Where no organization existed that could be used as the beginning of a League branch, contacts could be made through members of the National Board, who

---

[72] *Bulletin,* V, No. 1 (Nov., 1915), 10.

[73] *Bulletin,* VI, No. 4 (Nov., 1916), 8; "Secretariat," *Opportunity: A Journal of Negro Life,* VI (Mar., 1928), 88.

[74] Eugene Kinckle Jones, "The National Urban League," *Opportunity,* III (Jan., 1925), 14.

[75] Eugene Kinckle Jones, "Progress: The Eighteenth Annual Report of the Activities of the National Urban League," *Opportunity,* VII (Apr., 1929), 117; *Fortieth Anniversary Yearbook,* p. 32.

[76] *Fortieth Anniversary Yearbook,* pp. 32-33.

represented most of the principal cities, and friends of the League in organized cities.

In spite of its progress in program development, the League had only meager success in the establishment of branches prior to World War I. The annual report for 1913 listed only four affiliated cities, excluding New York. None of the affiliates engaged in program activities remotely comparable to the work being developed in New York. The Philadelphia affiliate was the League for the Protection of Colored Women, which limited its work primarily to traveler's aid and reformative assistance to women.[77] In St. Louis, the Committee for Social Service Among Colored People had a rather varied program but lacked formal organization and professional workers. Richmond, Virginia had a new organization in 1913, and the Norfolk work consisted of two traveler's aid agents, who were partially supported by the National League. Of these affiliates, only St. Louis and Philadelphia were still functioning in 1919.[78]

The mortality rate remained high among affiliates organized during the prewar years. There were twelve affiliated cities in 1916, but only six of these were still in affiliation in 1919. Lack of personnel and financial resources, as well as the types of organizations and their geographical location, partially account for the ephemeral nature of the League's early expansion efforts. The organization placed the blame primarily on the first set of circumstances. The annual report for 1912-13 stated: "The work of starting local organizations which will do creditable work has not been rushed, first because care was needed to avoid mushroom attempts, and second, because the National League has not yet had funds sufficient to supervise adequately such branch organizations and make sure that good work would be done."[79]

At the time that the League was organized, few people thought that the northward movement of Negroes would reach overwhelming proportions. The census of 1910 showed that 84 per cent of the Negro population still lived in the South. True there was a trend toward urbanization, but it appeared that the Negro might make

[77] A more balanced League program was conducted in Philadelphia when the Armstrong Association became an affiliate around 1915. This organization dated from the 1905-06 period. Its emphasis was on bettering industrial conditions.

[78] The interruption in Richmond was temporary, but Norfolk never developed an active branch.

[79] *Bulletin,* III, No. 2 (Nov., 1913), 9-10.

his home in southern cities. Of the forty-three cities having 10,000 or more Negroes in 1910, thirty-three were in the South. Three northern cities — Philadelphia, New York, and Chicago — were the destinations of most nonwhite migrants.[80]

Under these circumstances, it is not surprising that the National Urban League looked to the South as a possible area of expansion. Many of the early affiliates were in the South. Savannah, Augusta, and Atlanta in Georgia; Birmingham in Alabama; Memphis, Nashville, and Chattanooga in Tennessee — these and other southern cities contained large numbers of Negroes comprising a high percentage of the total population.

Yet, even the League's "conservative" social work approach was incompatible with southern views on the race question. The principle of interracial cooperation was basic to Urban League organizational structure, but in most southern cities it was virtually impossible to set up boards of whites and Negroes. In addition, these cities were not ready to meet even the mild social service demands made by League branches. Southern affiliates were limited in their choice of program areas, the composition of their boards, and their financial potential. Many of the prewar branches in the South were probably all-Negro–controlled organizations conducting primarily recreational and settlement type projects.

Nine of the fourteen affiliated cities listed by the League in 1916 were in southern or border states. Many of these branches had very hectic and checkered histories between 1916 and 1950 or went out of existence long before the latter year. The border cities of St. Louis and Louisville maintained continuous League connections. St. Louis, in particular, developed a very active and progressive League branch. The situation was different in states of the deep South. Only Atlanta and Memphis were listed as League cities in both 1916 and 1950. Memphis had difficulty in surviving,[81] while the so-called "Atlanta Plan" helped the League in that city to avoid the fate of other southern branches. The Atlanta League was run by two boards, one Negro and the other white. These groups met separately three weeks out of each month and held one monthly

---

[80] United States Department of Commerce, Bureau of the Census, *Negro Population 1790-1915* (Washington: Government Printing Office, 1918), pp. 87-107.

[81] *Fortieth Anniversary Yearbook*, p. 89; *Fiftieth Anniversary Yearbook*, p. 34.

joint meeting.[82] Affiliates in Nashville, Savannah, Augusta, Richmond, and Huntsville suffered periods of inactivity or went out of existence altogether. In contrast, only one of the five northern affiliates listed in 1916 ceased functioning.[83]

When war conditions brought a disposition in the South toward moderating racial policies, the National Urban League was committed to serving the urban North. The increased tempo of the Negro migration after 1915 caused concern in the South for its labor supply. The continuing flight of southern labor resources to the cities of the North exerted enough pressure to bring promises of some change in the conditions of Negro life. However, the seemingly inexhaustible demand for labor that accompanied the period of mobilization and war assured the Negro of an opportunity for employment in northern industry. With the choice between arbitrating racial matters in the South and taking advantage of the more promising opportunities for service presented in the North, the Urban League turned its attention to the greater potential offered in the northern city.

A list of new Urban League branches founded between 1915 and 1919 reads like a roll call of America's industrial centers of that period. Chicago, Pittsburgh, Columbus (Ohio), Detroit, Cleveland, Newark, and Milwaukee entered the ranks of Urban League cities during this period. Employers in these cities were offering every inducement to attract Negro workers from the South, but the increasing concentration of rural nonwhite migrants intensified problems in both race relations and industrial relations. The Urban League was expected to help fill labor requirements and facilitate the integration of nonwhites into the industrial labor force. This brought added emphasis on the industrial program and placement activities. On the other hand, the League branch took a leading role in orienting the new migrant to urban life. The historical development of one Urban League, that in Chicago, typifies the problems, challenges, successes, and failures encountered by the Urban League movement in these northern cities.

---

[82] *Bulletin,* IX, No. 1 (Jan., 1920), 6.

[83] Indianapolis, Indiana was listed as an affiliated city in 1916 but was not listed after 1918.

2

THE FOUNDING YEARS, 1915-18

Four years after the founding of the National Urban League, efforts began to extend the organization's work into Chicago. This was an important step in the League's program of national expansion. For Chicago, the nation's second city in total population, could provide a base of operations for expansion into the Middle West and parts of the West. A successful branch in Chicago would be a model for branches in this region, just as the New York branch was for the East. Like New York, Chicago had a growing Negro population circumscribed in choice of occupation, snubbed by organized labor, and relegated to housing in the most undesirable sections of the city.

Yet, in the years 1914 to 1918 Chicago conditions were in a state of flux. The war in Europe stopped the flow of immigrant labor, which had previously filled the jobs in plants and factories. In addition, many immigrants returned to their homelands during the war, creating a labor shortage in the North at the time that industry began expanding to meet the increased demands of wartime. This labor shortage brought a flood of Negro migrants from the South into Chicago, resulting in new and intensified problems in race relations and in industrial relations. On the other hand, Chicago rivaled New York in the dedication and aggressiveness of its confraternity of social workers and municipal reformers. There were also philanthropist and industrial groups, who formed potential sources of support. These conditions gave League officials reason to assume that their program would be well received. They had only to convince those who could provide moral and financial support that a League branch could make a definite contribution to the adjustment of racial problems.

The preliminary steps taken to mobilize support for a Chicago Urban League were characteristic of the personal methods which dominated early procedures in the Urban League. In the beginning there was no attempt to enlist a large public following. Attention was given to gaining the confidence and support of key individuals, those who exercised leadership roles in groups that could help in program activities or in meeting financial needs. In fact, the direction and control of the League remained in the hands of this select group. They became the board of directors and formulated the policies and goals of the branch. This is not to say that the League made no bid for public favor. On the contrary, the Urban League movement has always been concerned about its public image. Through a continuing public relations campaign, the movement tried to gain public acceptance. To a large extent, its program depended upon volunteer workers; and while it was more convenient to have large donors, a fair percentage of the budget came through small contributions. However, the first step was to "sell" the Urban League ideal to people of influence, who could in turn enlist others for the cause.

Eugene Kinckle Jones, the associate director of the National Urban League, and L. Hollingsworth Wood, the national president, took the initiative in preliminary contact work. In November, 1915, Jones visited Chicago in the interest of the League's work. The *Chicago Defender* announced that he was coming "to make inquiries into the social work being done in this city and to determine whether there is a place in this community for such activities as this organization fosters."[1] During this visit, Jones met with a small group of white and Negro leaders at the City Club to acquaint them with the purposes and program of the Urban League. Other meetings were held throughout 1916. In these meetings the applicability of the League's work to Chicago conditions was discussed and a nucleus of supporters recruited. Jones and Wood made several trips to Chicago during 1916 to address meetings of interested individuals, to make personal contacts, and to prepare the way for a preliminary organization.[2]

---

[1] *Chicago Defender,* Oct. 30, 1915.

[2] *Ibid.,* Jan. 15, 1916; Feb. 9, 1918; Chicago League on Urban Conditions Among Negroes [Chicago Urban League], *First Annual Report, 1916-17*

Through these efforts, a number of individuals were motivated to work for the establishment of a Chicago Urban League. From the beginning, there was at least one advocate of the movement in the city. Sophonisba P. Breckinridge, a member of the faculties of the University of Chicago and the Chicago School of Civics and Philanthropy, had been a member of the National Urban League's Board of Directors for several years. Miss Breckinridge was quite active in social work and reform activities; and as dean of the School of Civics and Philanthropy,[3] she was well known in social work and reform circles. She and her co-worker at the University of Chicago and the School of Civics, Edith Abbott, attended the discussion groups and probably played a leading role in arranging for some of these meetings.[4] The majority of white participants in the 1916-17 period came from the ranks of the social workers and their friends. Among them were Amelia Sears, at that time Superintendent of the Juvenile Protective Association, and Celia Parker Woolley, the founder of the Frederick Douglass Center. Mrs. Woolley, a retired Unitarian minister, spent the last fourteen years of her life "in uplift work among the Negroes" on Chicago's South Side.[5] Other white supporters included Judge Edward Osgood Brown — who was active in the single tax movement and president of the Chicago Branch of the N.A.A.C.P.[6] — and Julian Mack — a judge on the United States Circuit Court, an active participant in Jewish welfare movements, and a confirmed Zionist.[7] Robert E. Park, professor of sociology at the University of Chicago, and Horace Bridges, leader of the Chicago Ethical Culture Society, were respectively the first and second presidents of the Chicago Urban League.

Advocates of a Chicago League had a dual function to perform

(Chicago: Chicago Urban League, 1917), p. 6. These reports will be cited hereafter by number and years covered in the report as *Annual Report*. Each report covered the work done during a fiscal year running from November 1 to October 31.

[3] The Chicago School of Civics and Philanthropy later became the University of Chicago School of Social Service Administration.

[4] Interview, Chicago, July 13, 1961. The names of persons interviewed will not be cited in footnotes. Some persons consented to interviews under the condition that they not be identified with opinions expressed or information revealed. Records of these interviews are in the files of the author, and all interviewees are listed in the bibliography.

[5] Obituary, *Broad Ax* (Chicago), Mar. 16, 1918.

[6] *Ibid.*, Apr. 3, 1915.

[7] M. R. Werner, *Julius Rosenwald: The Life of a Practical Humanitarian* (New York: Harper and Brothers Publishers, 1939), pp. 90-91.

when meeting with the leaders of Negro organizations. The League would need a certain amount of cooperation from these leaders and their organizations in recruiting volunteers and in fund raising. At the same time, there was a certain reticence among Negro leaders about helping to build up a new agency that might take over the program of their own institutions or compete with them for influence and philanthropic support. These personal fears had to be assuaged or at least held in abeyance to forestall active opposition.[8]

The affable and socially ambitious physician and Surgeon-in-Chief of Provident Hospital, George Cleveland Hall, was one of the first Negro leaders to actively support the establishment of a League in Chicago. As a reward for his efforts, he joined Miss Breckinridge as the second Chicago member on the national board of directors. Hall took an active part in almost every conceivable type of Negro betterment activity, except the N.A.A.C.P., and he was even listed as a member of this organization. He had been friendly with Booker T. Washington and used this relationship to good personal advantage. His connection with Washington brought him the backing of Julius Rosenwald and other Chicago supporters of Tuskegee Institute.[9] No matter what motives — status seeking, a sincere interest in racial advancement, or both — actuated Hall's Urban League work, he was a definite asset in the founding of the Chicago Urban League.

Robert S. Abbott, editor of the *Chicago Defender,* also gave early and continuing support to the movement. He opened both his news columns and his editorial page to Urban League publicity. On the occasion of Jones's second visit, in January, 1916, Abbott ran an editorial endorsing the League and urging unity among Negroes to facilitate the development of a Chicago branch.[10]

Other Negro founders and adherents were less well known outside

---

[8] Interview, Chicago, July 13, 1961.

[9] See *Who's Who in Colored America, 1928-1929: A Biographical Dictionary of Notable Living Persons of African Descent in America,* ed. Joseph J. Boris (New York: Who's Who in Colored America Corp., 1929). Dr. Hall's connection with Booker T. Washington and his use of these connections were discussed by Helen Buckler in *Doctor Dan: Pioneer in American Surgery* (Boston: Little, Brown and Company, 1954), pp. 236-243, 245-258, *et passim.* An interviewee related how he had witnessed Hall in action during the selection of Booker T. Washington's successor at Tuskegee. Hall helped to swing Chicago support, especially that of Julius Rosenwald, away from the obvious choice, Emmett Scott, to Robert R. Moton, who was finally selected.

[10] *Chicago Defender,* Jan. 15, 1916.

of Chicago at that time. With the possible exception of Albert B. George, an attorney who became Chicago's first Negro municipal judge, they were approached primarily because of their organizational connections. The Young Men's Christian Association was represented by Alexander L. Jackson, executive secretary of the Wabash Avenue Branch and friend of Dr. Hall. Joanna Snowden-Porter, Elizabeth Lindsey Davis, and Jessie Johnson provided representation from the Negro women's clubs, while Bertha Mosely, who was "prominent in circles of young people," spoke for this group. Through meetings at the Abraham Lincoln Center, the Frederick Douglass Center, the Y.M.C.A., and other South Side locations, every effort was made to reach the key individuals in Negro organizations.[11]

In spite of Abbott's admonitions in the *Chicago Defender* and the work of Jones and Wood, it took twelve months of preparation before a sufficient number could "get together on the proposition" to set up an organization. Later in the year, another Negro publication joined in supporting the Urban League and urged immediate action in organizing a Chicago branch. This appeal declared:

> The city of Chicago, with its fifty thousand colored people lacks one essential sign of progress. It has no active branch of the National League on Urban Conditions Among Negroes.
>
> We are certain that there is need for fresh air funds, rest homes, big brother and big sister movements and other benefits derived from an Urban League. We appeal to both the citizens of Chicago and the directors of the national organizations.
>
> You know the necessity for such. Then why the delay?[12]

Finally, on December 11, 1916, a group met with Eugene Kinckle Jones and T. Arnold Hill, the national organizer, at the Wabash Avenue Y.M.C.A. to start the process of organization. Those present were: A. Kenyon Maynard, resident at Chicago Commons and a member of the faculty of the Chicago School of Civics; Mrs. Alice J. Caldwell, Charity Section, City Federation; R. L. Hazlett, Chicago Boy Scouts of America; C. C. Haradon, Stock Yards District, Chicago Boy Scouts of America; Miss Clotte E. Scott, Berean Center; Miss Jennie E. Lawrence, Superintendent, Phyllis Wheatley Home; Mrs. Joanna Snowden-Porter, Chicago Federation of

[11] Interview, Chicago, July 13, 1961.

[12] *The Champion Magazine* (Dec., 1916), p. 171, clipping in the Julius Rosenwald Papers, University of Chicago Library. Cited hereafter as Rosenwald papers.

Colored Women's Clubs; Mrs. J. O. Lee; Mrs. Francelia Colby, Civic Woman's City Club; Arthur A. Gould, Juvenile Protective Association; Mrs. June Purcett-Gould; Mrs. William Carry, Baptist Women's Congress of Chicago; Mrs. Georgetta Ashburn, Evanston; Mrs. Irene Goins; Mrs. Katherine M. Briggs, United Charities; Miss Ella M. Bland; Alexander L. Jackson, executive secretary, Wabash Avenue Y.M.C.A.; and George Cleveland Hall, presiding.[13]

At this meeting Jones discussed the work of the National Urban League and "suggested that a permanent organization be affected at once." He had brought T. Arnold Hill to Chicago to guide the new organization through the first few months of its formation. Hill was to help raise the necessary funds for the first year's budget and outline a program. Although most of the principal supporters were absent, this session is considered the organizational meeting.[14] However, the details of organization were left to subsequent meetings.

Another general session and the first meeting of the executive board were held at the Wabash Avenue Y.M.C.A. on January 10, 1917. Hall acted as temporary chairman during the meeting of the executive board, and T. Arnold Hill was acting secretary. Hill announced that thirteen of the fifteen board members provided for in the constitution had been elected.[15] Lasting only thirty minutes, this first official meeting was mainly informational in nature. Sections of the constitution were read for the instruction of the board and the proposed plan of work was reviewed. In addition, the budget for the first year was read "for the information of the Board."[16]

The most important task facing the new organization was raising the funds required to get the program under way. The degree of success achieved in raising $3,000, the amount needed for the first year's operations, would give some indication as to how well the League was being received in Chicago. It was necessary, therefore,

---

[13] Minutes of the National League on Urban Conditions Among Negroes, Dec. 11, 1916, cited in Dorothy Counse, Louise Gilbert, and Agnes Van Driel, "The Chicago Urban League," June 18, 1936 (unpublished study in the files of the Welfare Council of Metropolitan Chicago), pp. 2-3.

[14] *Ibid.*

[15] Julian W. Mack to William C. Graves, Jan. 27, 1917, Rosenwald Papers; Minutes of the First Meeting of the Executive Board of the Chicago League on Urban Conditions Among Negroes, Jan. 10 [1917], copy in Rosenwald Papers.

[16] *Ibid.*

to broaden the base of moral support for the organization as a prerequisite for obtaining financial support. T. Arnold Hill was a fortunate choice for the job of guiding the Chicago Urban League during this formative stage. When he first came to Chicago in December, 1916, it was intended by the National Urban League that he stay only one month.[17] It was decided later that three months would be needed "to obtain assurances of financial support." Consequently, Hill's stay was to be extended two months,[18] but the allotted three months stretched into a tenure of eight years. Before coming to Chicago, Hill had been on the National Urban League staff almost two years. Like Eugene Kinckle Jones, he was a native of Richmond, Virginia, where both men attended Wayland Academy and Virginia Union University, though not during the same years.

Well suited by personality and dedication for his Chicago assignment, Hill followed the person-to-person approach to good advantage in building the new branch. Soon after his arrival, he went to the office of Horace J. Bridges, leader of the Chicago Ethical Culture Society, with a letter of introduction from Felix Adler of New York, a member of the National Urban League Board and founder of the Ethical Culture Society. In later years, Bridges recalled that he was impressed by Hill "and the social ideal he so ably expounded." Bridges characterized Hill as "one of the most capable, indefatigable, and efficient executive personalities" he had ever met.[19]

Hill used the people who had become committed to the League idea during the November, 1915 to December, 1916 period to reach other individuals. George C. Hall and Alexander L. Jackson were his chief Negro contacts. They were probably responsible for his introduction to C. Wilbur Messer, general secretary of the Y.M.C.A. of Chicago. Messer sent Hill a letter of endorsement, which he in

---

[17] Minutes of the National League on Urban Conditions Among Negroes, Dec. 11, 1916, in Counce, Gilbert, and Van Driel, "The Chicago Urban League," p. 3.

[18] *First Annual Report, 1916-17,* p. 6.

[19] Horace J. Bridges, "The First Urban League Family," in Chicago Urban League, *Two Decades of Service* (Chicago: Chicago Urban League, 1936), pages not numbered. Bridges' memory failed in respect to many of the details of the founding period. His chronology was inaccurate on Hill's visit to his office, which he placed "late in 1915." Hill did not come to Chicago until December, 1916.

turn used in approaching others.[20] Edward Osgood Brown provided him with a letter of introduction to Charles G. Dawes — who was president of the Central Trust Company but later more noted for the "Dawes Plan" for reparations settlement and who in 1924 became Vice President of the United States. Brown said that his letter was to help Hill to get "to know and advise with representative men in Chicago whom he thinks would be interested in the conditions which confronted his people."[21] After Hill had advised with him, Dawes was persuaded to make a fifty-dollar contribution to the League's work. In addition, Hill discussed his plans with Arthur J. Francis of the Chicago Community Trust, James G. K. McClure, president of McCormick Theological Seminary, Mrs. Louise deKoven Bowen of the Juvenile Protective Association, and others who were "in touch with social problems." "All of whom," Hill said, "expressed favorable opinions of our program of work and methods of administration, and felt that Chicago offered a field for practical work along our line."[22] A most fortunate conversion to the Urban League cause was that of William C. Graves, the confidential secretary to Julius Rosenwald.

It was Rosenwald's financial assistance that enabled the Chicago Urban League to meet its obligations during the first year. Soon after the first board meeting, Hill wrote Rosenwald, through Graves, requesting financial support. The letter contained a detailed recital of the progress made up to that time in perfecting organizational structure and in obtaining financial support. Documentary evidence was included in the form of minutes, letters of endorsement, lists of pledges and contributions, and clippings from newspapers and magazines. After several pages of explanation, the purpose of the letter was stated. Rosenwald was asked to contribute $1,000, which constituted a third of the budget for the first year. Before making his decision, Rosenwald had Graves write letters to Julian W. Mack, George C. Hall, A. K. Maynard, Miss S. P. Breckinridge, Horace J. Bridges, Robert E. Park, and Miss Amelia Sears inquiring as to their future intentions as members of the Urban League Board. Each of these individuals was informed that Rosenwald "is inclined, because of your apparent connection with this movement and the connec-

[20] C. Wilbur Messer to T. Arnold Hill, Jan. 5, 1917, copy in Rosenwald Papers.

[21] Edward Osgood Brown to (Charles G.) Dawes, Dec. 14, 1916, copy in Rosenwald Papers.

[22] Hill to Julius Rosenwald, Jan. 19, 1917, Rosenwald Papers.

tion of others in whom he also has special confidence, to contribute $1,000 a year toward the proposed budget, but before reaching a final decision he would like to know whether he is correct in assuming that you really are interested and that your interest is one that can be relied upon as abiding in an effort to make the proposed work successful."[23] Meanwhile, Graves and Hill conferred on the situation in person and by telephone.

Apparently, the majority of the replies were satisfactory. Only Judge Mack stated his reservations in writing. While expressing interest in the League and a belief that the "people on the board will work," Mack felt that the possibility that he would soon leave Chicago made it impossible for him to "accept the moral responsibility" that Graves's letter "would seem to impose."[24] On February 24, Graves was able to inform Hill and the favorably responding board members "that Mr. Rosenwald will take great pleasure in contributing $1,000 toward the first year's budget . . . provided said budget in the total sum of $3,000 is underwritten by responsible subscribers."[25] The condition attached to this pledge created a problem for the organization. There was an immediate need for funds, and there was little likelihood that $2,000 in subscriptions would be received in the near future. In fact, at the time Rosenwald's help was solicited, only $353 in "reliable pledges" had been made.[26]

Relief was received when Rosenwald amended his offer in April, 1917. Under the new terms, the League would not have to get its entire budget subscribed before receiving payments on the Rosenwald pledge. The amended offer provided for payments on the basis of contributions received by the League from other sources. Rosenwald would match the funds collected on the basis of one dollar for every two dollars received.[27] These receipts had to be substantiated by submitting a list of contributors with each request for matching funds.

The donations of white business and professional people accounted for the success of the first financial campaign. Substantial contri-

[23] Graves to selected members of the proposed board of the Chicago Urban League, Jan. 23, 1917, Rosenwald Papers.
[24] Mack to Graves, Jan. 27, 1917, Rosenwald Papers.
[25] Graves to Hill, Feb. 24, 1917, Rosenwald Papers.
[26] Contributions and Reliable Pledges Made to the Chicago League on Urban Conditions Among Negroes [Jan., 1917], Rosenwald Papers.
[27] Hill to Graves, Apr. 7, 1917; Graves to Hill, Apr. 10, 1917, Rosenwald Papers.

butions were received from the Manufacturers Association, the Chicago Community Trust, and the Pullman Company; and contributions ranging up to fifty dollars came from individuals. Of the $3,131.60 received in contributions and membership fees, $2,811.45 came from fifty-seven white members and friends. Moreover, the greater part of an additional $260 to help finance special projects — a study of Negro migration, operation of a settlement, and transportation funds for workers — was furnished by the Carnegie Peace Foundation and an industrial concern.[28]

In general, Negroes were not very generous in their financial support to the League's first budget. While constituting almost 75 per cent of the members and contributors, they gave only about 10 per cent of the money raised. Just $320.05 was contributed by 155 Negro individuals and groups. If the $100 contributed by the Baptist Women's Congress and several individual gifts above five dollars are deducted, the average donation was quite small.[29]

Although Hill worked diligently in trying to unite the diverse Negro organizations in support of the League, he had only partial success. There were a multiplicity of organizations in the Negro community professing "race betterment" as one of their purposes, but many of them neglected this purpose in pursuit of "the more immediate satisfaction of literary and social meetings." A number of these groups were adjuncts to churches and, therefore, narrow and denominational in outlook.[30] Others were social clubs whose members were quite conscious of their social positions or lack of it.

The divergence among Negro organizations is usually attributed to a difference in philosophical orientation. An effort is made to divide Negroes of this period into two groups — the followers of Booker T. Washington and the followers of William E. B. Du Bois. While white leaders could support both the National Association for the Advancement of Colored People (N.A.A.C.P.) and the Urban League, Negroes of some influence usually made a choice as to the group with which they preferred to be identified. Jane Addams was a member of the national board of directors of the N.A.A.C.P. and a supporter of the Urban League, and Edward O. Brown was

[28] *First Annual Report,* 1916-17, pp. 12-13.
[29] *Ibid.,* p. 12. Lists of contributors showing the amount each gave are in the Rosenwald Papers.
[30] See Junius B. Wood, "Colored Race Needs Better Conditions," *Chicago Daily News,* Dec. 27, 1916. The activities of Negro organizations were regularly reported in the *Chicago Defender.*

president of the Chicago branch of the N.A.A.C.P. and a founder of the Chicago Urban League. But in the case of Negro leaders, the goals of an organization often had to take second place to its public image in their determination as to whether or not to give it active support. This was often a question of self-interest. To advance in their chosen occupations many of these leaders needed the backing of influential whites. George C. Hall's identification with Booker T. Washington had helped him in his struggle for control of Provident Hospital and had gained for him the confidence of several influential white people in Chicago. The members of the Manufacturers Association, officials of the Chicago Community Trust, and businessmen like Rosenwald contributed more willingly to Negro groups led by what they considered "practical" men, such as Hall, than to causes espoused by an "idealist" like Charles E. Bentley, the Negro dentist who was active in the N.A.A.C.P. and an opponent of Hall.[31]

However, in his bid for Negro support, Hill had to contend less with philosophy than with personal ambitions and jealousies. Churches operated employment agencies and were contacted by those needing certain types of labor. This service to its members enhanced the reputation of a church. Many of the small settlements operated employment offices and received their main support through these activities. The settlements, churches, and many social clubs also engaged in civic and welfare activities. These services were used as the basis for their appeals for contributions. The Urban League, with its call for coordinated work and with its emphasis on improving industrial conditions, seemed to pose a threat to many of the existing agencies. Nevertheless, Hill approached the heads of Negro organizations to enlist their cooperation. During one week in January, 1917 he talked to the presidents of sixty clubs.[32] The *Chicago Defender* joined in this appeal for cooperation. In an editorial entitled "Getting Together," the editor urged the social clubs, churches, and other organizations to join with white friends of the Negro in raising funds for the League. The Appomattox Club, an

[31] *Chicago Daily News,* Dec. 27, 1916. Buckler (*Doctor Dan,* pp. 231-258) discussed the rivalry between the Bentley group and Hall's supporters at Provident Hospital. Bentley was, for a number of years, secretary of the Provident Hospital Board. This struggle and the broader implications of the Bentley-Hall conflict were related to this writer by an interviewee who had been a friend of Hall.

[32] Hill to Rosenwald, Jan. 19, 1917, Rosenwald Papers.

upper-class social club, was called upon to set an example in cooperation for other organizations.[33]

Women's groups made the most enthusiastic response to these appeals. The Baptist Women's Congress had a representative, Mrs. William Carry, at the organizational meeting and contributed $100, the largest single contribution from a Negro group. But, more important from a moral standpoint was the support given by the leaders of the Chicago Federation of Colored Women's Clubs. This was one of the first groups to endorse the League. Its leaders were active in the preliminary organizational work and were represented on the board of directors by Mrs. Jessie Johnson and Mrs. Joanna Snowden-Porter.[34] Younger club members went out soliciting League memberships. Mrs. Irene McCoy Gaines recalled that she turned in the first memberships obtained in the Negro community.[35] Funds obtained through these membership dues, however, constituted only a small fraction of the total income.

In spite of their enthusiastic support, the leaders of the women's clubs were not adverse to participating in a bit of internal dissension. Before it was decided that T. Arnold Hill would remain in Chicago as executive secretary, there seems to have been some difficulty in reaching agreement on who would fill the position. Mrs. Joanna Snowden-Porter tried unsuccessfully to get Graves and Rosenwald to influence the committee in its selection. Graves refused Mrs. Porter an interview and tactfully explained his position.

> Mr. Rosenwald and I have no official connection with the Chicago Branch of the National League on Urban Conditions Among Negroes now being organized. We, therefore, would not feel justified in trying to influence the Officers or Committee, or whoever has the responsibility of selecting an Executive Secretary, especially when we realize the delicacy and difficulty of the task before them of choosing one who has had sufficient experience in matters of this kind and is in other ways fitted for the particularly difficult task of creating an organization of many diverse elements and of bringing them into harmonious and helpful relations.[36]

Nevertheless, the threat of internal conflict at this early stage probably motivated the decision to leave Hill in Chicago. After this

[33] *Chicago Defender,* Feb. 10, 1917.
[34] *First Annual Report, 1916-17,* p. 2; Albon L. Foster, "Twenty Years of Interracial Goodwill Through Social Service," in *Two Decades of Service.*
[35] Interview with the author.
[36] Graves to Joanna Snowden-Porter, Feb. 9, 1917, Rosenwald Papers.

decision had been made, Graves wrote to Hill: "It is with great pleasure that I note you are to remain in Chicago."[37]

Early in 1917 the League was ready to establish an office and commence program operations. From December, 1916 to the end of February, 1917 Hill had carried on his activities from the Wabash Avenue Y.M.C.A., where he lived.[38] Then, on March 1, 1917, office space was rented at 3303 South State Street, and the executive secretary and a stenographer moved into these quarters.[39] By the end of the fiscal year, October 31, 1917, the staff had increased to five and the executive secretary contemplated a greatly enlarged budget.[40]

After eight months of program activities, the League was in a much better position for raising its budget for 1917-18 than it had been the first year. One of the first appeals again went to Julius Rosenwald. Hill informed Graves that the finance committee had decided to run the fiscal year from November 1 to October 31. Consequently, the organization would need funds to operate during the period October 31, 1917 to January 1, 1918. Since all contributions for the first year had been made after January 1, the organization did not want to approach these people again until after January 1, 1918. The committee, therefore, requested that Rosenwald contribute $1,000 immediately and pledge an additional gift equal to one-half of all money above $3,000 raised during the fiscal year.[41]

The second budget was more than twice as large as the first, but the increase was "only an apparent one." The first budget had been formulated on the basis of an estimated yearly expenditure of $4,700. However, the organization was in actual operation only eight months. This second budget of $6,749 had in reality only increased the estimated expenditure by $2,149.[42]

Graves conveyed Hill's request to Rosenwald and added a strong personal endorsement. "I am satisfied," Graves wrote, "that this organization is up and coming and doing a work of value to our community." He continued:

---

[37] Graves to Hill, Sept. 25, 1917, Rosenwald Papers.
[38] Interview, Chicago, July 13, 1961.
[39] *First Annual Report, 1916-17,* p. 6; *Chicago Defender,* Mar. 2, 1918.
[40] *First Annual Report, 1916-17,* p. 12.
[41] Hill to Graves, Nov. 1, 1917, Rosenwald Papers.
[42] *Ibid.*

It is bringing cooperation from scores of Negro civic and philanthropic organizations which have been working at cross purposes and with much jealousy. It has received the migrants from the South, has advised them, has helped them secure homes and has found work for them. It has been their constant friend and advisor. On the other hand, it has been of assistance to many employers whose forces have been reduced by employes volunteering and being drafted for military service. It has opened kinds of employment hitherto closed to Colored people.[43]

Graves climaxed his presentation by announcing that Jane Addams, in whom Rosenwald had great confidence, had agreed to become a director and that Graves himself was joining the board "to inform myself for you and because of my deep interest in these problems and my desire to do what I can to help." Still, Graves could not bring himself to recommend that Rosenwald comply with the League's request. He recommended instead a contribution equal to one-third of all money collected on a budget not to exceed $7,000, to be paid in pro rata installments.[44] Rosenwald, however, decided that he would give $250 for every $500 collected, with a limit of $3,000 to be paid in this manner.[45]

The success of this second fund drive surpassed expectations. A few individuals, including Victor F. Lawson of the *Chicago Daily News,* did not renew their gifts,[46] but new and increased contributions more than made up for these losses. In addition to increased individual contributions, more business concerns, such as the packing plants, made substantial donations. The number of Negro contributors increased, and at least one individual sponsored an "entertainment" for the benefit of the League. When the fiscal year ended, there were 498 members, and contributions totaled $7,324.50. Funds contributed for special purposes brought total income up to $8,419.10.[47]

In March, 1918, the League had the good fortune to obtain rent-free office space. Mrs. Celia Parker Woolley — founder, head resident, and guiding spirit of the Frederick Douglass Center — invited the League to move its headquarters into the Center, located at

[43] Memorandum from Graves to Rosenwald, Nov. 23, 1917, Rosenwald Papers.
[44] *Ibid.*
[45] *Ibid.,* autographic notation by Rosenwald; Graves to Hill, Nov. 30, 1917, Rosenwald Papers.
[46] Victor F. Lawson to Hill, Sept. 18, 1918, Victor F. Lawson Papers, Outgoing Letters, Personal Series, Newberry Library.
[47] *Second Annual Report, 1917-18,* pp. 13-15.

3032 South Wabash Avenue. The first floor of the three-story structure became the League's headquarters. This provided ample space for the five staff members and enough additional room to hold meetings and conferences. In theory the League and the Frederick Douglass Center were to share the quarters, but the Center was becoming inactive, and after Mrs. Woolley's death, the League began using the entire building.[48]

The philosophy actuating the program activities of the Chicago Urban League was, generally, that of the national organization. The objectives of the Chicago branch as stated in its constitution and certificate of corporation were verbatim statements of the purposes of the National Urban League. Like the National League, this branch emphasized in these documents its intention to coordinate existing agencies, to engage in research, and to undertake "all kinds of work for improving the industrial, economic, and social conditions among Negroes."[49] In seeking support for the establishment of a branch in Chicago, the practical applications of these purposes had been presented in terms of the work in New York. Chicago was promised an organization whose policies would lead to "better relationship between the two races," better playgrounds and places of recreation for children, boys' and girls' clubs, and assistance to the delinquent and the indigent.[50]

Yet, a statement of philosophy and procedure was needed which more specifically reflected conditions in Chicago. In 1917 and 1918, Chicago was confronted with a mass influx of Negroes from the South, attracted by the promise of lucrative employment in industry. So long as the war continued, this labor supply was welcomed, at least by industrial interests. But, as the war drew to a close, apprehension began to develop as to what would happen as industry retrenched and servicemen returned to augment the rapidly increasing labor force. This was the general situation facing the Chicago Urban League during the first two years of its existence, its formative years.

---

[48] *Ibid.*, p. 5; *Chicago Defender*, Mar. 2, 1918. The Frederick Douglass Center was not listed by the Association of Commerce and Industry after 1915 as an organization endorsed to solicit contributions. See Chicago Association of Commerce and Industry, *Contributor's Handbook: A Classified List of Local Civic, Health and Welfare Organizations* (published annually).

[49] Certificate of Corporation; Not for Profit, June 13, 1917, in the Office of the Secretary of State, Springfield, Illinois; Constitution, art. II.

[50] See *Chicago Defender*, Oct. 30, 1915; Jan. 15, 1916; Feb. 10, 1917.

Robert E. Park, the first president, formulated the generally accepted interpretation of the League's philosophy and function in Chicago.[51] This interpretation, based upon Park's conception of the Negro's status in the Chicago milieu, became the philosophical basis for programs of the Chicago Urban League. Park was considered an authority on Negro problems. He had done educational work among Negroes for several years before joining the University of Chicago faculty, and at Chicago he was involved in the study of sociological problems in cities. Yet, his work revealed him to be fatalistic and rather pessimistic in his view on the future of the Negro in America.[52] In assessing the Chicago situation and the League's role in 1917 and 1918, Park compared the Negro's plight to that of the immigrant. The immediate concern of both groups, he felt, were matters dealing with "work and wages, health and housing, the difficulties of adjustment of an essentially rural population to the conditions of a city environment, and to modern life." Thus, it was the League's primary function to do for the Negro what other organizations were doing for European immigrant groups. Park realized that there were differences between the circumstances facing the immigrant and the Negro, but these differences held advantages, as well as disadvantages, for the Negro. Being "to the manner born" and "a citizen without a hyphen," there was no question as to his loyalty in wartime. Here was a dependable supply of labor, which the League would assist employers in utilizing and at the same time "widen the industrial opportunities of the colored man and woman." The most obvious disadvantage encountered by the Negro was race prejudice, resulting in discrimination and segregation. Even this, Park thought, could be used to some advantage. Prejudice "created a solidarity and a unity of purpose" among Negroes "which might not otherwise exist." A purpose of the Urban League was, then, to convert this "liability into an asset" by directing "the energies roused by racial antagonism into constructive channels."[53]

In fulfilling its social service role, Park assigned the League three primary functions. First, it would increase the effectiveness of the

---

[51] See Horace J. Bridges, "The First Urban League Family," in *Two Decades of Service*.

[52] Gunnar Myrdal, *An American Dilemma: The Negro Problem and Modern Democracy* (New York: Harper and Brothers Publishers, 1944), pp. 1049-51.

[53] *First Annual Report, 1916-17*, pp. 3-4.

welfare work performed by the many "rather primitive" Negro organizations by providing them with "a body of authentic fact." The League would also stand between the Negro and regular city welfare agencies. It would interpret the Negro to the boards and the administrators of these agencies in order that they might give adequate service to the Negro migrants. Third, the League would acquaint the Negro with the services provided by public and private agencies. It would evaluate their needs and direct them to the agency equipped to help them. Park, however, thought that the key to the whole situation was research. "Efficiency," he said, "rests, in the long run, upon knowledge."[54]

The approaching termination of the war brought a slight modification in Park's interpretation of the League's role. He felt that basically the organization's functions would not change. For, there was still "a great restlessness among the masses of the Negro population," which would keep them moving into northern cities. Therefore, the orientation of migrants would remain the fundamental task facing the League. On the other hand, the war "disturbed the equilibrium of the races." Uncertainty and confusion prevailed as to what effects the great wartime principles would have on race relations in the United States. The returning soldiers and continuing migration would make the period of postwar reconstruction a difficult time. The most fundamental problem would be labor. Park felt that all other problems were "intimately bound up with" the labor question. Reconstruction would be a period of transition in which the Negro would have to compete with immigrants and native whites to hold the employment gains made during wartime. To meet this situation, he counseled patience, wisdom, and a humane spirit, in addition to knowledge. But research remained of primary importance in his philosophy of the Chicago Urban League's role. Of this function he said: "It is a fact of general observation, which has been confirmed by two years' experience in Chicago, that the most important service that one individual or group of individuals can perform for others is to give them the means of helping themselves. It is this service which the Urban League, through its department of records and research, is seeking to render to the Negro of Chicago."[55]

The program activities of the first two years stressed research, co-

---

[54] *Ibid.*, p. 5.

[55] *Second Annual Report, 1917-18,* pp. 3-4.

ordinated social services, and industrial relations. While he was president, Dr. Park took the initiative in developing the organization's research facilities. Under his general direction, a bureau of investigations and records was established. He secured a grant of $300 through the University of Chicago to finance a part-time worker in this bureau.[56] In July, 1917, this work began under Charles S. Johnson, who was at that time a student at the University of Chicago. The League undertook the assemblage of a file of information on Negro life in Chicago and throughout the country. This file of clippings, reports, surveys, and other materials was intended to aid the staff in interpreting Negro life and to provide information for individuals and agencies on various aspects of the race question. Another important function of the bureau was to supplement collected materials by conducting original investigations.[57]

The League initiated a number of research projects and cooperated with other organizations in conducting several. An early project was the examination of the Juvenile Court records of Negro delinquents to ascertain the principal charges brought against Negro children. This research was the prelude to more direct action. In 1918 the organization became involved in the cases of five boys being tried in Juvenile Court. There was alleged mistreatment of these boys while they were in the custody of the police and juvenile authorities. While little doubt existed as to the boys' guilt of thefts charged to them, the League was interested in exposing "the treatment given colored boys and girls by the police department and other officials with whom delinquents must come in contact."[58] The evidence collected on police brutality was forwarded to the Police Committee of the Chicago City Council and the Civil Service Commission for action. In addition, a conference was held to devise methods of prevention and correction of "delinquency and dependency among Negro children."[59] Further inquiry was made into the question of juvenile welfare through a study of 104 boys who left

---

[56] Hill to Graves, July 6, 1917, Rosenwald Papers.

[57] See Counse, Gilbert, and Van Driel, "The Chicago Urban League," pp. 6-7; *First Annual Report, 1917-18,* p. 7; Foster, "Twenty Years of Interracial Goodwill Through Social Service," in *Two Decades of Service; Third Annual Report, 1918-19,* pp. 4-5.

[58] *First Annual Report, 1916-17,* p. 7; *Second Annual Report, 1917-18,* p. 9; *Chicago Defender,* June 22, 1918.

[59] *Second Annual Report, 1917-18,* p. 9; National Urban League, *Bulletin,* VII, No. 4 (Aug., 1918), 7. The latter publications will be cited hereafter as *Bulletin,* with distinguishing volume, number, and date.

school. This study aimed at determining the effectiveness of truant officers in Negro communities.[60]

Several studies of housing conditions resulted from work with migrants. At the League's suggestion, a student at the School of Civics and Philanthropy investigated living conditions among migrants in two blocks on Wabash Avenue. The League's housing investigations were usually conducted to facilitate finding lodging for people who came to the agency for assistance. Data was gathered on the exorbitant rents charged in Negro sections of Chicago, and an attempt was made to compile a list of available housing. These projects motivated efforts to interest individuals and companies in the construction of "decent houses at reasonable rentals." Concerns employing large numbers of Negroes were encouraged to provide adequate housing for their workers, with facilities for recreation and welfare programs.[61]

The most extensive investigations in which the Chicago Urban League was involved surveyed conditions outside of Chicago. The Central Council of Social Agencies in Milwaukee invited the Chicago League to do a survey of conditions among Negroes in that city. This investigation was completed and reports of the findings sent to the press and to civic leaders. Shortly thereafter, a League branch was organized in Milwaukee to help alleviate the conditions revealed in this report.[62] During the same period, Charles S. Johnson was placed at the disposal of Emmett J. Scott to assist in a study of Negro migration. This investigation was financed by the Carnegie Endowment for International Peace. Johnson was assigned the state of Mississippi and centers in Missouri, Illinois, Wisconsin, and Indiana. He visited his assigned areas and wrote a report of his findings, which Scott used, along with the reports of other investigators, to write his monograph on the migration.[63]

In spite of the stress placed on research, this was the most dispensable part of the League's program. It was generally dependent upon special grants and the availability of a suitable director of research doing graduate work at the University of Chicago. After

---

[60] *Bulletin,* VII, No. 4 (Aug., 1918), 7.

[61] *Ibid.; First Annual Report, 1916-17,* p. 7; *Second Annual Report, 1917-18,* p. 9; *Bulletin,* VII, No. 3 (Jan., 1918).

[62] *Second Annual Report, 1917-18,* p. 9; *Bulletin,* VII, No. 4 (Aug., 1918), 7.

[63] Emmett J. Scott, *Negro Migration During the War* ("Carnegie Endowment for International Peace: Preliminary Economic Studies of the War," No. 16; New York: Oxford University Press, 1920), p. v.

only a year with the League, Charles S. Johnson went into the Army; and during the year he was away, the department of records and research, as the work was called after 1918, ceased to function. When Johnson returned, he spent only four months with the League before taking another position. His work was carried on for two months by a substitute, then another period of inactivity followed.[64]

The war and the migration created a great demand for welfare services. The League's stated policy was to refrain from giving direct relief in competition with agencies better equipped to provide such services. Whenever possible it would act as a "clearing house," referring clients to the proper agencies for the assistance they needed. Only where no agency existed to meet a given need would the League seek to provide direct assistance.[65] It was sometimes impossible, however, to avoid straying into the province of other organizations. And too, as an agency which stressed cooperation, the League often accepted assignments from other organizations which did not have facilities convenient to the Negro community and, thereby, acted as a branch office for another agency.

During the formative years, the League geared its welfare program to the needs of the migrants. This service began when the migrant first entered the city. A worker stationed at the railroad terminal gave directions to the homes of relatives or friends, or where no previous arrangements had been made, the worker sent new arrivals "to proper homes for lodging." Cards were distributed urging all "new comers" to take their problems to the League office, and club women were recruited to go into the homes with "verbal advice" as to things the migrants should do and know. In the first year, some 6,000 persons were counseled through public meetings, where they heard "general advice, health talks, and admonition."

This orientation of the newcomers was the primary purpose of the League's civic work. Finding suitable housing accommodations was the greatest problem in this phase of the program. As the migration continued, the housing resources of the Negro community were severely taxed. Landlords could rent any hovel, without making improvements, at an exorbitant rental. The situation seemed so bad in 1917 that the League announced pessimistically that:

> The housing problem is urgent. The most that the League has been able to do this far has been to find decent lodgings, to assist in finding

[64] Counse, Gilbert, and Van Driel, "The Chicago Urban League," pp. 7-8.
[65] *First Annual Report, 1916-17,* p. 9; *Second Annual Report, 1917-18,* p. 5.

houses and to help tenants dissatisfied with poor quarters to find better ones. Lodging accommodations for more than 400 individuals were personally inspected by several women volunteers. It is impossible to do much else short of the construction of apartments for families and for single men.[66]

Temporarily thwarted by the barriers of prejudice and discrimination which proscribed the areas available to Negroes for homes, the agency turned its attention to living conditions within the ghetto. A community worker was employed to go into the churches attended by migrants and instruct the communicants in thrift, civic pride, personal hygiene, deportment, and other civic virtues. This worker also visited the homes of the newcomers with her "practical message," which called "a spade a spade" in order to touch "the heart of the careless, indifferent and troublesome man and woman." The churches and volunteers, especially from the women's clubs, helped in this work.[67] To encourage civic pride block organizations were started in neighborhoods inhabited largely by migrants. This early block plan seems to have been broader in purpose than the block clubs organized in later years. The block work in 1917 and 1918 aimed "to give system and organization to welfare work" among those living in the block.[68] In later years this work was primarily concerned with the care of homes and neighborhoods.

Many public and private agencies came to the League for assistance in their work among Negroes. These agencies usually sought information about the newcomers and methods of dealing with them. The Social Service Department of Cook County Hospital consulted the League on its Negro cases and finally employed a Negro visitor to handle such cases. Women and girls who arrived in the city with travel problems were referred to the League by the Traveler's Aid Society, and the Chicago Department of Public Welfare obtained information on Negroes to facilitate its work. During the influenza epidemic of 1918, the Red Cross distributed food through the League's office.[69]

In the welfare field, the League did its most constructive and original work in its service to children. A children's department was established in 1918, and a worker was added to the staff to initiate

[66] *First Annual Report, 1916-17,* p. 10.
[67] *Second Annual Report, 1917-18,* pp. 9-10.
[68] *Bulletin,* VII, No. 4 (Aug., 1918), 7.
[69] *Second Annual Report, 1917-18,* pp. 6-7; *Broad Ax* (Chicago), Dec. 21, 1918.

this program. The need for such work became apparent during a conference on juvenile delinquency sponsored by the League, during the trial of the five boys defended by the organization, and through numerous complaints from mothers, organizations, and the courts about juveniles who were involved in matters not handled by existing organizations. This department engaged primarily in preventive work. While adjustments were attempted in cases of petty crime, the principal objective was to "analyze thoroughly" the causes of these actions in order "to recommend and effect preventive measures to decrease the number of cases of this type." Reformative measures were planned for juveniles released from state training schools, and these youths were "assisted into proper environment and employment." Further preventive work was done through the public schools. Here the children's department tried "to increase attendance, to improve deportment and scholarship, and to work with the families of incorrigible and backward children."[70]

The establishment of day nurseries, another project in the area of child welfare, was a cooperative venture. In 1918 the Chicago Association of Day Nurseries appointed a committee to organize and run three day nurseries for Negro children. Because of the League's role in promoting this project, T. Arnold Hill was made secretary of the committee. By August $4,800 of the required $12,000 had been raised, and one nursery was in operation at the Wendell Phillips Settlement on the West Side.[71]

By taking over the supervision and support of the Wendell Phillips Settlement, the League incorporated settlement work into its program of civic improvement. The board of directors of this settlement asked the League, in 1917, to take over its operation. From that time until 1923 it remained a part of the League's activities. In addition to nursery care, the settlement provided a meeting place for clubs and organizations in the West Side area and sponsored a program of social and civic activities.[72]

The League also offered its services to organizations engaged in war activities and individuals affected by the war. In the first category was the work performed for the War Camp Community Ser-

---

[70] *Second Annual Report, 1917-18,* p. 10; *Third Annual Report, 1918-19,* p. 6.

[71] *Second Annual Report, 1917-18,* p. 6; *Bulletin,* VII, No. 4 (Aug., 1918), 8.

[72] Counse, Gilbert, and Van Driel, "The Chicago Urban League," pp. 12-13; *Bulletin,* VII, No. 4 (Aug., 1918), 8; *First Annual Report, 1916-17,* p. 8.

vice. The League was active in the operation of the South Side Soldiers' and Sailors' Club. It secured the site, selected the personnel, and organized an advisory committee from among Negro groups. Similar services were rendered in the establishment of a club at Rockford, Illinois.[73] The Red Cross used League facilities for its war-related activities. Station Sixteen of the Red Cross operated from League headquarters, where volunteer workers prepared Christmas boxes for soldiers.[74] In addition, an effort was made to relieve individual suffering. Many wives and dependents of servicemen were left without sufficient means of support. Where possible, the League sought relief for these cases through other agencies and tried to limit its direct assistance to finding employment for needy dependents.[75] But, at Christmas in 1918, volunteer workers under Mrs. Olivia Ward Bush Banks, the League's community worker, solicited funds for Christmas baskets and distributed them directly to needy families.[76]

The most explicitly stated objective of the Urban League movement has been the improvement of economic and industrial conditions. In spite of the publicity given research and welfare activities, the Chicago Urban League depended largely upon its industrial work for the creation of favorable sentiment toward the organization. In fact, many research and welfare projects resulted from industrial activities or were used to facilitate the work in the industrial department. Although Chicago offered a fertile field for employment work during World War I, there were many difficulties involved in trying to raise the status of Negro labor. Three major obstacles barred significant progress. The first of these involved the Negroes themselves. Negro workers clamoring for jobs were, in most cases, new arrivals from the rural South. They had few skills adaptable to industrial pursuits and were not accustomed to the discipline, restraint, and regularity of routine demanded in factories and plants. In the second place, employers who had never before used Negro labor — and these were greatly in the majority — were reluctant to experiment with these workers. They claimed to fear financial loss resulting from inefficient labor, or they offered the excuse that white workers would leave if asked to work with Negroes. This position by employers was reinforced by the third obstacle, organized labor.

[73] *Second Annual Report, 1917-18,* p. 6.
[74] *Broad Ax* (Chicago), Dec. 21, 1918.
[75] *Ibid.,* Nov. 3, 1917.
[76] *Ibid.,* Dec. 28, 1918.

The unions in Chicago had been adamant in their refusal to accept Negroes freely into membership. This discriminatory policy kept many occupations closed to Negroes and retarded or prohibited their advancement in others.

In 1917 the Chicago Urban League was trying to work on three industrial fronts simultaneously. Sometimes this entailed serving at least two masters, the employer and the Negro worker. The employer had to be convinced that it was to his advantage to use Negro labor and that most of his fears were unfounded. When the League was able to sell an employer on its point of view, the agency's reputation depended upon the successful assimiliation of Negro workers into that employer's plant. To a great extent, the organization then became the agent of the employer. It tried to insure him against inefficient, indolent, and troublesome workers. A successful experiment meant an example to place before other employers, increased stature for the League, and probably a sizable contribution from the employer concerned. On the other hand, the League's principal allegiance was to its Negro clients. While their cause advanced with each new barrier breeched, there was always the danger that they would be exploited. Consequently, the League had to be cautious lest in molding Negro workers into suitable subjects for employment experiments, it made them susceptible to exploitation and even facilitated that exploitation.

Meanwhile, organized labor could not be ignored. While some Negro leaders felt that the Negro's first loyalty should be to the employer — for this was his most assured way of entering new areas of employment — others thought that the unions offered the greatest promise for the future. The League based its activities on both immediate and long-range objectives. Employers could provide jobs immediately and financial support for the agency. Yet, through persuasion, education, and pressure, organized labor had to be convinced that the exclusion of Negroes was against the best interest of the labor movement. In 1917 and 1918, conflicts between Negroes and organized labor were at a minimum. The severe labor shortage gave employers little choice as to whom they would hire. And, with jobs in such plentiful supply, the entrance of Negroes on the lower levels of industry seemed to pose no threat to craft unions. Where the number of Negroes increased in unionized industries, such as the stockyards, efforts were made to bring them into the unions.

In spite of the limited types of occupations open, there was a steady demand for Negro labor. The decreasing supply of immigrant labor brought an opportunity for Negroes to fill numerous jobs in plants and factories. The League's representative visited plants, called employers on the telephone, and contacted them in writing to obtain their consent for the League to supply workers. In many instances, the officials of plants in which Negroes had not previously worked were persuaded to hire them for the first time.[77] The League also became involved in the adjustment of these workers to their new jobs. For the organization never forgot "to urge upon its applicants the necessity for strict application to duties, punctuality, efficiency and proper deportment." In plants employing large numbers of Negroes, the League recommended the use of welfare secretaries to "assist in adjudicating difficulties affecting Negroes in and outside of the plant." These welfare secretaries were also placed by the League and thus gave the agency a good contact within the plant. During its first eight months of operation, the League placed 1,792 applicants, and between November 1, 1917 and October 31, 1918, jobs were found for another 6,861.[78]

Finding openings for women presented the most difficult problem. Of over 8,000 placements made in 1917 and 1918, only about 3,000 were women, even though the number of women registering for employment exceeded the number of men.[79] Special efforts had to be made on behalf of women workers because even employers who had trouble finding workers were relucant to hire Negro women. Where these women were used, they were often placed in separate workrooms from white workers and assigned to separate lunch facilities and waiting rooms. In some jobs, like washing and polishing taxicabs, they were used to replace men. In addition, Negro women found employment during the war "in tobacco factories as strippers, packers and labelers, in garment factories, in button factories and box factories, as ushers in theaters, stock girls in some of the loop stores, and in a few cases as elevator operators."[80] The League felt that its most notable achievement on behalf of women workers was the part it played in placing Negro girls with Sears, Roebuck and Company. In 1918 this company hired 600 girls temporarily during

---

[77] *First Annual Report, 1916-17,* p. 9.
[78] *Ibid.,* p. 10; *Second Annual Report, 1917-18,* p. 8.
[79] *Ibid.*
[80] Mary Roberts Smith, "The Negro Woman as an Industrial Factor," *Life and Labor,* VII (Jan., 1918), 7-8. See also Carl Sandburg, *The Chicago Race Riots, July, 1919* (New York: Harcourt, Brace and Howe, 1919), pp. 31-34.

the Christmas rush to do clerical work in the entry office. Sears also opened a "special division" in which it used 1,400 Negro girls. All of these employees "were passed upon by the League's employment service before being employed."[81]

Although organized labor had little effect on the League's employment activities during the war, Hill and other League officials were quite conscious of the danger of labor conflict along racial lines. They knew that someday the question of organized labor's attitude toward the Negro would have to be faced. The League announced that it "would welcome any effort tending to an amicable settlement of this vital problem."[82] Yet, little was achieved toward bringing general acceptance of Negroes in labor unions. Conferences were held between League representatives and officials of the Chicago and Illinois Federations of Labor, and the League advised the Women's Trade Union League during its campaign to organize Negro women in the stockyards.[83]

Nevertheless, instead of working through labor unions the League usually preferred to apply its social work methods to the problems faced by Negro employees. It was thought that the worker's interest could be safeguarded through the introduction of welfare secretaries into plants. Before making placements, the League investigated wage levels and methods of payment. Where these were considered unsatisfactory, the agency used its "influence to restrain individuals from applying to such places for employment."[84]

In January, 1918 the National Urban League called a conference on Negro labor. Out of this meeting came several resolutions, one of which called on "the American Federation of Labor for a fairer attitude toward the Negro." Another requested "the United States Department of Labor to appoint representative Negroes in the Department to handle matters affecting the welfare of Negro wage-earners in America." Following the conference, the Executive Council of the American Federation of Labor was approached, but the promises this body made had little effect on the general attitude of the A. F. of L. toward organizing Negroes.[85] However, other in-

[81] *Third Annual Report, 1918-19,* p. 4.
[82] *First Annual Report, 1916-17,* p. 10.
[83] *Second Annual Report, 1917-18,* p. 6.
[84] *First Annual Report, 1916-17,* p. 10.
[85] *Bulletin,* VIII, No. 1 (Jan., 1919), 11; Sterling D. Spero and Abram L. Harris, *The Black Worker: The Negro and the Labor Movement* (New York: Columbia University Press, 1931), pp. 107-111.

dividuals and organizations joined in the demand for Negro representation in the Department of Labor, and in 1918 a Division of Negro Economics was created within the Department. George E. Haynes, educational secretary of the National Urban League, became director of the new division, with district supervisors to carry on the work in various sections of the country. The National Urban League described the purpose of the Division of Negro Economics as follows: "To aid in the proper distribution and stabilization of Negro labor and to see as far as possible that Negro workingmen are given a square deal in wages and hours, in opportunity for advancement, in choice of occupation according to their natural interests and aptitudes and in conditions under which they work and live."[86] Since the Division had no coercive powers, it was restricted to the same methods — education, persuasion, and moral pressure — that the League used in pursuing almost identical objectives. This similarity of purposes and methods almost caused conflict between the new governmental agency and the Chicago Urban League.

Several months before the Division of Negro Economics was organized, the Chicago Urban League had commenced a very beneficial arrangement with the United States Department of Labor. In March, 1918 the Department of Labor assumed responsibility for the League's employment office, while leaving it under the supervision of the League. The clerks employed by the League became "examiners of the U.S. Employment Service at a larger salary," and before the end of the year, two additional workers were added. A fringe benefit that came with this arrangement was the right "to use franked envelopes when corresponding in regard to employment." Besides supervision, the Urban League furnished office space and telephone service. In October, upon the League's recommendation, a second employment office was opened and three more government-paid employees placed under the League's supervision.[87]

Meanwhile, the Division of Negro Economics began to elaborate its organizational framework. George E. Haynes took office in May, 1918, and the following month secured the appointment of Forrester B. Washington, former Urban League fellow and executive secretary of the Detroit Urban League, as district supervisor for Michigan and Illinois. These states were separated in September,

[86] *Bulletin,* VIII, No. 1 (Jan., 1919), 13.
[87] *Second Annual Report, 1917-18,* pp. 5, 8; *Chicago Defender,* Mar. 16, 1918; Oct. 19, 1918.

and Washington was sent to Chicago to develop the work in Illinois. He held a conference of Negro workers, white employers, and white workers in Springfield, Illinois, and from this meeting a state advisory committee, with local committees throughout the state, was launched. During the Springfield Conference, a committee on general conditions of Negro labor was appointed. This committee's report stated that Chicago had the greatest influx of Negroes and, consequently, conditions there were most in need of attention.[88]

The presence of this new organization was a matter of grave concern to T. Arnold Hill. Being an official agency of the Department of Labor, there was a possibility that it might take over the employment services delegated to the Chicago Urban League. This would have been a severe blow to the League's industrial program. Hill took his problem to William C. Graves. Graves suggested that Hill call a meeting of the Chicago Urban League Board of Directors, and in the meantime, he wrote L. Hollingsworth Wood urging action from the national level to forestall this threat to the Urban League movement. Graves reported to Wood that League secretaries throughout the area were concerned because Haynes's new agency seemed unwilling to cooperate with League branches. However, the crux of the matter was a fear that the Chicago Urban League would lose government support of its employment office. After outlining the general threat to the Urban League movement, Graves came to the real issue in question:

> In view of the value of the relation existing between the Chicago League and the U.S. Employment Service, I should appreciate your opinion as to the wisdom of requesting Dr. Haynes not to disturb the work of the League as now carried on in Chicago, unless he can show a method that will be an improvement.[89]

Wood was reluctant to bring the National Urban League into this controversy, but Graves was persistent. He had followed his letter with a telegram. Wood replied in a telegram and wrote a letter setting forth his position in detail. He agreed to present the matter to the steering committee of the National Urban League, but he felt that the problem was more complicated than Graves realized. Wood suspected that Haynes was jealous of Eugene Kinckle Jones and thought Haynes felt that Wood usually backed Jones when

[88] U.S. Department of Labor, Division of Negro Economics, *The Negro at Work During the World War and During Reconstruction,* by George Edmund Haynes (Washington: Government Printing Office, 1921), pp. 68-69.
[89] Graves to Wood, Sept. 20, 1918, Rosenwald Papers.

there was disagreement. "Consequently," Wood said, "I do not want to inject any more of this problem than I can help into the situation at Chicago." Furthermore, Wood considered the Chicago controversy a local problem, and he was "not sure that the atmosphere of a local discussion" was the "best one in which to decide the whole national issue." The situation regarding League branches and the Division of Negro Economics differed from city to city. Some Leagues were not well enough developed to do the type of work being done in Chicago. Wood also realized that in his new job Haynes could not cater to any specific group in a city. As the head of a governmental agency, he had to try to mobilize groups of varying opinions behind his work. On this point, Wood stated:

> You will realize, of course, that the Urban League group in any community is not the one most difficult to satisfy by the Labor Department, but rather the so-called "Advancement Group," who are more vociferous and inclined to act on theory rather than on the facts of a situation. I will consult the Executive Secretary of the Advancement Association [N.A.A.C.P.] privately in regard to this and see if we can arrive at some consensus of opinion which would be of value.[90]

Not satisfied with the response made by Wood, the Chicago group decided to resolve the situation in its own way. Haynes was invited to a meeting of the Chicago Urban League Board of Directors, without being informed that the "Federal labor–Urban League situation" would be discussed. When the League directors revealed the purpose of the meeting, Haynes "justly resented" their methods. Graves tried to save the situation by inviting Haynes and Washington to talk with him and George C. Hall at Graves's home after the board meeting. This conversation was more successful. As Haynes was leaving, Graves remarked, "Now we understand each other. The differences are brushed aside and what we understand is that we are going to cooperate each with the other here in Chicago and its manufacturing suburbs as to Government employment of Colored labor during the war emergency."[91] Haynes agreed that he had every intention of cooperating with the League, but he also felt free to use any other resources available to him. The ubiquitous George C. Hall put the finishing touches on the matter. After departing from Graves's home, Hall obtained Haynes's assurance that he and Forrester Washington would be guided by the advice of Hall and Graves in their labor policies in Chicago and its environs.

[90] Wood to Graves, Sept. 27, 1918, Rosenwald Papers.
[91] Graves to Wood, Oct. 2, 1918, Rosenwald Papers.

After the signing of the Armistice on November 11, 1918, terminating World War I, the Chicago Urban League was confronted with more fundamental problems than jurisdictional disputes with other agencies. A course had to be charted for postwar operations. Yet, there was uncertainty as to what peace would bring. Returning soldiers would be seeking jobs and the migration from the South was continuing. Would there be enough openings for all of these workers? And what of the job security of Negroes who had replaced whites during the wartime labor shortage?

In retrospect, an incident which occurred just two days after the Armistice was signed seems prophetic of the new era. On November 13, R. H. Aishton, Regional Director of Railroads for the Northwest, issued an order prohibiting the employment of Negroes as firemen, hostlers, switchmen, brakemen "or in any service not heretofore open to them [or] to take the places of white men."[92] Both the National Urban League and the N.A.A.C.P. worked to have the order withdrawn. John R. Shillady, executive secretary of the N.A.A.C.P., protested directly to William G. McAdoo, Director General of Railroads. The Urban League, on the other hand, used its indirect method of personal influence. A group of the national directors wrote to George Foster Peabody requesting that he use his influence in Washington, D.C. to get the order revoked. Although McAdoo had the order withdrawn, the fact that it was issued was indicative of the postwar situation facing Negroes in the industrial field.[93]

Although the postwar prospects were not bright, the League had succeeded during the war years in making itself a part of the Chicago scene. T. Arnold Hill's tact and persuasiveness had attracted a considerable number of supporters among influential groups. And, even with the very limited financial resources available, the League had made important contributions toward helping to facilitate the

[92] R. H. Aishton to North-Western Railroads, Nov. 13, 1918, quoted in Wood and others to George Foster Peabody, Nov. 25, 1918, Rosenwald Papers.
[93] It is impossible to assign credit to any particular individual or group for bringing about McAdoo's withdrawal. The Chicago Urban League is given credit by M. R. Werner (*Julius Rosenwald,* p. 268). However, the evidence does not support this contention. See Wood and others to Peabody, Nov. 25, 1918; Horace J. Bridges to Graves, Dec. 3, 1918; Peabody to Bridges, Nov. 29, 1918; Bridges to Peabody, Dec. 3, 1918; Peabody to Bridges, Dec. 9, 1918; Bridges to Graves, Dec. 12, 1918; Bridges to Peabody, Dec. 12, 1918. The role of the N.A.A.C.P. is revealed in Edward O. Brown to Graves, Dec. 13, 1918, which quotes in full correspondence between John R. Shillady and William G. McAdoo. Copies of these letters are in the Rosenwald Papers.

social and economic adjustment of migrants. The agency had, however, overwhelmingly committed itself to employment services as the principal feature of its work. Because it was founded largely as a result of the demand for Negro workers during a period of industrial prosperity, this emphasis on industrial relations was probably inevitable. This program feature allied the League with the employing class and made it dependent upon this group for financial support. The big question facing the organization when the war ended was whether or not employers would continue their financial support when economic conditions became less prosperous.

3

VIOLENCE AND UNCERTAINTY, 1919-24

At the close of World War I, the Chicago Urban League had to make its first major adjustments in policies and program. The organization had become thoroughly committed to wartime operations. Its program was geared to industrial placement and counseling and to the orientation of migrants. But when peace came there was no longer a steady demand for labor, and the migrant was increasingly considered an unwelcome intruder. In addition, the accumulated tensions and sublimated passions of the war years burst forth in racial conflict and industrial strife.

The uneasy truce between organized labor and management was terminated. Labor was determined to consolidate the gains it had made in increased membership and bargaining power and to accelerate its rate of growth. On the other hand, management, now that it had fulfilled its patriotic duty of maintaining peak production during wartime, was anxious to be rid of the labor union incubus. As the economy fluctuated up and down between 1919 and 1924, the Negro worker was the first to experience the effects of curtailment and the last to enjoy the fruits of revival. His position was assured only in those industries where, because of his traditional distrust of organized labor, he would be a deterrent to unionization. The Urban League — dedicated to the economic advancement of the Negro and dependent upon business for support — had to follow a constrained and opportunistic course in its industrial work. Furthermore, the organization was caught in the maelstrom of social and political readjustment in postwar Chicago.

Soon after the war ended the League was called upon to change its policy in regard to migration. Instead of welcoming the newcomer and trying to orient him to urban life, the agency was asked to discourage his coming and to urge Negroes in Chicago to accept the southern planters' invitations to return South. The pressure for a change in policy became so great that T. Arnold Hill placed the matter before the Chicago Urban League's board of directors. This body felt that a national policy was needed and suggested that representatives of all Urban League branches meet to formulate a policy on migration and labor.[1] Hill informed the national president, L. Hollingsworth Wood, about the situation in Chicago and of the Chicago board's suggestion concerning the institution of a national policy. Wood expressed surprise that the Chicago League was being pressured to advise Negroes to return South, since no such pressure was being exerted in the East. His attitude was mixed. He felt that if the League "could be known as advising Colored people to return to the Southern states" it would improve the organization's "prospects of a sympathetic hearing from the white people of the South." But, he also realized that this approach would hurt the organization in its work with southern Negroes.[2]

The fact that the Chicago branch tried to pass the problem up to the National Urban League was indicative of its complexity. Sentiment was divided among both Negroes and whites. While Negroes were hopeful of better conditions — growing out of the idealistic concepts propounded during the war and at the peace conference — and proud of the role they had played during the war, they were also becoming resentful and bitter. They were hearing of discrimination and injustices perpetrated against Negro soldiers in the United States and abroad.[3] Lynchings, mob violence, and riots erupted in both the North and the South during the first months of peace. Although the "Old Settlers" in the Chicago Negro community resented the presence of the Negroes who migrated during the war and opposed actual migration, more intense race consciousness growing out of postwar disillusionment motivated virtual una-

[1] Board of Directors Minutes, May 13, 1919, cited in Dorothy Counse, Louise Gilbert, and Agnes Van Driel, "The Chicago Urban League," June 18, 1936 (unpublished study in the files of the Welfare Council of Metropolitan Chicago), p. 13.

[2] L. Hollingsworth Wood to T. Arnold Hill, May 19, 1919, copy in Julius Rosenwald Papers, University of Chicago Library.

[3] See U.S. Dept. of Labor, Division of Negro Economics, *The Negro at Work During the World War and During Reconstruction,* by George Edmund Haynes (Washington: Government Printing Office, 1921), p. 29.

nimity of belief among all classes in the principle that the Negro should have the same freedom of movement as any other American.[4] A stand by the Urban League in seeming negation of this principle would have alienated Negroes in the North, as well as in the South.[5]

There was also diversity of opinion among whites. Those who were feeling the pressures of Negro competition for living space, jobs, and political preferment and those employers who no longer needed their Negro workers would have liked to be rid of the migrants. These groups encouraged labor agents from the South who appealed to the migrants to return to the southern plantations. Some of the daily papers urged Negroes to heed these appeals and helped to arouse anti-Negro sentiment by their sensational reporting of news concerning Negroes. The largest employers of Negro labor, however, were opposed to stopping the flow of migrants into Chicago. Meat-packing industries and the steel concerns were resisting organized labor's efforts to unionize their plants. These industries knew that by employing a large number of Negroes they would have an element in their plants that would not readily enter the unions. In addition, a steady supply of Negro labor coming into Chicago would be a ready source of strikebreakers in case the unions resorted to walkouts. The Chicago Association of Commerce also opposed efforts to stop the migration and to start a countermigration to the South.[6] Other white people, especially some of those in the reform groups, simply believed in the principle of freedom of movement.

The League did not want its stand on migration to appear as an endorsement of the views of either labor or management. These groups were generally on opposite sides of the migration question. Even though management's attitude seemed more favorable to the

---

[4] For a discussion of the attitude of the "Old Settlers" — Negroes who lived in Chicago before World War I — toward the migration and the mixture of facts and myths on which their opinions were based, see St. Clair Drake and Horace R. Clayton, *Black Metropolis: A Study of Negro Life in a Northern City* (New York: Harcourt, Brace and Company, 1945), pp. 73-76.

[5] George Edmund Haynes, in "The Negro at Work: A Development of the War and a Problem of Reconstruction," *American Review of Reviews,* LIX (Apr., 1919), 391, expressed the Negro intellectuals' attitude on the principle of freedom of movement when he said: "The present migration northward is only an acceleration of a movement from the rural districts to Urban centers, and from South to the North, that has been going on for half a century. The acceleration, however, has driven deep into the consciousness of the Negro masses the perception that a man's freedom means his opportunity to move from place to place, to find a better job, and to secure a higher standard of living and greater liberty of conduct."

[6] U.S. Dept. of Labor, *The Negro at Work,* pp. 27-29.

Negro, it would not have been politic for the Urban League seemingly to espouse publicly the cause of either group. Negro leadership was generally suspicious of organized labor, but there was a growing sentiment that the Negro worker should accept labor's proffered olive branch and try to change its racial attitudes and policies from within the labor movement.[7] The League may have supplied strikebreakers on occasion; even so, it certainly did not want to be known as a strikebreaking organization. Its objective was to act as a mediator between the Negro worker and management on one side and the Negro worker and labor on the other. In this role the League wanted to get the best possible consideration for the Negro worker from both sides. During this period, however, the organization found itself in the equivocal position of trying to be friendly to both labor and management at a time when it was necessary to choose sides. Nevertheless, in the years 1919-24 the choice was not too difficult; for the immediate best interest of both the Negro worker and the League seemed to be with management. The craft unions in meat-packing and steel were no match for the forces management were able to array against them.

It was no easy task for the Chicago Urban League to set a course through this maze of controversy. L. Hollingsworth Wood conferred with Eugene K. Jones, director of the National League, and they decide to place the Chicago migration problem before the National Urban League's executive committee. They also suggested that the question be considered in a meeting of Urban League representatives in attendance at the forthcoming session of the National Conference on Charities in Atlantic City.[8] Before the League's policy on migration and labor could be clarified, the temper of race relations in Chicago was drastically altered by the eruption of violence.

On July 27, 1919 Chicago "forgot her conscience and went rioting." A Negro boy strayed across the imaginary line dividing the "Negro" and "white" waters of Lake Michigan at the Twenty-ninth Street beach. Whites threw stones and the boy drowned. This incident was the spark that activated the latent hostilities which had accumulated throughout the war years. Within hours after the first clash, the riot had spread to other sections of the city. When order

---

[7] See, for example, *Chicago Defender,* Feb. 9, 1918; Apr. 26, 1919.
[8] Wood to Hill, May 19, 1919; Eugene K. Jones to Hill, May 19, 1919, copies in Rosenwald Papers.

was restored on August 2, with the help of the state militia, 38 persons were dead, 537 had been injured, and about 1,000 were "homeless and destitute." Chicagoans were shocked into an awareness of the race problem in their city.

Causes of the riot were rooted in the failures to make adjustments necessitated by a greatly increased Negro population. From a group of several thousand domestic and service workers, leavened by a small group of government employees and professionals, Chicago's Negro population had grown by 1919 to over 100,000, with representation in almost every occupational classification listed in the census. The housing space in the prewar Black Belt became inadequate to accommodate this mounting population, and the only relief came through gradual infiltration into neighboring white areas. These "invasions" created tension and resulted in sporadic bombings and skirmishes. In politics the Negro community supported William Hale Thompson and his faction of the Republican party and gave its wholehearted support to Mayor Thompson's re-election in the hard-fought campaign of April, 1919. The Chicago Commission on Race Relations reported that "the bitterness of this factional struggle aroused resentment against the race that had so conspicuously allied itself with the Thompson side." Although Thompson was "wrong" on every issue considered important by the reform groups, he was "right" on the one issue that governed the Negro vote. He recognized and catered to the aspirations of the Chicago Negro for political recognition.[9]

During the riot the Chicago Urban League devoted its efforts to the restoration of order, to the relief of suffering, and to agitation for constructive measures for preventing the recurrence of such conflicts. League headquarters became a Red Cross relief distribution center, providing food for needy families who could not leave the area to reach their jobs. In addition, the Urban League

made food surveys of the entire Negro area, printed and distributed thousands of circulars and dodgers urging Negroes to stay off the streets, refrain from dangerous discussions of the riot, and co-operate with the

[9] The Chicago race riot of 1919 received the most objective and thorough study of any racial conflict of this period. The riot, its causes, and their implications for race relations in Chicago were exhaustively treated in the Chicago Commission on Race Relations, *The Negro in Chicago: A Study of Race Relations and a Race Riot* (Chicago: The University of Chicago Press, 1922). See also Drake and Cayton, *Black Metropolis,* pp. 65-67, 346-351; Carl Sandburg, *The Chicago Race Riots, July, 1919* (New York: Harcourt, Brace and Howe, 1919).

police in every way to maintain order. The League sent telegrams to the governor and mayor suggesting plans for curbing disorder, organized committees of citizens to aid the authorities in restoring order, and served as a bureau of information and medium of communication between the white and Negro groups during the worst hostilities.[10]

When Jewish merchants became alarmed over the possibility that lack of income in the Negro community could lead to the looting of their stores, the League served as one of the pay stations where the meat-packing plants arranged to make unpaid wages available to their workers.[11]

The riot temporarily awakened public awareness to the dangers of unrelieved racial tensions. Before hostilities had ceased, the representatives of social, civic, and professional organizations from the city at large were meeting to seek possible solutions to the problems confronting Chicago. Such a meeting was held on August 1 at the Union League Club. The participants called upon Governor Frank O. Lowden to appoint "an emergency state committee to study the psychological, social and economic causes underlying the conditions resulting in the present race riot and to make such recommendations as will tend to prevent a recurrence of such conditions in the future." A committee of six — among whose members were T. Arnold Hill and William C. Graves — was appointed to "wait upon" the governor and to work for his acceptance of the recommendation for a state committee.[12] Governor Lowden, in compliance with this recommendation, appointed the Chicago Commission on Race Relations. St. Clair Drake and Horace Cayton in their significant study of Negro life in Chicago gave some indication of the importance of this commission's work when they said, "For the next twenty years its suggestions set the pattern of activity for such civic groups as the Urban League, the YMCA, and various public agencies. The Commission's report was the first formal codification of Negro-white relations in Chicago since the days of the Black Code."[13] Some of the Urban League's pride in the Commission's work came from the fact that materials from League files were used during the investigations, and the League's director of research, Charles S. Johnson, served as the Commission's associate executive secretary.

The riot did not settle the problems of migration and anti-Negro

---

[10] Chicago Commission on Race Relations, *The Negro in Chicago,* pp. 45-46.
[11] *Ibid.,* pp. 43-44.
[12] *Ibid.,* p. xv.
[13] Drake and Cayton, *Black Metropolis,* p. 69.

union policies. The National Urban League conference meeting in Detroit in October, 1919 tackled these twin problems. Since efforts were being made to involve the organization in the migration issue, some action was necessary; but the League did not want to limit its usefulness by committing itself completely to either side of the question. To avoid this, the conference reaffirmed the League's determination to work for the best social and economic interest of the Negro and to cooperate with any group which offered broader opportunities and better conditions. In essence the policy enunciated in Detroit favored continued migration and permanent residence in the North. The principles outlined by the conference were national in scope; yet, their application centered largely in Chicago. It was left to T. Arnold Hill and the Chicago board of directors to assess conditions and to determine how this policy would be applied to specific situations.[14]

Following the riot, southern labor agents worked with renewed vigor to recruit Negro workers. The South was experiencing a labor

[14] The resolutions on migration adopted in Detroit were as follows:

"Regarding the migration of Negro labor from the South to the North, we affirm it is the right and duty of every man to seek more promising opportunities and a fairer measure of justice wherever he believes they can be found.

"We shall continue to discover and create industrial opportunities for Negroes and to serve as a bureau of information to the Negro who seeks wider opportunities in industry, and to employers seeking a new and dependable supply of labor.

"Regarding the efforts of southern planters and business men on the plea of improved conditions, to secure the return of Negroes, we shall be glad to investigate such reported and promised conditions and to publish our findings for the benefit of Negroes who desire the information. They can decide for themselves whether they should return.

"We stand ready to cooperate with responsible, fair-minded organizations or bodies of men, in the North or the South, whenever they publicly announce, for districts in which they have known influence, policies which we feel justified in accepting as guarantees:

"1. That working and living conditions of Negroes will be fair and decent.

"2. That transportation accommodations for Negroes will be equal to those provided for white people.

"3. That adequate educational facilities will be provided for Negroes.

"4. That the Negro will be given fair treatment, and be protected in buying and selling.

"5. That the life and property of every Negro will be protected against all lawless assaults.

"6. That the Negro will be assured of equal justice in the courts.

"We also believe that the Negro should be assured of all of his other constitutional rights." Published in "National Urban League Adopts Strong Platform," *Life and Labor,* IX (Nov., 1919), 294-295.

shortage in 1919. By this time the continuing exodus of farm workers was being acutely felt in Mississippi, Louisiana, and Tennessee. It was from these states that the largest number of migrants came to Chicago or through Chicago to other midwestern cities and towns. So these states looked to Chicago for Negro workers to return to the turpentine industries and to the cotton, rice, and sugar cane fields. The Mississippi Welfare League — an organization formed to bring Negroes back from the North — sent its agent to Chicago. Louisiana was represented by a committee from the New Orleans Chamber of Commerce and the director of the state department of immigration. In spite of favorable publicity in some northern papers and a well-planned propaganda campaign, the agents had little success in convincing Negroes to return south. The Mississippi Welfare League's agent left disappointed but escorted back a carefully selected "commission" of Chicago Negroes to "study" and report on the allegedly amicable conditions in the South.[15]

The Chicago Urban League strongly opposed the work of the labor agents. The organization announced in its annual report for 1918-19 that it was continuing the work of adjusting migrants to "metropolitan conditions." It viewed the economic emergency created by the labor shortage in the South as providing "an opportunity for impressing upon the South the necessity for a fundamental reform of those conditions against which the departure of these thousands of Negroes was a protest."[16] To counteract the testimony given by the "commission" which went South from Chicago, the League obtained statements on conditions in their respective states from Negroes in Mississippi and Louisiana. These statements, ridiculing both the "commission" and its report, were published in the *Chicago Defender*,[17] and they were included in an article Hill wrote for the *Survey*. Hill felt that the Negro was justified in remaining in the North. He was not surprised that the South could not attract Negroes since "the promises of fairer treatment and unrestricted economic development are powerless because they are barren. Negroes know they are barren. The good intentioned white persons of the South in serious moments confess their own impotence to deal

[15] *Chicago Defender*, Sept. 27, 1919; T. Arnold Hill, "Why Southern Negroes Don't Go South," *The Survey*, XLIII (Nov. 29, 1919), 183-185; *Third Annual Report, 1918-19*, pp. 3-4.

[16] *Third Annual Report, 1918-19*, pp. 2-3.

[17] *Chicago Defender*, Sept. 27, 1919.

with community problems. They are, unfortunately, as helpless as Negroes themselves in changing conditions."[18]

By 1923, however, the League was forced to modify its position. Faced with depressed economic conditions and an increased tempo of migration, opinion in Chicago was overwhelmingly in favor of curbing the influx of southern Negroes. Its association with the newcomers caused some people to withdraw their support from the League. The organization tried to clarify its position in the annual report for 1922-23. In his introductory remarks the president of the Chicago Urban League, Horace Bridges, stated:

> Some people think we are engaged in persuading Southern Negroes to come here. *That is not true at all, and never was true.* On the contrary, whenever business is slack here, we send warnings throughout the South informing Negroes that work is not available in Chicago.[19] [Italics in original.]

Another section of the report emphasized the League's attempts at being impartial on the question, without departing from its principles. Here it was stated that:

> We have been asked by five delegations from the South to persuade their labor to return. We have taken advantage of their distressed condition to impress upon them the actual causes for the desire on the part of their workmen to forsake their native home. . . . We have offered opportunity to Southern planters to talk directly to the men, and we have shown them original letters from individuals . . . stating . . . their objections to the social and economic systems of the South. . . . In no case has the League handled or advised shipments of Negroes South; and likewise *it has refrained from influencing them to move to Chicago.*[20] [Italics in original.]

Concomitantly with its consideration of policy on migration, the League had to reassess its procedures in dealing with organized labor. Negroes had never received a friendly reception from the unions in Chicago. During the war this attitude on the part of labor did not completely close employment opportunities in skilled trades; but after the war when jobs became less plentiful, labor's exclusion policy began to have serious effects on Negro employment opportunities. Early in the postwar period the Chicago Urban League tried to formalize its methods of dealing with the question of

---

[18] Hill, "Why Southern Negroes Don't Go South," p. 185. See also an article by Hill in the *Chicago Defender,* Feb. 17, 1920. The editor of the *Defender* applauded Hill's more militant tone in an editorial on May 15, 1920.

[19] *Seventh Annual Report, 1922-23,* p. 3.

[20] *Ibid.,* pp. 9, 11.

the Negro worker and organized labor. The board of directors passed the following resolutions on this subject:

It is the general sense of this Board, first: that whenever we are attempting to introduce Negro workers into trades in which white workers are unionized, we urge Negroes to join the unions.

Second, that when we are introducing Negro workers into industries in which workers are not unionized, we advise Negroes, in case an effort is made to unionize, to join with their fellows.

Third, that we strongly urge organizers of all unions in industries which may be open to colored labor, not only to permit, but actively to assist in incorporating Negroes into the unions.

Fourth, in cases where Negroes are prevented from joining the union, the League reserves to itself complete liberty as to the advice it will give to the person under its influence.[21]

There was considerable confusion of opinion as to the best course for the Negro worker to follow in relation to the unions. Early in 1918 one Chicago Negro leader had called upon Negro workers to organize and iron out "preliminary confusion" among themselves in order to present "a solid front" to the A. F. of L. and its leaders. It was felt that this was the only way to hold the gains made during the war.[22] After the war, the editor of the *Defender* revealed the extent of the Negro's dilemma in an editorial condemning both management and labor. It was pointed out that the Negro was expected to give loyal support to the labor movement, but the few unions which accepted him fought for the Negro's "rights only when it was to their interest." On the other hand, in spite of the Negro's loyalty to management, he had not received a square deal from capital either. After their usefulness as strikebreakers ended, management usually released its Negro workers. The editorial stated that the Negro had been placed in the position "of choosing between two evils." The editor concluded: "If it is to our economic, social and political interest to join with organized labor now, it should not make the least bit of difference to us what was their attitude toward us in the past, even if that past was as recent as yesterday." He implied that it was to the Negro's best interest "to join with organized labor."[23] George E. Haynes rationalized the

[21] Quoted in Counse, Gilbert, and Van Driel, "The Chicago Urban League," pp. 14-15.

[22] M. O. Bousfield, "Union Labor and the Race," *Chicago Defender*, May 4, 1918. Bousfield, a physician and businessman, later became the first Negro president of the Chicago Urban League.

[23] Editorial, *Chicago Defender*, Apr. 26, 1919.

Negro's lack of enthusiasm for unions by maintaining that the Negro "naturally inclines toward conciliatory agreements to prevent industrial strife, rather than toward conflict and peace conferences after industrial war."[24]

The Chicago branch wanted the National Urban League to strengthen local policies on labor by formulating a national platform. Although a majority of the representatives attending the conferences of the National Urban League usually favored unionization, some local branches tried to remain neutral or were openly antagonistic to organized labor.[25] In the Detroit conference of 1919 these differences were reconciled in a set of resolutions which received unanimous acceptance. These resolutions were patterned after those passed by the Chicago board. Horace Bridges said that he and William C. Graves worked together on the national statement and tried to formulate a policy that was "clearcut and unambiguous, yet not needlessly provocative." Bridges gave himself credit for the final wording.[26] These resolutions stated:

> Employers have heretofore given Negroes meager opportunities for advancement, and the wages and labor conditions of Negroes have been far below the American standard.
>
> Organized labor has given Negroes scant consideration and often no encouragement.
>
> But, in spite of the grinding of the Negro between these upper and lower mill-stones, his faithfulness and industry, in taking advantage of the opportunity the war brought, have forced him upward into new branches of skilled labor. . . .
>
> We believe in the principle of collective bargaining, and in the theory of cooperation between capital and labor in the settlement of industrial disputes and in the management of industry. But, in view of the present situation, we advise Negroes, in seeking affiliation with any organized labor group, to observe caution. We advise them to take jobs as strike breakers only where the union affected has excluded colored men from membership. We believe they should keep out of jobs offered in a struggle to deny labor a voice in the regulation of conditions under which it works.
>
> But, we believe the Negroes should begin to think more and more in the terms of labor group movements, so as ultimately to reap the benefit of thinking in unison. To this end we advise Negroes to organize with white men whenever conditions are favorable. Where this is not possible they should band together to bargain with employers and with organized labor alike.

---

[24] Haynes, "The Negro at Work," p. 391.

[25] See *Chicago Defender,* Feb. 9, 1918.

[26] Horace J. Bridges, "The First Urban League Family," in Chicago Urban League, *Two Decades of Service* (Chicago: Chicago Urban League, 1936).

With America and the whole world in labor turmoil, we urge white and black men, capital and labor, to be fair and patient with each other while a just solution is being worked out.[27]

It is not surprising that this statement was unanimously accepted. There was little possibility that any conceivable local policy could not be justified under one or more of its recommendations. Those who advocated efforts by Negroes to join existing unions could claim that conditions were favorable. Proponents of all-Negro unions, on the other hand, could say that conditions were not favorable. Where no unions at all were desired, it could be maintained that caution was being observed. Since most unions excluded Negroes, it would not be difficult to justify strikebreaking, even where the struggle was for a voice in the regulation of working conditions. In the final analysis, the choice as to what policy a local League would follow was still left to the branch concerned. The consequences growing out of local decisions would depend upon how sagaciously the local situation had been analyzed.

The labor and industrial picture was of particular concern to the officials of the Chicago Urban League. Industrial work was the foundation of the whole program. Research and welfare services were secondary to the campaign to place Negro workers in suitable jobs and to open broader economic opportunities to them. Moreover, in 1919 very little was being done in the area of research. Soon after Charles S. Johnson, the League's director of research, returned from the army, he took a leave-of-absence to become associate executive secretary of the Chicago Commission on Race Relations. When the work of this commission was completed, Johnson accepted a position with the National Urban League. In 1921 the Chicago League tried to "revitalize" its department of research; but throughout this period, the research function of this branch was largely neglected.[28] Such welfare services as advising migrants, operating the Wendell Phillips Settlement, and working with delinquent and dependent children were continued. The scope of these services and the emphasis placed on them, however, depended upon the agency's financial fortunes; and the volume of contributions received was largely dependent upon the demand for and the acceptance of the League's industrial services. In brief, the uncertain economic con-

[27] "National Urban League Adopts Strong Platform," *Life and Labor,* p. 295.
[28] *Fourth Annual Report, 1919-20,* p. 10; *Fifth Annual Report, 1920-21,* p. 6.

ditions in Chicago between 1919 and 1924 determined the nature and scope of the League's program activities from year to year.

During the early months of 1919, the outlook for Negro workers was very bleak. The demand for Negro labor declined sharply immediately after the war. Instead of the 1,700 to 1,800 placements each month made by the League's employment office during the war, only 500 placements were made in April, 1919.[29] The plight of women workers was particularly serious. When plants producing war goods began receiving cancellations of orders, they started releasing their women employees. In the majority of plants in Chicago, Negro women were the first to go.[30] Moreover, the employment situation was complicated by the entrance of some 10,000 Negro soldiers into the labor market.

The League tried to adjust its work to the changing conditions. It cooperated with the United States Employment Service, the Division of Negro Economics, and the Illinois Employment Office in trying to place men returning from military service.[31] The League launched a special financial campaign and raised $2,000 to employ an industrial secretary. William E. Evans, the industrial secretary, was sent into nearby towns seeking jobs for the growing number of unemployed workers. He went to Battle Creek, Flint, and Detroit, Michigan, and to parts of Wisconsin and Illinois. His efforts met with some success. On one occasion a group of 300 men were sent to an army camp as civilian laborers.[32] At this critical juncture in the employment picture, the League lost government support of its employment office. Congress failed to appropriate funds for the continuation of the United States Employment Service, which was operated through the Department of Labor. Consequently, on March 22, 1919, the League had to resume supporting its employment office.[33]

In April the economic situation began to improve, and Chicago enjoyed twelve months of relative prosperity. The improved conditions gave a boost to the League's industrial work. A campaign

[29] Sandburg, *The Chicago Race Riots,* p. 17.
[30] Forrester B. Washington, "Reconstruction and the Colored Women," *Life and Labor,* IX (Jan., 1919), pp. 3-4.
[31] U.S. Dept. of Labor, *The Negro at Work,* pp. 72-73.
[32] *Third Annual Report, 1918-19,* p. 3; Albon L. Foster, "Twenty Years of Interracial Goodwill Through Social Service," in Chicago Urban League, *Two Decades of Service.*
[33] *Third Annual Report, 1918-19,* pp. 2-3.

was started to seek new employment opportunities and stress was placed on industrial counseling. Negro women, especially those qualified to perform stenographic and clerical work, greatly benefited from the employment campaign. Montgomery Ward and Company — following the example of Sears, Roebuck — opened a special office in which it placed 600 Negro women as clerks and typists. Early in 1920 Montgomery Ward employed a member of the League's industrial staff, Mrs. Helen Sayre, to serve as welfare secretary in this office.[34] The Rand McNally Company was also persuaded to open a branch office, and several other firms considered the expediency of such a move.[35] However, the Chicago Telephone Company, one of the main targets in the employment drive, refused to consider using Negro girls as telephone operators.[36] There was also an increase in the placement of skilled men workers. Several firms — the American Car Shop, the U.S. Reduction Company, Terra Cotta Company, Ira Barnett and Company, and the Malleable Iron Company — hired such workers in various capacities. The International Harvester Company, which already had a large force of Negro workers, broadened the range of skilled operations open to them.[37]

Industrial counseling and the mediation of disputes involving Negro workers became a principal feature of the League's work. This new area of concern may have resulted partially from the decrease in requests for workers and the necessity of maintaining a program to justify the retention of the industrial secretary. But the League's interest in improving working conditions and in helping Negro workers to hold their jobs cannot be discounted as major factors in motivating this work. The League reported that "it became evident . . . that the failure of colored workers, in certain plants, to make suitable progress after what should be a long enough knowledge of the work required was due largely to the system, which prevented mutual understanding of the points of view of the em-

---

[34] Foster, *Two Decades of Service; Chicago Defender,* Feb. 14, 1920; Feb. 28, 1920.

[35] Report of the Industrial Department, June, 1920 (in the files of the League).

[36] Louise deKoven Bowen to B. E. Sunny, president of the Chicago Telephone Company, in Louise deKoven Bowen, *Speeches, Addresses and Letters of Louise deKoven Bowen, Reflecting Social Movements in Chicago,* comp. Mary E. Humphrey (2 vols.; Ann Arbor, Michigan: Edwards Brothers, Inc., 1937), I, 503-504; *Fourth Annual Report,* 1919-20, p. 8.

[37] *Ibid.,* p. 6.

ployers and the employees."[38] Counseling services provided opportunities for continuing contacts with employers who had used the League's placement services but no longer needed additional workers. In its role as counselor, the League's industrial department sent staff members into plants to investigate working conditions and to suggest remedies where necessary. Other cities were visited to study "plans for an apprentice school, for industrial housing, recreation, sanitation, welfare, and supervision of labor camps." Information obtained on these visits was incorporated into recommendations and submitted to Chicago industries. Industrial Secretary Evans spent considerable time conferring with foremen, supervisors, and officials in plants employing large numbers of Negroes.[39] The department tried to mediate questions involving wages and hours and to suggest solutions for unrest, inefficiency, and intolerable working conditions.[40]

In the latter half of 1920 Chicago felt the first pangs of economic depression. The Negro community was aware that prosperity was on the wane before it was generally felt in other sections of the city. Except for a few requests for women as domestic servants, the League's placement activities came to a standstill. As early as June, the mail order houses began closing their special offices employing Negro women. Considerable antagonism was aroused against one of the firms, because its Negro workers were released at a time when unemployment had not become general enough to be widely felt; and, moreover, an office was opening in another section of the city hiring white girls.[41] By the end of the year there was a general state of unemployment. During the final months of 1920, the industrial department centered its attention on urging Negroes who had jobs to hold on to them and to exhibit their merit through increased efficiency.[42]

Although unemployment was rife throughout the city, the Negro community suffered most. It was estimated that the number of Negroes unemployed reached 20,000. Many of these became homeless and destitute. Refused accommodations by the Salvation Army, the Y.M.C.A. (except for the Wabash Avenue branch), the Dawes Hotel, the Christian Industrial League, and other institutions fur-

---

[38] *Ibid.*
[39] *Ibid.*, p. 8; Report of the Industrial Department, June, 1920.
[40] *Ibid.*
[41] *Ibid.*
[42] *Chicago Defender,* Nov. 27, 1920; Dec. 4, 1920.

nishing lodging for the unemployed, this army of Negro indigents still would not except free transportation South. They preferred to sleep in the doorways, halls, and poolrooms of Chicago. "Police stations," Hill reported, "no longer able to accommodate them, turned them back into the street."[43] From Thirty-first Street several blocks north along the shores of Lake Michigan, a "village of the deserted" grew, where the unemployed constructed shelters of rocks and debris.[44]

Instead of being a dispenser of jobs, the Chicago Urban League's industrial department became a distributor of relief. Statistics on the number of placements made were replaced by accountings of the number of meals served and beds provided. Over 15,000 placements were made in 1919-20, but only 4,854 in 1920-21. The large number of women in this group indicates that many were in domestic service.[45] When in December, 1920 it became apparent that widespread suffering would result from the increased unemployment, the League took further steps to provide relief. Many public and private agencies either refused or were unable to provide assistance to unemployed Negroes. The League turned to the Negro community for help. A meeting of ministers, public spirited citizens, and representatives from social agencies and women's clubs was called to consider the situation. A citizens' committee was then organized. One group of Negro businessmen turned over to the League the proceeds from an entertainment, and the churches and women's clubs collected funds for food and beds. The packing companies donated meat, and several firms gave bread and other foodstuffs. Some churches were turned into lodging houses, while others became feeding stations. During this operation, the League acted as a "clearing house." To help "avoid duplication and to weed out undesirables," the Urban League "was allowed to receive and record the meals and beds of all persons who were thus helped."[46]

Depressed economic conditions did not deter southern Negroes from continuing their movement into Chicago. The South was also

[43] T. Arnold Hill, "Recent Developments in the Problem of Negro Labor," in National Conference of Social Work, *Proceedings* (Chicago: University of Chicago Press, 1921), p. 325; *Fifth Annual Report, 1920-21,* p. 5.
[44] *Chicago Defender,* Mar. 12, 1921.
[45] *Fourth Annual Report, 1919-20,* p. 6; *Fifth Annual Report, 1920-21,* p. 6.
[46] Hill, in National Conference of Social Work, *Proceedings,* pp. 324-325; Memorandum from Hill to members of the executive board, Feb. 25, 1921 (in the files of the League); *Chicago Defender,* Jan. 15, 1921; Feb. 26, 1921; May 14, 1921; *Fifth Annual Report,* 1920-21, pp. 5-6.

experiencing an economic slump. One migrant when told that there was no work in Chicago replied, " I also know that there is no work in Mississippi, and I had rather be out of work in Chicago than out of work in Mississippi."[47] The exigencies of the economic situation finally brought efforts by the League to discourage migration. Through the *Chicago Defender*, the League's industrial secretary appealed to Negroes in the South not to migrate. He described the hardships and suffering that prevailed and warned those who were contemplating coming to Chicago that they would probably be out of work for an indefinite period.[48] These appeals had little effect. In 1923 the League reported mournfully that "jobs which newcomers can handle are getting scarcer as the weeks go by and even larger numbers come to Chicago."[49]

While conditions generally remained grave between 1921 and 1924, the League was periodically able to place some people who came to its office. In 1921 and 1922 demands for workers came from the stockyards, steel plants, and other industries, and a number of requests for unskilled labor were received in 1923.[50] But the League expressed greatest satisfaction over the fact that most industries had retained a proportionate percentage of their Negro workers during the depression. The Nachman Springfilled Cushion Company, for instance, still had its force of Negro women in 1924.[51]

Many of the job openings of these years came as a result of industrial strife. Before the National Conference of Social Work in 1921, T. Arnold Hill took a rather noncommittal stand on the question of organized labor. He pointed out that mutual suspicion and fear existed between the unionist and Negroes and that Negro leaders were "still unagreed as to whether to encourage or impede unionizing" Negro workers. On the other hand, Hill felt that the more favorable stand taken by the American Federation of Labor in its Montreal Convention in 1920 was being reflected in its affiliated international unions. Hill expressed doubt as to the wisdom of separate unions, such as the Pullman Porters, because he feared that "whites and

---

[47] Hill, in National Conference of Social Work, *Proceedings*, p. 324.

[48] See, for example, W. L. Evans, "Unemployed Problems Menace to Chicago," *Chicago Defender*, Mar. 12, 1921.

[49] *Ibid.*, Aug. 25, 1923.

[50] *Opportunity: A Journal of Negro Life*, I (Feb., 1923), 32; I (May, 1923), 31.

[51] The *Broad Ax* (Chicago), Nov. 18, 1922; William L. Evans, "The Negro in Chicago Industries," *Opportunity*, I (Feb., 1923), 15-16; Helen B. Sayre, "Negro Women in Industry," *Opportunity*, II (Aug., 1924), 242-244.

blacks organized in separate unaffiliated bodies will, sooner or later, be on opposite sides of some important issue which ought to affect all alike." In general, Hill thought that "little practical progress" had been made in allaying the Negro's fear of unions; but he noted "with relief a more friendly feeling on the part of white workers organized and unorganized — a feeling which will make improbable widespread discord such as was anticipated."[52] Before the year ended, however, the delicate question of establishing a *rapprochement* between Negroes and unions was overshadowed, as far as the Chicago Urban League was concerned, by the more mundane problems of widespread Negro unemployment and of maintaining the support of the packing industry. An article in the *Defender,* based upon a National Urban League release, announced that in December, 1921 the League's job placement work had met with greater success. It was stated that "the chief factor in bringing about this increase in the percentage of applicants in Chicago was the stockyards strike which absorbed a large number of the unemployed." The article noted that "the strike was broken by both races in about equal proportions." Although the Urban League sent a total of 453 men and women to four packing plants and to sausage-casing companies, "the League did not assist several of the plants which requested workers for the reason that they had never before hired . . . [Negroes] and gave no assurance of permanent employment."[53]

In 1923 the League's industrial secretary openly boasted of the gains made by Negro workers during strikes. He said that Negroes had regained previously lost skilled positions in the stockyards during the strike of 1920-21. In addition, strikes in various industries during 1919 and 1920 had "resulted in promotions from unskilled to skilled positions in the plants of the International Harvester Company, Corn Products and Refining Company, and many other industries." Negroes also replaced whites in "the grey iron industry," as molders and foundry workers. New skilled positions were opened in the Chicago railroad shops during a strike in that industry. The industrial secretary maintained that strikes furnished the Negro his only assured road to advancement. He declared, "There is no reason to conclude that the Negro is by choice a strikebreaker any more than other men, but the fact is that in most instances where he has risen above the ranks of a common laborer, the strike has furnished

[52] Hill, in National Conference of Social Work, *Proceedings,* pp. 322-323.
[53] *Chicago Defender,* May 13, 1922.

the medium thru which his advancement is accomplished. To our notion, the policy of white unionists is more to blame than all else."[54] In justification of the League's part in supplying workers for the stockyards during the strike, Evans said:

> The writer recently heard a colored stock yards union workman bitterly denouncing the Urban League and the Y.M.C.A. for what he thought was their interference in the stock yards strike. His denunciation was as bitter and typically union as any the writer has ever heard, but the writer knew that with 20,000 Negroes unemployed over a period of a year in a great city like Chicago where at all times the struggle for existence is keen, that the calling of a strike was pure folly and that no force, social or otherwise, could have saved the situation to the union. If the statements of stock yards officials may be accepted, the strike-breakers were about equally divided between white and colored men who preferred the danger of a strike-breaker's position to the suffering incident to unemployment.[55]

The Chicago Urban League's fluctuating financial fortunes between 1919 and 1924 reflected Chicago's uncertain economic conditions and the diversity of public opinion in regard to migration, labor-management disputes, and the best means of achieving racial adjustment. Yet the economic depression did not have an immediate adverse effect on the League's finances. Greater concern about race relations, after the riot, brought increased contributions. In addition, the packers gave liberally to Negro agencies in order to secure support in their struggle against stockyard unions.[56] It was not until 1922 — when the unions had been defeated in both meatpacking and steel and the riot had lost its poignancy — that the League started to experience financial difficulty.

During 1918-19 the League had "a successful financial year." Contributions were over 100 per cent above those of the previous year. After the riot, men like Victor F. Lawson, editor and publisher of the *Chicago Daily News,* renewed their donations to the League.[57] Even though the number of contributors grew steadily, the organization was still dependent upon a very few individuals and groups for its principal support. In other words, the base of support remained narrow. The total income from contributions and membership fees in 1918-19 was $15,008.49. Of this amount, $12,906.05 was given by thirty-two donors. Thus, just over 3 per cent of the

[54] Evans, "The Negro in Chicago Industry," p. 15.
[55] *Ibid.,* pp. 15-16.
[56] Interview, Chicago, July 13, 1961.
[57] Lawson to Hill, Sept. 19, 1919, Victor F. Lawson Papers, Outgoing Letters, Personal Series, Newberry Library, Chicago, Illinois.

contributors furnished 87 per cent of the income. Even more significant was the fact that three contributors furnished nearly 50 per cent of the budget.[58]

Dependence upon a small group of large contributors created a number of problems. In the first place, it was hard to distribute income throughout the year and, thereby, to avoid "lean" months and "fat" months. For instance, it was usually well over in the fiscal year before enough money could be raised to match the greater part of Rosenwald's contribution, as required. When other large contributors deferred payments until the middle or towards the end of the fiscal year, there were serious administrative problems. These conditions made effective program planning difficult. As the demand for League services grew, there was no way to determine how many new obligations could be safely assumed. Support having steadily mounted each year since the founding of the League, those responsible for program planning usually took optimistic views of the organization's potential. The League's work was steadily expanded to meet the pressing social and economic needs of Chicago's Negro population. Financial expedients were used to get through the "lean" months.

February, 1920 was such a month. At the middle of the month, the League was unable to pay its bills. Harry D. Oppenheimer, a Jewish businessman and a very active Urban League board member, loaned the agency $800 to meet its obligations. But conditions did not improve by the end of the month. A few days before the payroll was due, there was no money available for salaries. Oppenheimer and Hill turned to Rosenwald for a loan to cover this emergency.[59]

Meanwhile, the organization tried to broaden the base of its support. New contributors were sought among both whites and Negroes. Victor F. Lawson's renewed zeal for the cause of racial adjustment, resulting from his membership on the Chicago Commission on Race Relations, served the League to good advantage. Not only did he make a personal contribution of $1,000 annually, he also tried to motivate other leading business and professional men to make contributions. Getting men like Lawson to engage in such

---

[58] *Third Annual Report, 1918-19,* pp. 7-8.

[59] Rosenwald refused to grant a loan but agreed to advance $500 on his contribution for that year. Harry D. Oppenheimer to William C. Graves, Feb. 25, 1920; telegrams from Graves to Rosenwald, Feb. 26, 1920 and from Rosenwald to Graves, Feb. 27, 1920; Graves to Hill, Feb. 28, 1920, Rosenwald Papers.

work was a part of the League's "comprehensive plan" for financing its work for 1920. Rosenwald allowed the use of his name in the recruiting of "other influential gentlemen." These men would "call a meeting with the view of placing the facts before others who, knowing them," would support the Urban League. Lawson had been approached through his pastor, John Gardner, who was a member of the League's board of directors.[60] Lawson responded immediately to this appeal and worked enthusiastically to help raise the League's budget.[61] An effort was also made to get a larger percentage of the budget from the Negro community. Robert L. Bradley, a Baptist minister from Detroit, came to Chicago to conduct the campaign among Negroes.[62] As a result of the more vigorous fund drive conducted in 1920, contributions totaling $21,547.42 were received.[63]

In spite of depressed economic conditions, a spirited fund campaign was planned and conducted during the next fiscal year — 1920-21. At least two influential board members, however, were inclined toward a review of the League's financial prospects before approving an enlarged budget. George C. Hall and William C. Graves called for a comparison of the Chicago Urban League's salary scale and budget with those of other branches. They were particularly interested in having the National Urban League assume a larger portion of T. Arnold Hill's salary.[64] Nevertheless, a budget totaling $30,000 was announced. Surprisingly, the League raised $27,943.71 during this year of economic depression. When the balance from the previous year was added, the organization's budget was oversubscribed.[65]

Although the drive did not officially open until April, a publicity campaign was launched among Negroes in early February. Throughout the fund drive, the *Chicago Defender* gave unlimited support to the effort to secure $10,000 from Negro contributors. Those who sponsored parties or other affairs to raise money were

---

[60] John Gardner to Lawson, Feb. 27, 1920, quoted in Lawson to Graves, Mar. 1, 1920, Lawson Papers.

[61] *Ibid.;* Lawson to Gardner, Mar. 1, 1920, Lawson Papers; *Chicago Defender,* May 22, 1920; May 29, 1920.

[62] *Ibid.,* May 22, 1920; May 29, 1920.

[63] *Fourth Annual Report, 1919-20,* p. 15.

[64] Statement by William C. Graves and George C. Hall, Dec. 8, 1920, Rosenwald Papers. Hill received fifty dollars per month from the National League for serving as western field secretary for the national organization.

[65] *Fifth Annual Report, 1920-21,* p. 11.

assured of good newspaper coverage.[66] The names of individuals and groups, such as the porters on a particular train who made contributions, were published with laudatory comments.[67] Still Negro contributions did not amount to the desired one-third of total income. These gifts totaled only $6,656.48, of which $1,743.95 was raised especially for unemployment relief.[68]

The success of the 1920-21 campaign was due to the efforts of Victor F. Lawson. In June, 1921 he composed a four-page letter of appeal asking selected citizens for financial contributions to the League. The appeal was based upon the findings of the Chicago Commission on Race Relations and the League's role in lessening racial tensions. Lawson said that his membership on the Commission had given him and "every other white member . . . a new understanding of the gravity of the situation with which we are dealing, and of the personal and inescapable responsibility on every citizen for his best contribution to a wise solution of this most difficult civic problem." He felt that the League had part of the answer to this problem. His letter concluded:

> In a word this race problem — the most difficult of all civic problems in a city of three million cosmopolitan population — is Chicago's problem, *Your* problem, mine. What are we doing about it? . . . Hereafter "let us have peace" — the peace of common justice and good will. Anything less is *dangerous.* To this end I ask your support — your continued support — of the work of the Chicago Urban League.[69]

The recipients of this letter were selected from the membership list of the Union League Club. Sixteen hundred names were selected and sent to T. Arnold Hill for the elimination of those who were already contributors. Hill was also sent a copy of the letter but was instructed to hold it in strict confidence. Lawson was afraid that if his letter were "duplicated by others" its effectiveness would be decreased.[70]

By July responses to this letter started coming in. Many of those who wrote took Lawson's advice and granted Hill an interview to give them an understanding of what the Urban League was doing.

---

[66] See *Chicago Defender,* Feb. 12, 1921; Feb. 19, 1921; Feb. 26, 1921.
[67] *Ibid.,* Apr. 2, 1921; Apr. 9, 1921; Apr. 16, 1921; Apr. 23, 1921; Apr. 30, 1921.
[68] *Fifth Annual Report, 1920-21,* p. 10.
[69] Letter of appeal from Lawson to selected citizens, June 15, 1921, Lawson Papers.
[70] Lawson to Hill, June 16, 1921; Lawson to Edgar A. Bancroft, chairman of the Commission on Race Relations, June 25, 1921, Lawson Papers.

Many of the letters contained checks in varying amounts. For several months Lawson's secretary regularly transmitted checks to Hill and notified him of appointments for interviews. In one letter Hill was sent checks totaling $500 from Samuel Insull, including contributions from the various components of his utilities empire.[71]

Ending 1920-21 with a balance of over $4,000, the League had high expectations for the next fiscal year. These expectations failed to materialize. The budget was set at $33,768.55, with hopes of raising around $30,000.[72] The National Urban League's extension secretary was brought to Chicago to "organize for the drive with the idea of getting more members and money among colored people."[73] The *Defender* again gave good editorial and publicity coverage of the drive,[74] but little success was achieved among Negroes. By October only $2,838.18 had been collected in the Negro community. In order to stimulate Negro giving, the *Defender* misleadingly announced: "White friends have given $20,000 of the total yearly budget this year." It was also stated that Rosenwald would give an additional $2,500 if $12,000, an impossible sum, was raised in three weeks.[75] For the first time in its short history, the Chicago Urban League failed to raise its budget. Both its white and Negro friends reduced their support. At the end of the year just $16,482.80 had been raised, but the organization had spent $25,295.53. This wiped out the balance from 1920-21 and left a deficit of $4,244.80.[76]

Program curtailment was in order; for the "lean" years had begun. "Modest curtailments" were inaugurated at the beginning of the fiscal year 1922-23, but they were too modest. Between February 15 and March 15 no money was available for salaries.[77] Although receipts for 1922-23 were larger than for 1921-22, expenditures again exceeded income; and the League's deficit rose to almost $8,000.[78]

[71] Lawson to Hill, Aug. 8, 1921. Throughout the period July to October letters conveying checks went from Lawson's secretary, W. Werner, to Hill. Copies of these letters are in the Lawson Papers. No record was found of the total amount received as a result of this appeal, but the volume of letters would indicate that it was a considerable sum.
[72] Hill to Graves, Feb. 21, 1922, Rosenwald Papers.
[73] Hill to Graves, Feb. 25, 1922, Rosenwald Papers.
[74] See *Chicago Defender,* Apr. 1, 1922; Apr. 8, 1922; Apr. 15, 1922; Apr. 29, 1922; May 6, 1922; May 13, 1922.
[75] *Ibid.,* Oct. 7, 1922.
[76] Memorandum on finances from Hill to members of the board of directors, Dec. 1, 1924 (in the files of the League).
[77] Hill to Graves, Mar. 16, 1923, Rosenwald Papers.
[78] *Seventh Annual Report, 1922-23,* p. 14.

In 1923-24, less than $13,000 was used to operate the agency. T. Arnold Hill expressed concern over the deterioration in the League's program resulting from inadequate financial support. He stated, "The Executive Secretary's time was almost wholly given over to the raising of funds. An inefficient Examiner handled our Employment Service for the greater part of the year, and cheap stenographic work had to be tolerated. In fact, the entire organization suffered loss of prestige and morale from which we can recover only when ample finances are available to pay salaries when due and to provide for necessary promotional expenses."[79]

Several weeks later Hill sounded more optimistic. He reported to Graves that the note signed by Bridges had been paid. Furthermore, the deficit had been reduced, and Hill felt "encouraged over the prospects of pulling out of debt within a comparatively short time."[80] His optimism, however, may have resulted from the prospect that he would soon be leaving Chicago and the Chicago Urban League.

Some of the League's "loss of prestige and morale" dated from Hill's excursion into politics in 1923. In that year, he ran for alderman. This act violated one of the cardinal principles of the Urban League movement. References to politics were scrupulously avoided in League philosophy and in statements on policy and purposes. This partially accounted for the organization's success in appealing to diverse groups. Although the aldermanic elections in Chicago were supposedly nonpartisan, the existence of political machines and numerous factions made the nonpartisan label of dubious significance. It was inevitable that Hill would be subjected to adverse publicity, as would the League incidentally.

Several things were involved in motivating Hill's decision to enter the aldermanic campaign. In the first place, he probably had reason to feel that there was a good possibility of his being elected. The reform forces were mustering for an all-out offensive against the Thompson machine in 1923. The people had been aroused by the graft and scandals made public during grand-jury investigations which resulted in indictments against members of Mayor William Hale Thompson's administration. The storm was so great that the Republicans were relieved when Thompson declined to run for another term. There was every indication that William E. Dever, the

[79] Memorandum on finances, Dec. 1, 1924.
[80] Hill to Graves, Dec. 26, 1924, Rosenwald Papers.

Democratic candidate, who had the backing of the reformers, would be elected.[81] It also seemed possible that aroused public opinion would bring the defeat of the aldermen who had given allegiance to the Thompson machine. One of the chief targets of the reform groups was Louis B. Anderson, the Negro alderman from the second ward. Anderson served as Thompson's floor leader in the City Council and was accused of protecting vice in his ward.[82] Hill was the reformers' choice to replace Anderson. With the Chicago Urban League in debt and being forced to curtail its activities, Hill was ready to move into a more promising field. He had the endorsement of the more influential and dependable supporters of the Urban League and felt no doubt that running for alderman was a safe way to move up from his Urban League position. In any case, his job with the League would not be in jeopardy.[83]

The Negro community, however, was not a strong territory for reformers. Vice and corruption were not the main issues in the minds of second ward voters. They were more interested in the status of the candidates as militant racial leaders. The Municipal Voters' League and the *Chicago Daily News* gave Hill strong endorsements, but the *Chicago Tribune* seemed mainly interested in discrediting Anderson. Hill was presented in the *Daily News* as the candidate of the "respectable colored citizens of the ward," who would free the area of "vicious resorts." Contrasting the two leading candidates, the paper said: "On the one hand voters are asked to support an alderman during whose council terms the ward has acquired its present injurious reputation, and on the other hand, they have a candidate who well represents the highest ideals and ambitions of his race."[84] But within the ward, Hill's support came mainly from women's clubs and groups who were uninitiated to the ways of politics. On the other hand, Anderson, an astute politician and an able lawyer, had the backing of organized political groups and the Negro press.

While the Hill group was talking about vice and decency,[85] the

[81] Lloyd Lewis and Henry Justin Smith, *Chicago: The History of Its Reputation* (New York: Harcourt, Brace and Company, 1929), pp. 441-443.
[82] Municipal Voters' League of Chicago, *Twenty-seventh Annual Preliminary Report,* 1923, p. 15.
[83] Interviews, Chicago, June 26, 1961; July 13, 1961.
[84] *Chicago Daily News,* Feb. 3, 1923; see also issues for Feb. 17 and 24, 1923. The Municipal Voters' League's endorsement of Hill was in the *Chicago Daily News,* Feb. 21, 1923. For the *Chicago Tribune's* position on Anderson see papers for Feb. 3 and 14, 1923.
[85] *Chicago Defender,* Feb. 10, 1923.

Anderson forces pressed the question of racial advancement. Anderson was pictured as the symbol of Negro political achievement in Chicago. In one Anderson release it was declared:

> The issue in the aldermanic contest of the second ward is plain. A false issue is raised by literary delegates, by the Urban league heels over head in politics. "We will clean up the Second ward," you are told.
>
> Backers of the fight against Louis B. Anderson are not interested in cleaning up the Second ward. The Second ward is as clean as the Gold Coast wards. Tales of immorality and degeneracy float out from the home wards of the reformers with the freedom of the perfume of the Yards [stockyards].
>
> The issue is not one of decency versus indecency, good versus bad, honor versus dishonor. The issue is Louis B. Anderson versus enemies of his Race and their tools in conspiracy to undo him so that it cannot be said that his Race, target of diatribe and ridicule, gives to Chicago a man of superior mind, of skill and power in intellectual combat.[86]

The *Chicago Defender* gave Anderson solid support.[87] The election resulted in Anderson's "overwhelmingly defeating the 'field of gold,' " with 6,360 votes. Hill placed a poor second with 2,572 votes.[88]

After running for office, Hill's usefulness to the Urban League in Chicago was impaired. His reputation suffered from rumors of personal indiscretion and "mudslinging" tactics that were employed to defeat him. He was no longer a "neutral" figure heading a non-aligned organization.[89]

Actually, the Chicago Urban League had reached the climax of its effectiveness and public appeal during the 1919 riot and the two years following this disturbance. At the end of World War I, the agency experienced a mild decline in support. This condition resulted largely from postwar industrial curtailments. Then, with the outbreak of racial violence, the League took on new meaning for Chicago leaders. They looked to it to provide "sane" leadership in the Negro community. The agency made recommendations and furnished materials and personnel to help in interpreting the conditions which fostered the riot. Increased public awareness of racial conditions was reflected in the financial support given the League. Another contributing factor to the League's well-being during the

---

[86] *Ibid.*, Feb. 24, 1923.

[87] *Ibid.*

[88] *Chicago Defender*, Mar. 3, 1923.

[89] Interviews, Chicago, June 26, 1961; July 13, 1961.

1919-21 period was labor unrest. Employers needed Negro labor to help thwart unionization, and they supported the League because it was a supplier of such workers. By 1922, however, conditions had changed. Public apathy concerning race relations had returned, and the unions had lost, temporarily, in their struggle with management. The League had not, and probably could not have, prepared for this situation. It continued, after 1921, to emphasize employment services, but there was little demand for Negro workers. It asked for public support of its work to adjust migrants to urban living, but migration became increasingly unpopular. The increased financial support of the riot period had been used for staff expansion, without giving consideration to revising program activities. So, between 1922 and 1924, decreasing income forced the League to make successive reductions in its staff and programs. By 1924, the agency had reached an advanced stage or decline. The year 1924 also marked the end of an era — the T. Arnold Hill Era — for the Chicago Urban League.

4

PRELUDE TO DEPRESSION, 1925-29

Early in 1925, T. Arnold Hill left Chicago to become secretary of the National Urban League's new department of industrial relations. This job was a promotion for Hill; moreover, it rescued him from the uncertain future facing the Chicago League.

Albon L. Foster was selected to replace Hill. This was a rather surprising choice. Since the executive secretaryship in Chicago was considered one of the more desirable posts in the Urban League movement, it was expected that a man of considerable experience in League work would be selected to fill this position. It is probable, however, that those who were knowledgeable about actual conditions in Chicago had no desire to hazard a change from their own jobs at that time. In any case, Foster was pleasantly surprised when Hill notified him that he was under consideration for the job.[1] Although Foster had four years of social work experience with the Y.M.C.A., he was a relative newcomer to Urban League work. Two years as executive secretary of the Canton, Ohio branch was the extent of his League experience.[2]

Foster's inexperience and lack of acquaintance with Chicago conditions were both assets and liabilities in beginning his new job. He was not burdened by adherence to the traditions and fading idealism of those who had founded the organization, who experienced the flurry of activity during the war and the riot, and who since 1922 had tried to revitalize a waning organization. On the

[1] Interview, Chicago, July 1, 1961.

[2] *Ibid.; Opportunity,* III (July, 1925), 221; VI (Mar., 1928), 86-87; *Chicago Defender,* Oct. 2, 1943.

other hand, as a newcomer, Foster could not gain immediately the acceptance and confidence which Hill had earned by force of personality and eight years of dedicated service. Several board members felt that under any new executive the organization would discontinue operation within a year.[3]

T. Arnold Hill and Albon L. Foster differed in several ways. Both men were sincerely dedicated to the principles of the Urban League movement, but they differed in personality and methods of administration. Foster lacked Hill's diplomacy and broad point of view, but he had attributes which suited him for the role he was to play in Chicago. Hill was strongly committed to the interracial concepts of the League movement; Foster preached interracial conciliation but showed deep faith in the Negro upper-class doctrine of racial solidarity. Hill was nationally known in social work circles and greatly respected by officials of the National Urban League; Foster was virtually an unknown. Hill had felt that his career was being jeopardized through the declining fortunes of the Chicago League; but Foster saw the move from Canton to Chicago as a promotion. Hill was at his best in person-to-person contacts; Foster seems to have preferred group situations. Hill could work with cliques, such as the George C. Hall–William C. Graves influence, and still maintain his perspective; Foster tried to work within the League's formal organizational framework, as he saw it, and his departures from this procedure lacked adroitness. The new executive secretary, like the former one, was a man of seemingly limitless energy and great determination. These were qualities sorely needed to administer the Chicago Urban League in 1925.

Getting the money to carry on an effective program was the League's major problem. From its founding to about 1922, employment services and the adjustment of migrants were the main features of the organization's work; but after 1922, these activities no longer excited public enthusiasm. Even during the prosperity of the late 1920's there was no great demand for Negro labor; and new job opportunities came only at irregular intervals. The League's program could not be built around the placement of several hundred domestic servants and the opening of a few new positions each year. Yet, there were no obvious choices to replace industrial relations and work with migrants as basic program features. Chicago was having a period of relative racial peace. Memory of the riot of 1919

[3] Interview, Chicago, July 1, 1961.

no longer pricked Chicagoan's civic conscience, and gangsterism had replaced race relations as the chief concern of civic leaders and reformers. Under these conditions, the League's income was not sufficient to maintain a dynamic organization. Program activities and financial support were interdependent. Without good financial support it was virtually impossible to maintain a forceful program; and without a vigorous program it was difficult to dramatize the need for funds.

Foster tried to utilize his small staff and limited finances to stimulate renewed public awareness of the problems faced by Negroes in Chicago. With a staff of just three professional workers — one in the department of civic betterment and two in the department of industrial relations — program possibilities were very limited. Four staff members, including the executive secretary, could do very little toward ameliorating the condition of Chicago's large Negro population. Foster realized the limitations imposed by these meager resources and tried to supplement his staff with volunteer workers. The first move in this direction was an effort to enlist lay participation in the work of the League departments. A plan recommended to the board in 1921 was revived to achieve this objective. In 1921 the executive committee had suggested the formation of an advisory council with subcommittees for each department. Departmental subcommittees would "study and recommend to the Board of Directors, appropriate action in each field" and "assist in practical work assigned" by the board.[4] In 1925, this plan was modified and put into effect. Noncoordinated advisory committees were organized for the two functioning departments. A nineteen-member committee on civic betterment and an eleven-member committee on industrial relations were established. These groups consisted of both board members and nonboard members.[5] As its next step, the League tried to recruit women volunteers to "assist in raising funds" and to serve on various subcommittees "concerned with carrying out program objectives."[6]

Under Foster, the Chicago Urban League's program during the late 1920's became distinctly promotional in nature, with the im-

[4] Report of the Executive Committee to the Board of Directors, Sept. 29, 1921, quoted in Dorothy Counse, Louise Gilbert, and Agnes Van Driel, "The Chicago Urban League," June 18, 1936 (unpublished study in the files of the Welfare Council of Metropolitan Chicago), p. 16.

[5] *Tenth Annual Report, 1925-26,* p. 3.

[6] The *Broad Ax* (Chicago), Apr. 18, 1925.

provement of race relations as the basic theme of program operations. The traditional program areas — industrial relations, research, civic improvement, and coordinating welfare services — were maintained; but the projects pursued were designed to have more publicity appeal than ameliorative value. The League needed publicity to create a favorable image of itself. Unfortunately, publicity oriented activities which could have furnished the means for accomplishing the League's traditional objectives — improving the social and economic conditions of Negroes — came to be looked upon as ends in themselves. An interracial dinner, organization of an interracial committee, speeches attacking an evil, or League representation on a board or commission — such activities were heralded as definite accomplishments. In some cases they were, but most of the activities had no definite objectives beyond the general cause of better race relations.

The *Chicago Defender* expressed the prevailing Chicago Urban League point of view in an editorial commending the agency on its annual dinner in 1928. The editor declared:

> No better spirit of interracial good will has ever been manifested in this country than that shown Monday night when enlightened members of two races in Chicago sat together and discussed at length the best methods of bringing about a better understanding among themselves. After all, the race problem in America is the problem of ignorance. When men and women are in ignorance of their neighbors and their hopes, ambitions and aspirations, they are unsympathetic toward them. As long as they do not know, they cannot understand.
>
> The meeting, sponsored by the Urban league of Chicago, at which those interested came together as friends and brothers, is the kind of which America is so much in need. There should be more of them, not so much for the purpose of discussing racial problems as for the purpose of getting acquainted. There can be no doubt that those who participated in this affair have enriched their lives by the extent to which they were capable of understanding. And their influence will be felt where it will do most good.
>
> The dinner was an excellent testimonial to the growing feeling of good will between the races and the Urban league is to be congratulated on making this possible, if for nothing else.[7]

Yet it was not the "enlightened" and the "interested" who were most in need of the League's educational work. Interracial dinners and interracial committees for the purpose of achieving general changes in attitudes toward Negroes, although laudable, were ques-

[7] *Chicago Defender,* Nov. 24, 1928.

tionable uses of the League's meager staff and financial resources. Such activities, however, made good copy in the Negro press. They also provided a channel of communication between the "better" class of white people and the aspiring young professional men and businessmen in the Negro community.

The League's research work was an example of the public relations orientation of its program. The use of facts obtained through research as the basis of its operation was fundamental in Urban League philosophy. Nevertheless, the Chicago Urban League was without a director of research for long and frequent intervals. When in 1926 the executive secretary appealed to the board of directors to re-establish the department of research, he based his request primarily on the public relations function of this work. "The League suffers from the lack of publicity which the Department of Research has in the past provided," the secretary said. He continued: "The temporary discontinuance of this Department has prevented us from rendering an effective and efficient service to students and other organizations that call upon us as the one authoritative service on Negro matters, for information and advice."[8] Since the organization was having financial difficulty at this time, funds were not available for a director of research. Any studies undertaken had to be conducted by the departments of civic improvement and industrial relations.[9]

These departments conducted several studies, and they cooperated with other organizations in making additional investigations. The League obtained volunteers for a survey of the near West Side made by the University of Chicago and the Institute for Juvenile Research, but the League had no part in the supervision of the study.[10] The civic department made "studies of day nurseries, of summer camps, and of several neighborhoods." What the League called its "most important neighborhood study" covered the two blocks bounded by Thirty-third and Thirty-fifth Streets on Calumet Avenue. The material collected in these studies were used for "a discussion of the housing situation" in a housing conference conducted by the Woman's City Club. Pictures made during housing investigations

---

[8] Secretary's Report to Board of Directors, 1926, quoted in Counse, Gilbert, and Van Driel, "The Chicago Urban League," p. 8.

[9] *Tenth Annual Report, 1925-26,* p. 20.

[10] Secretary's Report to Board of Directors, 1926, cited in Counse, Gilbert, and Van Driel, p. 8.

were formed into an exhibit on bad housing conditions.[11] The industrial department recruited volunteers to canvass 275 business establishments on Chicago's South Side "for the purpose of securing more openings for high school boys and girls." In announcing the findings of this survey, the League made one of its first statements on the principle of merit employment. This statement also contained an implicit avowal of the need for racial solidarity. The League's report stated: "While there may be those who regard it a personal matter as to whom a privately conducted business shall employ, the Urban League believes that employers should think in terms of merit, and should employ any person qualified to perform the required task, regardless of color, race or creed. Particularly should this be true of those firms which are dependent upon a particular race for existence and success."[12] It was this philosophy upon which the *Chicago Whip,* a militant Negro newspaper, based its campaign several years later to force white South Side businesses to employ Negroes. Aside from reflecting the views of the executive secretary and some other League officials, this statement showed an awareness of the growing "Negro consciousness" on the South Side.

In January, 1928 the Chicago Urban League was able temporarily to re-establish its department of research. This new department, however, did not undertake investigations upon which to base program activities. Its chief contribution to the League's work was publicity and the prestige that came from the League's association with the University of Chicago in financing the department. The new director of research, E. Franklin Frazier, was already engaged in his study of the Negro family in Chicago as a research assistant at the University.[13] As part-time director of the League's department of research, Frazier continued his project. The League furnished him office space, access to the materials it had available, and a small salary. It could boast of joint sponsorship, with the Local Community Research Committee of the University, of a study of Negro life in Chicago.[14] Then, too, E. Franklin Frazier had already received some recognition as a Negro sociologist. He had conducted

[11] *Eleventh Annual Report, 1926-27,* p. 11.
[12] *Ibid.,* pp. 11-12.
[13] E. Franklin Frazier, *The Negro Family in Chicago* (Chicago: the University of Chicago Press, 1932), pp. xiii-xv.
[14] *Chicago Defender,* Jan. 14, 1928; *Opportunity,* VI (Aug., 1928), 248; *Thirteenth Annual Report, 1928-29; Twelfth Annual Report, 1927-28.* The pages in these reports were not numbered.

several investigations, studied in Denmark, published articles in various periodicals, and served as director of the Atlanta School of Social Work.[15] The League capitalized on his name to secure newspaper space in its campaign to keep the agency before the public. The arrangement between Frazier and the League was probably mutually beneficial, but the League's greatest gain was from the additional publicity and prestige. League support was not crucial to the completion of the study. Frazier's findings, which were later published, would have been available, in any case, through the University of Chicago. Upon completion of his work in 1929, Frazier's connection with the League ended, and he left Chicago to join the faculty of Fisk University.[16]

The work of the department of civic betterment was severely handicapped by insufficient personnel. A broad program — including a thrift campaign, a better health drive, the organization of neighborhood clubs, and a referral service for welfare cases — was undertaken. This department's work, however, was rather superficial; for it was beyond the capabilities of a department consisting of one professional worker to execute such a wide range of activities.

Most of the civic department's work was promotional and educational in nature. During the thrift campaign meetings were held in which South Side businessmen explained "simple facts in their respective fields to the surprisingly large number of people" who were "ignorant of the most simple methods of thrift."[17] Other speakers were recruited to "carry the message of thrift to thousands in churches, lodges, clubs and places of employment."[18] Similar methods were used in promoting better health. Both individuals and organizations were asked to assist in the health campaign during designated months.[19] By securing the services of a number of speakers from different organizations, the department maintained a speakers bureau to furnish year-round talks on thrift and health. The subjects covered by these speakers were later expanded to include "all phases of the so-called race problem."[20] Little success was achieved in the League's effort to organize neighborhood clubs. Lacking the staff personnel to perform this work, the organization

[15] *Twelfth Annual Report, 1927-28.*
[16] *Thirteenth Annual Report, 1928-29.*
[17] *Chicago Defender,* Jan. 23, 1926.
[18] *Ibid.,* Jan. 9, 1926.
[19] *Ibid.*
[20] *Chicago Defender,* Apr. 3, 1926.

tried unsuccessfully to get the existing neighborhood clubs to undertake this task.[21] On various occasions the department of civic betterment did help to dramatize the housing and social needs of the Negro community to other groups. Tours of the slum districts were conducted for students from colleges and universities and the members of civic clubs.[22] The League also participated in agitation for additional park facilities on the South Side[23] and in protesting the segregation of Negro pupils in the schools of Morgan Park.[24]

In October, 1927 the civic department secured help in its work from the South Side store of a large Chicago furniture company. The second floor of the League's headquarters was furnished as "a model apartment for the demonstration of economics and household arts." Furniture for the four-room apartment was provided by the L. Fish Furniture Company. This was the beginning of a questionable relationship between the League and this business firm. The League's executive secretary said that the apartment was established to demonstrate to those who were forced to live in substandard housing "the methods for making an ugly, ill-kept flat into a decent appearing home."[25] This area of the League's building was also used by classes in "domestic science," coming from the public schools in the neighborhood and by the League's department of industrial relations for the purpose of training domestic workers.[26] In 1928 the L. Fish Company provided $100 to be distributed by the League to the winners of an essay contest on the subject "Better Homes and Better Health." In addition, Nahum D. Brascher, L. Fish Company's Negro public relations man, was allowed to work very closely with the League's staff. The annual report for 1928 even listed Brascher as a member of the League's staff, with the added note that he was "loaned by L. Fish Furniture Company."[27]

There was some suspicion that the furniture company's motives were not altogether charitable in maintaining its relationship with the League. The editor of the *Chicago Defender,* who was also a director of the League, commended the work being done by the League and the furniture company in their campaign to improve

---

[21] *Tenth Annual Report, 1925-26,* p. 18.
[22] *Chicago Defender,* July 24, 1926.
[23] *Tenth Annual Report, 1925-26,* pp. 7-8.
[24] *Chicago Defender,* Jan. 15, 1927.
[25] *Ibid.,* Oct. 29, 1927.
[26] *Twelfth Annual Report, 1927-28.*
[27] *Ibid.* See also *Chicago Defender,* Nov. 24, 1928.

home conditions in the Negro community. But the editorial implied that commercial considerations were present in this community betterment work.[28] A former League official said that Brascher's work was designed to increase Negro patronage of the L. Fish store.[29] The Urban League's board of directors took cognizance of this situation in its January, 1929 meeting. The board was informed by the executive secretary "that there was no intention on the part of the League Staff to lend itself to the promotion of any commercial enterprise." He felt "that both the model apartment and the essay contest had helped materially in the efforts of the Civic Department to emphasize better home conditions and health." Nevertheless, the board "warned the staff members against forming any entangling alliances or in any way permitting the work of any department to be so closely identified with commercial enterprises as to leave any question as to the motive."[30] The civic department continued its relationship with L. Fish Company and in February announced plans for the 1929 essay contest.[31] The department had little choice but to continue this arrangement. For the past two years the meager civic betterment program had been centered around the "model apartment" and the essay contest.

The industrial department also worked under very adverse conditions. Throughout the predepression years, unemployment was prevalent in the Negro community. In deference to this department's past pre-eminence, it was assigned two of the organization's four professional staff workers. Continuing efforts were made to place Negro workers, but the dearth of demand for labor left the industrial staff little to do except engage in explorative activities, many of which had dubious significance in relation to the League's goals. For instance, in 1925 and 1926 the industrial department, along with the civic department, was engaged in organizing "Educational Clubs" among domestic servants and in plants employing Negro workers. These clubs had as their purpose the promotion of "health, thrift, recreation and other educational programs for the workers."[32]

Few industrial gains for the Negro could be listed by the League for the fiscal year ending in October, 1926. The organization stated

---

[28] *Ibid.*, Aug. 4, 1928.
[29] Interview, Chicago, July 1, 1961.
[30] Minutes of the Board of Directors, Jan. 3, 1929, copy in Salmon O. Levinson Papers, University of Chicago Library.
[31] *Chicago Defender*, Feb. 2, 1929.
[32] *Tenth Annual Report, 1925-26*, p. 15.

that "signs of continued depression" had existed throughout the year. The industrial department's only "real achievement" was the establishment of the departmental advisory committee which had among its membership representatives of leading Chicago organizations — such as the Illinois Manufacturers Association, the Men's City Club, and the Union League Club. Efforts were made to place Negroes with the Chicago utility companies, with the Great Atlantic and Pacific Tea Company stores as managers, and with the Bell Telephone Company; but the only success in industrial placement was the securing of a few additional jobs with several concerns which already had large Negro labor forces. The greatest demand was for women to work in laundries and as domestics. In these two fields 1,536 placements were made as compared with 517 in other jobs.[33]

During the winter of 1927 the League turned its attention to the relief of the destitute unemployed. In January representatives of social agencies were called together to form a joint committee on unemployment and emergency relief. This group appealed to the public for clothing and food for the unemployed. The League also assisted in the supervision of an emergency lodging house, which was established through the influence of Alderman Louis B. Anderson to accommodate the overflow from the Municipal Lodging House.

Early in 1927 the Chicago branch obtained the cooperation of the National Urban League in an effort to bring the plight of Negro labor to public attention. The Chicago organization sponsored a "Negro in Industry Week" during the week of April 3 to persuade industries and business enterprises to make new skilled and semi-skilled jobs available to Negroes.[34] The League announced that the activities of this week were designed to accomplish the following aims:

(1) To arouse public thinking on the low status of Negroes forced upon them by lack of occupational opportunity, (2) to impress upon Negroes the necessity for training and thorough application to the jobs they now hold, as a means of widening employment opportunities for them, and demonstrating the capacity of the race, and (3) to get jobs for colored

---

[33] *Ibid.*, pp. 11-14.

[34] The industrial relations department of the National Urban League, under T. Arnold Hill, started the observance of "Negro in Industry Week" in 1926. In that year campaigns were conducted in Philadelphia and Boston. In addition to Chicago, Baltimore and Columbus (Ohio) planned campaigns for 1927. See T. Arnold Hill, "The Negro in Industry, 1926," *Opportunity*, V (Feb., 1927), 63.

men and women in occupations and business houses that do not now offer employment, or which afford little chance for advancement.[35]

Leading staff members of the National Urban League came to Chicago to participate in the conferences and meetings scheduled during the "Negro in Industry" campaign.

In conjunction with this observance, the League started a drive to get white businesses operating in the Negro community to employ Negroes in clerical positions. The industrial department had made a survey in 1925-26 of industries employing Negro workers and found that employment in the fields then open to Negroes was relatively stable, but there were "scarcely any possibilities of sudden employment increases."[36] The League then turned to white businesses in the Negro community as possible sources of new jobs. Before the agency began its survey to determine the "facts" of the situation, a statement was released to the press which declared that "more than 75 per cent of the money spent by Race residents on the South side goes to South side merchants who are in most cases of the white race." At the same time it was announced that a joint citizens' committee was being organized to assist in the drive to place high school boys and girls in South Side stores.[37]

Under the auspices of the League's joint committee for the employment of Negro workers on the South Side, the industrial department began a survey in January, 1927 to substantiate the contention that Negroes were not employed in most South Side businesses.[38] An article in the *Defender* stated:

It has been generally felt for some time that the owners and proprietors of South Side businesses should give more employment to Race people and that positions which carry responsibility should be open to them. Although porters and maids are employed in large numbers there are entirely too few cashiers and office clerks and the league will lay special emphasis on the securing of that type of employment.[39]

---

[35] *Eleventh Annual Report, 1926-27,* p. 10; *Chicago Defender,* Feb. 19, 1927.
[36] *Tenth Annual Report, 1925-26,* p. 13.
[37] *Chicago Defender,* Jan. 1, 1927. It was an idiosyncrasy of the editor to substitute the word "Race" wherever the word "Negro" would have appeared in his paper.
[38] A similar project was conducted by the Urban League of New York City in 1926. There a joint committee for the employment of Negroes in Harlem was formed. With the support of the Negro press, the New York City League tried to place workers in stores catering to Negroes. See Ira DeA. Reid, "Industrial Problems in Cities — New York City," *Opportunity,* IV (Feb., 1926), 69; Hill, "The Negro in Industry, 1926," p. 63.
[39] *Chicago Defender,* Jan. 15, 1927.

The survey was conducted by the League's industrial secretary, H. N. Robinson, with the assistance of a former League staff member, Mrs. Mary R. Smith, and a graduate student at the University of Chicago, W. H. Bolton. The study of the situation was largely a formality; for it was already generally known that Negroes were not used by these concerns in clerical positions, and the League was already preparing to launch its campaign. Volunteers were being recruited and organized to make a store-to-store canvass, and people with clerical training were urged to register with the League to fill the anticipated openings.[40]

The League's involvement in the South Side employment campaign marked a departure from its usual methods of operation. Interracial cooperation was the keynote in most League projects, but this drive was clearly a manifestation of Negro militancy. Although the League's phase of the project used persuasion in attempting to open new jobs, this was primarily a Negro project directed against whites. The joint committee was composed of representatives of Negro organizations and representatives from the Negro press. It was also a project with mass support in the Negro community. Even the aldermen from wards with large Negro constituencies found it expedient to give their endorsements and assistance.[41]

Although the employment drive was scheduled to close with the observance of "Negro In Industry Week" in 1927, the League continued this program for almost two years. A number of South Side firms did open new jobs to Negroes. Early in 1928 the Standard Oil Company placed one of its stations under Negro attendants and promised to turn over other stations to Negroes if this experiment succeeded.[42] Before the end of the year, Negro clerks were employed by the Silver Dollar Store, the Great Atlantic and Pacific Tea Stores, the Spiegel Furniture Store, and several other retail businesses.[43] The most heralded breakthrough came with the opening of the South Center Department Store. This store began operation with Negroes comprising one-third of its employees and soon raised this proportion to one-half. The League proclaimed this a "practical

[40] *Ibid.*, Jan. 15, 1927; Jan. 29, 1927.
[41] *Ibid.*, Mar. 5, 1927.
[42] *Ibid.*, Mar. 31, 1928; *Twelfth Annual Report, 1927-28.*
[43] *Chicago Defender*, Dec. 22, 1928; Dec. 29, 1928; Albon L. Foster, "Twenty Years of Interracial Goodwill Through Social Service," in Chicago Urban League, *Two Decades of Service* (Chicago: Chicago Urban League, 1936).

experiment in race relations." It was felt that South Center's success in integrating its 114 employees was a refutation of the traditional arguments — unavailability of efficient Negroes for such positions and the refusal of whites to work with Negroes.[44]

At the same time that these gains were being made, losses were occurring in other places. One concern moved from the Negro community into another area and dismissed its thirty-five Negro employees.[45] A pencil factory also dismissed 120 Negro workers when it moved from the South Side. Laundry employees were released in a downtown department store, and a hospital dismissed its Negro maids in all but one section of the institution. Other concerns dispensed with the use of Negro porters, elevator operators, and restaurant workers. One of these businesses stated that it wished "to experiment with white help" in the work being done by Negroes, and the hospital was suspected of instituting a complete policy of segregation in its facilities.[46] In early 1929 the Standard Oil Company released the Negro attendants it had employed and replaced them with white workers. The company said that during slack periods men with seniority were given preference in employment.[47]

Depressed economic conditions after 1929 did not end the South Side job campaign, but the initiative in this movement passed from the League into more radical hands. The *Chicago Whip,* an aggressive Negro weekly, spearheaded the second phase of this drive. Under the slogan "Spend Your Money Where You Can Work," this paper urged Negroes to boycott stores and businesses which did not employ them. Through boycotts and picketing, some 2,000 jobs were opened in South Side stores.[48] This movement was very popular and well supported by the masses of Negroes. The aggressive nature of this phase of the campaign, however, caused conservative organizations and those dependent upon white support to withhold active participation. Yet, they gave moral support whenever possible. The League's executive secretary said in later years that his organization endorsed the campaign.[49] Nevertheless, boycotts and

---

[44] *Twelfth Annual Report, 1927-28.*
[45] *Chicago Defender,* Dec. 22, 1928
[46] *Twelfth Annual Report, 1927-28.*
[47] *Chicago Defender,* Feb. 9, 1929.
[48] St. Clair Drake and Horace B. Cayton, *Black Metropolis: A Study of Negro Life in a Northern City* (New York: Harcourt, Brace and Company, 1945), pp. 84, 743.
[49] Foster, in *Two Decades of Service.*

picketing were not Urban League methods, and the League was very susceptible to reprisals from the white community. Even the *Chicago Defender,* in spite of earlier boasts of its activities in this area,[50] had to consider the reaction its active support might bring from white advertisers.[51]

The quixotic nature of many League program activities probably resulted from the organization's precarious financial condition throughout this period. When T. Arnold Hill left Chicago, the League had a deficit of over $3,000. Before taking office, the new executive secretary had been led to believe that the organization was out of debt. Some reduction in the deficit occurred, but this was achieved by having several regular contributors make advances on their pledges.[52] No fund drive was conducted in 1924-25; the only income came from renewals by past contributors.[53] The League had small increases in income each year between 1926 and 1929, but it was not until 1929 that the organization ended the fiscal year without a deficit. Efforts were made, by juggling the financial statements appearing in annual reports, to conceal the organization's true financial status.[54]

The League conducted well-publicized financial drives in the Negro community each year. Leading Negro business and professional men provided leadership. Negroes were asked to contribute $10,000 and were told that "white friends" had guaranteed $20,000.[55] No announcements were made of the amounts finally contributed by Negroes. However, a part of the League's income each year came from benefits — dances and other entertainments — patronized by Negroes.[56] The amounts coming from this source varied from slightly over $1,000 listed in the 1927 financial statement to almost $3,000 reported in 1929.

In October, 1926 the board of directors decided to follow the example of the National Urban League and the two New York City

---

[50] See, for example, *Chicago Defender,* Mar. 31, 1928.
[51] Drake and Cayton, *Black Metropolis,* p. 412. It is commonly believed that the withdrawal of advertising and other pressures resulting from this campaign forced the *Whip* to discontinue publication.
[52] Interview, Chicago, July 1, 1961.
[53] *Chicago Defender,* Feb. 20, 1926; *Tenth Annual Report, 1925-26,* p. 20.
[54] *Ibid.,* p. 21; *Eleventh Annual Report, 1926-27,* p. 14.
[55] See *Chicago Defender,* Feb. 20, 1926; Mar. 6, 1926; Apr. 23, 1927; May 7, 1927; Apr. 27, 1929; May 25, 1929; The *Broad Ax* (Chicago), Feb. 20, 1926; Apr. 3, 1926.
[56] The *Chicago Defender,* Nov. 10, 1928, reported one such benefit dance.

branches and try to raise a three-year sustaining fund.[57] The Chicago board adopted the recommendations of its budget committee that a regular fund drive be organized for the fiscal year 1926-27 and that planning start for a campaign beginning in October, 1927 to raise a $60,000 sustaining fund.[58] Final board approval for the sustaining fund drive was given during a meeting on October 7, 1927. It was decided to raise the goal to $75,000 and to run the drive for one month. Board members were asked to submit the names of persons who might assist in the campaign and to accept "the responsibility for securing in cash and pledges a substantial amount."[59] Alfred K. Stern, Julius Rosenwald's son-in-law, acted as general director of the fund drive. During the opening period, several large pledges were obtained to provide the initial impetus for the campaign. Alfred K. Stern and Robert S. Abbott each pledged $1,500; Anthony Overton, a prominent Negro businessman, pledged $1,200; and the president of the League, Elbridge Bancroft Pierce, pledged $1,000. It was also announced that Julius Rosenwald promised to give a sum equal to 10 per cent of all funds subscribed by others.[60] A month after the scheduled closing date of the drive, however, only about $12,000 had been subscribed.[61] Several board members were delinquent in soliciting their quotas of $1,500 in cash and pledges, and some members of the board even neglected to make personal pledges.[62] According to a former League official's appraisal of the campaign: "It was not too successful."[63] Yet the organization's annual income for the last two years of this period did average over $20,000.[64] A portion of the increased income of these years came from pledges made during the sustaining fund drive.

On the eve of the depression, the League received a severe blow

---

[57] On May 15, 1926 the National Urban League, the New York City Urban League, and the Brooklyn Urban League began a joint campaign for $350,000 to finance the work of these three organizations for a period of three years. By July over $200,000 of this amount had been raised. (Editorial), "Sustaining the Urban League Movement," *Opportunity,* IV (June, 1926), 173-174; (editorial), "The Urban League Campaign," *ibid.,* IV (July, 1926), 207-208.

[58] Albon L. Foster to Salmon O. Levinson, Oct. 9, 1926, Levinson Papers.

[59] Foster to Levinson, Oct. 8, 1927, Levinson Papers.

[60] *Chicago Defender,* Nov. 19, 1927; Dec. 31, 1927; Jan. 28, 1928.

[61] *Ibid.,* Dec. 31, 1927.

[62] Foster to Levinson, Dec. 3, 1927, Levinson Papers.

[63] Interview, Chicago, July 1, 1961.

[64] The League's listed income by fiscal year was: 1925-26 — $15,089.71; 1926-27 — $17,356.87; 1927-28 — $22,296.74; 1928-29 — $25,195.75.

to its financial security when Julius Rosenwald withdrew his support. A number of changes took place in the management of Rosenwald's philanthropy between 1925 and 1929. Prior to 1928, the Rosenwald Fund had limited its activities to the distribution of funds for Negro education in the South, and William C. Graves had acted as a one-man foundation in handling Rosenwald's other philanthropic activities. Graves relied heavily upon George C. Hall for guidance in making his recommendations to Rosenwald for contributions to Negro organizations. This situation changed in 1928 when the Rosenwald Fund was reorganized and given control of all philanthropic giving. Meanwhile, Graves retired and moved to California.[65] Edwin R. Embree became president of the Rosenwald Fund, but Alfred K. Stern exerted considerable influence on the Fund's policy regarding the Chicago Urban League. For Stern was the Rosenwald "representative" on the League's board of directors after Graves's retirement. Under the new setup, the diminutive George R. Arthur, executive secretary of the Wabash Avenue Y.M.C.A., became the chief adviser on Negro affairs. It was Stern, advised by Arthur, who initiated the move to withdraw Rosenwald support from the League.

Stern's action seems to have been motivated more by personal considerations than by the shortcomings of the League's program. Former members of the League staff and board members who knew Stern characterized him as opinionated, dictatorial, and insistent that others defer to his ideas.[66] Even so, they felt that, in his own way, Stern was sincere in his efforts for Negro advancement. A part of Stern's disillusionment resulted from the cool reception given one of his favorite projects. He advocated merging the National Association for the Advancement of Colored People and the National Urban League. Under Stern's plan, Will W. Alexander, a white southern liberal, would have headed the combined organization. Eugene Kinckle Jones, as Alexander's assistant, would have supervised programs for the Negro's economic improvement.[67] This plan received little consideration from either of the organizations concerned. Stern also met several reverses on the board of the Chicago Urban League. It was reported that he delivered an "ultimatum,"

---

[65] M. R. Werner, *Julius Rosenwald: The Life of a Practical Humanitarian* (New York: Harper and Brothers Publishers, 1939), pp. 320, 334-335.
[66] Interviews, Chicago, Aug. 7, 1961; July 29, 1961; Aug. 1, 1961.
[67] *Ibid.*, Chicago, July 29, 1961.

which the board ignored, against hiring E. Franklin Frazier as director of research. His complaint was probably against employing a man to work on a personal research project; for, at that time, Stern did not know Frazier.[68] On another occasion, the League's board passed a resolution censuring Billings Hospital at the University of Chicago for its policy toward Negroes. The University of Chicago received substantial support from Rosenwald, and Stern took exception to the League's criticism of this institution.[69] There were a series of seemingly minor incidents which had the effect of turning Stern against the League and particularly against its executive secretary. Many of Stern's criticisms of the League's work were justified, but his attitude was more likely to destroy the organization than to make it a more effective agency.

The first indication that contributions from Rosenwald were in danger of being discontinued came during the 1928-29 fund drive. Before making the annual contribution from the Rosenwald Fund, Edwin R. Embree asked Rosenwald for clarification as to the policy to be pursued in regard to the League. Embree maintained that the much heralded promise to pay 10 per cent of the three-year sustaining fund had not been made. Rather, the agreement had been to contribute 10 per cent of the budget for the fiscal year 1927-28. Nevertheless, the officials of the League were depending upon the continuation of this subscription, and the executive secretary had reported to the Rosenwald Fund "that he had been led to believe that the subscription would run for three years." In addition to this misunderstanding, Embree was faced with Stern's attitude toward the League. On this subject Embree wrote:

> Mr. Alfred Stern, who is one of the directors of the Chicago Urban League, is, as you know, not at all satisfied with its work or with its present Director [executive secretary]. . . . Mr. Arthur, while admitting most of Mr. Stern's criticisms, believes that the work can be reorganized, a better group of directors assembled, and if it continues to seem desirable, a new Director appointed. Mr. Arthur thinks that to accomplish this (which we all agree is desirable) Mr. Stern should stay on the board of directors and you should continue your subscription, at least for another year.[70]

So, with Rosenwald's personal approval, Embree informed the pres-

[68] *Ibid.*
[69] Interview, Chicago, Aug. 7, 1961.
[70] Memorandum from Edwin R. Embree to Rosenwald, Jan. 17, 1929, Rosenwald Papers.

ident of the League that unless the League's work seemed "much more effective" by the end of 1929, Rosenwald would probably discontinue his support.[71]

Naturally, this letter from Embree was a shock to League officials. Elbridge Bancroft Pierce, the Chicago League president, replied personally to the points raised by Embree. He first tried to rebut the contention that Rosenwald had not made a three-year subscription. Then, he turned to the question of the effectiveness of the League's work. Pierce suspected that Stern was behind this move to discredit the organization with Rosenwald. His letter stated:

> I am sincerely distressed to know that Mr. Rosenwald is not completely satisfied with the present work of the League. I knew that Mr. Stern was not and have talked with him at some length and tried to get action on many constructive criticisms which he has offered. Perhaps I may add to you confidentially and frankly that it has been difficult to know exactly what Mr. Stern wishes to have done because at each Board meeting or personal interview with him, it seemed to me he had a different idea as to the branch of our work on which chief emphasis should be laid.

Pierce took "entire responsibility" for the policy and operations of the League. He agreed with Stern that the board needed more businessmen and fewer professional men and women social workers among its members. Pierce offered to withdraw from his position "in favor of any one else who can give more time, ability and experience" to the work.[72]

Embree's letter did spur the League's board into action. The Chicago Urban League was placed in the paradoxical position of preparing for the depression by expanding its industrial department. In spite of irrefutable evidence, gathered by the League itself, that employment opportunities were virtually nonexistent, the board made a last minute attempt to impress the Rosenwald group by expanding its industrial department. The board approved a plan for adding another member to the industrial staff and for the expenditure of additional funds in this work.[73] The executive secretary announced that the League's work would be extended into "the great Calumet industrial district and in all of the outlying communities in which Negroes live and work in reasonable numbers." Alonzo C. Thayer left his position as executive secretary of the Pittsburgh Urban League to become director of the Chicago League's indus-

[71] Embree to Elbridge B. Pierce, Jan. 23, 1929, Rosenwald Papers.
[72] Pierce to Embree, Feb. 1, 1929, Rosenwald Papers.
[73] *Thirteenth Annual Report, 1928-29.*

trial department. The former director, H. N. Robinson, and his assistant remained in the department as Thayer's assistants.[74]

Yet, Stern was not appeased at the end of the fiscal year. He remained adamant in his determination to block financial support to the League. Stern said that although there had been "some talk about how the program . . . could be made effective . . . no tangible results can be found." The employment of Alonzo C. Thayer was termed of no significance in improving the industrial program. Stern felt that Thayer was the wrong man for the job. Thayer was accused of being "opinionated and antagonistic in his attitude to executives in plants" and guilty of making "tactless statements." Stern concluded:

> It is my opinion, in which Mr. Embree and Mr. Arthur concur, that the proper thing for us to do is to recommend your [Rosenwald's] withdrawing local support, and what little support the Fund gives to the national organization. This is likely to give them a sufficient jolt to bring about some changes in the personnel of the national and local organizations.[75]

According to one former League official, Stern included the National League in his campaign after an unsuccessful attempt to get Eugene K. Jones to remove the Chicago executive secretary.[76] In any case, by October, Stern was charging that the National League was not "properly covering the field of work in which they are operating" and that Jones was incompetent to fill the position of national director. In the whole Urban League movement, Stern knew of only one "capable man." He was James H. Hubert of the New York City Urban League. His good standing probably resulted from the fact that he was having "considerable difficulty with the national organization."[77]

In a very caustic memorandum to Rosenwald concerning the Urban League, Stern attacked the board of directors and warned Rosenwald of the pressure that would be exerted on him to block his withdrawal of support. "As it is now constituted," Stern said, "the Board is made up largely of social workers and ministers and is dominated by a few women. Mr. Pierce has not shown any force-

---

[74] *Chicago Defender,* Oct. 19, 1929. Thayer had previously served on the staff of the Chicago Urban League under T. Arnold Hill.

[75] Memorandum from Alfred K. Stern to Rosenwald, Oct. 15, 1929, Rosenwald Papers.

[76] Interview, Chicago, July 29, 1961.

[77] Memorandum from Stern to Rosenwald, Oct. 15, 1929.

fulness or courage in handling the problems which have come up. You should be prepared, if you withdraw your support, to have pressure brought to bear on you against such action, by not only the Jewish members of the Board, including particularly Mr. Harry D. Oppenheimer, and Mrs. Emile Levy, but also by Dr. Bridges, Amelia Sears, Jane Addams, and Mary McDowell."[78]

Unfortunately, Stern had his way. At the end of October he reported that he was resigning from the League board of directors,[79] and Embree notified Pierce that Rosenwald would not make a contribution for 1929-30.[80] Both Pierce and Foster tried to get personal interviews with Rosenwald to give the League's side of the controversy, but neither was able to see him during 1929.[81] After he had persuaded Rosenwald to stop his contributions, Stern carried his campaign against the League a step further. He and George R. Arthur tried to get other foundations and business firms to stop making contributions. Fortunately, this part of the attack met with little success, but the depression almost completed the work of destruction which Stern started.

Although the League's program during this period was generally unimpressive, the organization did not deserve to be destroyed. Chicago needed an Urban League. In the general sphere of race relations, the agency was making a contribution. This contribution, however, was almost impossible to evaluate. It was relatively easy to present records of placements made and new openings obtained during periods of prosperity, and to describe them in terms readily understandable to the public. Because of the public appeal of employment services, the League was reluctant to curtail its work in this area. Yet, in periods of slack employment, such as the late 1920's, the number of jobs available did not justify broad programing in industrial relations. Those responsible for League planning knew that changes were needed to make the agency's work more effective, but the types of changes required were not apparent. By using its small staff and limited financial resources to explore a variety of projects, the League tried to discover new areas of pro-

[78] *Ibid.*

[79] Memorandum from R. S. Rubinow to Stern, with notation from Stern to Rubinow, Oct. 28, 1929, Rosenwald Papers.

[80] Embree to Pierce, Oct. 28, 1929, Rosenwald Papers.

[81] Pierce to Rosenwald, Oct. 31, 1929; Rosenwald to Pierce, Nov. 4, 1929; Foster to Rosenwald, Nov. 29, 1929; Pierce to Rosenwald, Dec. 9, 1929, Rosenwald Papers.

gram emphasis. This exploratory activity often resulted in the League's "spreading itself too thin" and in seeming confusion of objectives. It was not difficult for people like Stern to find shortcomings in the organization's work, but neither this group nor the League's loyal adherents could suggest effective means of strengthening the agency's program. It was unfortunate that at this critical juncture the organization lost the support, financial and moral, of one of its oldest and most consistent supporters — Julius Rosenwald.

5

THE DEPRESSION DECADE, 1930-40

The Great Depression threatened the social and economic structure of Negro life in Chicago. All sections of the city suffered, but the Negro community was hit hardest. This was the first area to feel the full impact of economic dislocation. Early in the depression, over one-half of the Negro employables were out of work; for they were the first to lose their jobs and the last to secure new employment, even in work created by governmental bodies. The banks on the South Side failed earlier than others in the city, resulting in the loss to Negro depositors of millions of dollars in savings. Business and professional interests dependent upon Negro patronage were in danger of impending bankruptcy. Investments in homes were lost; and landlords, many of whom were also in dire straits, had hundreds of impecunious families evicted and their possessions placed upon the streets. The Negro masses grew restless and looked to their leaders for positive action to stem the swelling tide of disruption.

The Chicago Urban League took the initiative in mobilizing the community for private relief activities. As a first step, in September, 1930, an effort was made to raise an emergency relief fund. Negro politicians gave their services as speakers for a mass meeting. Attendance was good, but the meeting was not a financial success.[1] Two months later, the League called a conference of South Side organizations and offered its services for the coordination of relief efforts by the churches, clubs, and social welfare agencies.[2] Many of these groups, especially the churches, organized special relief activi-

[1] *Chicago Defender,* Sept. 27, 1930.
[2] *Annual Report, 1930-32,* p. 22.

ties; but none, including the League, was equal to the situation confronting them in 1930. The churches and other all-Negro institutions were largely dependent upon the poverty stricken masses for support. After enduring the ravages of depression for almost a year, the Negro community was incapable of relieving its own distress. On the other hand, the Urban League, which could usually depend upon outside assistance, was hampered in its work by the prevailing view in Chicago on the nature of the depression.

The general public was unwilling to face the reality that a crisis existed. Lulled into a sort of fool's paradise by the press and the pronouncements of business and political leaders, the people expected the imminent return of prosperity. Chicago, like the rest of the country, engaged in hopeful waiting. No action was deemed necessary to correct this temporary malfunction in the economy. Soon the wheels of industry would be turning again, and the unemployed would be back at work. Meanwhile, distress was considered a personal matter and relief a private responsibility.[3] In late 1930, however, it became evident that private relief-giving agencies were floundering under the burden of the tremendously increased demand for their services. Governor Louis L. Emmerson called a conference to consider this problem. During this conference a Commission on Unemployment was formed to raise funds for distribution to private agencies. Nearly five million dollars was collected in 1930-31 and over ten million the following year,[4] but these sums were below the minimum needs for this period. Priority was given in the distribution of funds to casework organizations providing relief to families and dependent children.

During this period, the Urban League had difficulty in maintaining enough financial support to continue in operation. Not being an established relief-giving agency, it was at a disadvantage in the competition for private philanthropy. When Julius Rosenwald withdrew his support in 1929, the organization lost its most dependable source of income. In spite of repeated remonstrances from League officials, Rosenwald would not reconsider this decision. In addition

[3] Harold D. Lasswell and Dorothy Blumenstock, *World Revolutionary Propaganda: A Chicago Study* (New York: Alfred A. Knopf, Inc., 1939), pp. 26-27.

[4] Frank Z. Glick, "The Illinois Emergency Relief Commission," *The Social Service Review,* VII (Mar., 1933), p. 23; Samuel A. Goldsmith, "Financing Social Work in Chicago," *Social Service Yearbook* (Chicago Council of Social Agencies, 1935), p. 107.

to the direct monetary loss, Rosenwald's action caused others to question the organization's effectiveness.[5] Horace J. Bridges told Rosenwald that "the indirect consequences — the loss of confidence in the League's personnel and programme naturally caused to other possible helpers by your action, and the discouragement to those of us who are responsible for its management — are simply immeasurable."[6] In 1930 it was impossible for the League to meet its obligations. A bank loan was secured to pay staff salaries in August, but two months later, no further payments had been made.[7] The League closed the fiscal year with an "exceptionally large deficit"; and when time came for the annual drive in 1931, the United Charities was also trying to raise funds for a relief center in the Negro community. So, the League decided to postpone its drive until later in the year.[8]

By the end of 1930, the Urban League's work was virtually at a standstill. The department of civic improvement had been abolished because of insufficient funds;[9] and although the industrial staff remained intact, employment services were suspended. Under the cooperative arrangement with the University of Chicago, the agency retained its research department. When E. Franklin Frazier completed his study of the Negro family, another University of Chicago graduate student, Earl R. Moses, became the League's director of research. Moses was engaged in a study of juvenile delinquency among Negroes, which, like Frazier's study, had only an indirect relation to the League's program. His study did, however, provide materials for conference discussions and other public relations activities. In addition, this department assumed responsibility for the speakers bureau, formerly under the department of civic improvement, and offered adult education classes in "Negro History" and "Race Relations."[10]

Some features of the League's program and the nominal services of its staff personnel were saved temporarily through participation in the lodging program for the homeless. Large numbers of transients and jobless men roamed the streets of Chicago, sleeping in parks, hallways, and wherever else shelter could be found. Citizens

---

[5] Henry Horner to Julius Rosenwald, Apr. 22, 1930, Rosenwald Papers, University of Chicago Library.
[6] Horace J. Bridges to Rosenwald, Oct. 3, 1930, Rosenwald Papers.
[7] *Ibid.*
[8] *Chicago Defender,* May 30, 1931.
[9] *Annual Report, 1930-31,* p. 20.
[10] *Ibid.,* p. 6; *Chicago Defender,* June 21, 1930; *Annual Report, 1930-32,* pp. 13-16.

became concerned over this situation and demanded that facilities be established to get these men off the streets. This concern, however, was not entirely for the welfare of the men. The authors of one study concluded that "the unesthetic appearance of beggars and the danger of crime and violence were the principal motives in the development of more facilities for the care of homeless men."[11] In any case, this was work in which the League had experience, and the problem was considered important enough to merit financial support from the Governor's Commission on Unemployment. So, the Urban League staff became lodging house operators. A special committee of the Governor's Commission was formed and placed under the League's control to handle lodging facilities on the South Side. Alonzo C. Thayer, the industrial secretary, served as its executive secretary. During the cold months of the period 1930 to 1932, from one to three shelters and a feeding station were operated for varying intervals.[12]

Private relief efforts and the shelter program did little to stay the ferment in the Negro community. Led by hard-pressed business and professional men, the masses gave hearty support to the *Chicago Whip's* "Spend Your Money Where You Can Work Campaign." At first the *Whip's* editor felt that white businesses in the Negro community would be "driven by sheer necessity to open up the avenue for earning a living to black people." When economic self-interest failed to change employment practices, pressure was advocated. From 1929 to 1931, boycotts and picketing were employed against numerous white businesses on the South Side.[13] More ominous, however, was the resurgence of Communist activity. The restless masses were, by 1930, ready to listen to any group with a program for action. In spite of harassment by the Police Department's "Red Squad," Negroes, in large numbers, attended mass meetings and participated in protests and demonstrations. Even the churches showed little opposition to the Communists' work.[14]

At least one useful purpose was accomplished through Commu-

[11] Edwin H. Sutherland and Harvey J. Locke, *Twenty Thousand Homeless Men: A Study of Unemployed Men in the Chicago Shelters* (Chicago: J. B. Lippincott Company, 1936), pp. 191-192.
[12] *Annual Report, 1930-32,* pp. 16-23; *Chicago Defender,* Dec. 27, 1930; May 30, 1931; Sept. 5, 1931.
[13] St. Clair Drake, *Churches and Voluntary Associations in the Chicago Negro Community,* Report of a W.P.A. Project (Chicago, Dec., 1940), pp. 247-251. (Mimeo.)
[14] *Ibid.,* pp. 259-261.

nist agitation. It served as a catalyst, stirring the city from its lethargy. It awakened Chicago to the dangers inherent in unrelieved suffering, focused attention on the unemployment crisis, and forced public recognition of the inadequacy of private relief.

Although the events motivating this change in outlook were probably cumulative, the climax came on August 3, 1931. An eviction riot occurred on that date which resulted in three Negro deaths and injuries to many onlookers, demonstrators, and policemen. While speakers from the Communist-connected Unemployed Councils exhorted a crowd in Washington Park, a landlord, accompanied by three municipal court bailiffs, was going to his apartment house several blocks away to legally evict an elderly Negro woman. Informed of this impending eviction by one of the speakers, the crowd moved en masse to the scene. Policemen arrived to disperse the crowd of some 2,000 persons, and a riot ensued.[15]

The Communists took full propaganda advantage of this incident. Immediately after the riot, the Chicago Communists began an effort to capitalize on the tensions revealed. The city was flooded with leaflets calling upon "The Workers of Chicago" to demand the death penalty for the "murderers of the workers." Other appeals followed, urging workers to unite behind the Communist Party as "the only political party of the working class."[16]

The most effective demonstrations, however, were those staged during the funeral for the riot victims. Two of the bodies were turned over to the Communists for mass services. The Negro Communist center on South State Street was impressively prepared, and on August 6, the bodies were brought into this building to lie in state. In the two days they were there, some 25,000 people came to the hall. Then, on the day of the funeral nearly 15,000 lined the streets along the route of march. Communist banners and placards were liberally scattered throughout the procession. The Negro community responded favorably to these demonstrations. Applications for membership in the Unemployed Councils reached 5,500 within three weeks and Communist party applications over 500.[17]

---

[15] Accounts of this incident, which agree in essentials but differ in some details, are found in Paul E. Baker, *Negro-White Adjustment: An Investigation and Analysis of Methods in the Interracial Movement in the United States* (Pittsfield, Mass.: Sun Printing Co., 1934), pp. 106-109; Drake, *Churches and Voluntary Associations,* p. 261; Lasswell and Blumenstock, *World Revolutionary Propaganda,* pp. 196-197.

[16] Lasswell and Blumenstock, *World Revolutionary Propaganda,* pp. 197-200.

[17] *Ibid.,* pp. 201-204.

What was Chicago's reaction to these events? The city was on the verge of panic. News of the riot brought a realization of the widespread unrest. The twin dangers of Communism and race riots loomed in the public mind, and Chicago became aware that an emergency existed. Furthermore, "the fact burst upon the public consciousness that unemployment and the ills occasioned by it were *public* rather than *private* responsibilities. The breaking-point was the bloody riot of August 3. . . . From this point on, unemployment was never viewed as a purely individual responsibility."[18]

Measures were taken to relieve the immediate situation. A moratorium was declared on evictions, and the city borrowed $50,000 to provide work-relief for those in dire need. Steps were also taken to overcome discriminatory practices on the part of the relief-giving agencies. But, by the end of 1931, both public and private relief coffers were empty, and the relief problem was turned over to the state.

On February 1, 1932, a special session of the state legislature convened to deal with the relief problem. Bills were passed in record time, creating the Illinois Emergency Relief Commission (I.E.R.C.) and appropriating almost $19,000,000 for relief throughout the state. In Chicago the Joint Emergency Relief Fund of Cook County (formerly the Governor's Commission on Unemployment and Relief) acted as an agent of the I.E.R.C. and distributed public funds to private agencies.[19]

Later in 1932, funds were borrowed to supplement state allotments. The I.E.R.C. obtained $3,000,000 from the Reconstruction Finance Corporation in July, and the city of Chicago received $5,000,000 from the same source in September. These funds were adequate to relieve the more severe cases of suffering. Consequently, evictions declined sharply, and the number of families receiving relief rose to 168,000.[20]

It took the New Deal to create a new, though delicate, equilibrium. Fluctuations in relief programs continued and the Negro community was a good barometer of these changes. Negroes tried to adjust to the new state of things. With little hope for early reentry into private industry, they came to look upon the federal government as the guardian of their economic security. By 1939,

[18] *Ibid.*, p. 30.
[19] Glick, "The Illinois Emergency Relief Commission," pp. 23-33.
[20] Drake, *Churches and Voluntary Associations*, pp. 243-244.

Negroes constituted 40 per cent of those receiving direct relief and 32.4 per cent of persons employed by the Works Projects Administration. Fully one-third of all Negroes in Chicago received some form of relief.[21]

But what was the significance of these developments to the Chicago Urban League? The events of the early depression served to revive a measure of adherence to the principles established by the Great Migration and the race riot of 1919: that Chicago could ignore tensions and maladjustment in the "Black Belt" only at the risk of serious social disorder; and that so long as the problems relegating Negroes to an inferior status in society remain unsolved, channels of communication are needed between the molders of opinion in the white community and those in the Negro community. Since white leaders were basically conservative in outlook — in that they opposed abrupt or radical changes, especially in race relations — they sought the views of like-minded Negro leaders and organizations. But, it usually took crises and the pressures of groups demanding immediate or revolutionary changes to convince them that some alterations were required. At such times, rather than consult those who brought the pressure to bear, they turned to Negro leaders who advocated conciliatory methods. The Urban League was considered the "citadel" of "accepted" leadership. The need for such leadership motivated the founding of the Chicago Urban League during the Great Migration, promoted increased confidence in its efficacy during the race riot of 1919, and led to its revitalization during the last half of the depression decade.

The eventual effects of the early depression upon the League were not clearly apparent at the time of their occurrence. While Chicago was being aroused from its illusions, the Chicago Urban League seemed in the final stages of moribundity. Nevertheless, League officials struggled valiantly to keep the organization alive. Throughout the years 1930-34, they tried to keep the League's traditional purposes before the public.

With the staff devoting much of its time to the operation of lodging houses, volunteers were recruited for regular activities. Such workers were especially useful during "Vocational Opportunity Week" — an annual observance originated by the National Urban League to focus attention on different aspects of the Negro's industrial plight. National staff members and officers were made available

[21] *Ibid.*, p. 244.

to give general direction, serve as speakers, and conduct conferences, but of greater importance was the involvement of large numbers of local people. Negro business and professional people and members of the working classes helped during these observances as individuals and through their clubs and churches. Even though the caliber of programs deteriorated, "Vocational Opportunity Week" and similar special events were valuable in the League's struggle for survival.[22] Aside from the extent to which their stated objectives were accomplished, these activities raised the stature of the organization in the Negro community. The depression expediency of using more volunteers brought greater understanding and acceptance of the organization's purposes, methods, and programs.

As another means of supplementing the work of the staff, more active participation by board members in program activities was sought. Directors were asked to seek membership on policy-making bodies and advisory committees to public and private agencies, especially those concerned with relief. It was felt that League board members would provide representation sympathetic to the Negro. They could also serve as valuable links with groups throughout the city and help in securing sponsors and participants for interracial conferences and meetings.

There was a serious problem involved, however, in getting their cooperation. The League's board of directors was overloaded with individuals who gave only the prestige of their names and disassociated League membership from their other activities. Directors were needed who would give service, as well as prestige; inactive members had to be weeded out, with care being taken to maintain their good will. The method employed was revealed in a letter to a director who was being removed from the board. He was informed that "with the particular need this year [1931] for additional activity on working committees to be largely made up of Board members, it has seemed wise to create an Advisory Board on which we may retain those loyal friends to whom we may occasionally need to turn for suggestions, but who are so crowded in other ways that the committee work would be impossible."[23] The advisory board plan allowed

[22] For reports on the observances of "Vocational Opportunity Week" in Chicago, see *Annual Report, 1930-32,* pp. 17-21; *Chicago Defender,* Mar. 8, 1930; Apr. 26, 1930; May 3, 1930; Mar. 7, 1931; Apr. 25, 1931, Apr. 16, 1932.

[23] Elbridge B. Pierce to Salmon O. Levinson, Oct. 20, 1931, Salmon O. Levinson Papers, University of Chicago Library.

the League to keep a connection with these people and still use their names, while removing them from the board and securing more active replacements.

Still, the agency's position remained precarious. From 1930 to 1932, the organization operated principally on funds provided for lodging facilities. When public funds became available to private agencies through the I.E.R.C., the League continued its shelter work. It "loaned" its staff to the Commission and continued to provide sleeping facilities and meals for homeless men and women. Then, in the spring of 1933, another step was taken in the transition from private to public responsibility for relief. A policy was instituted that "public funds should be administered by public agencies," thereby forcing the League out of shelter work.[24] Since these facilities were to remain in operation under public control, the League staff members working in them had the choice of going on the public payroll or remaining in salaryless positions with the League. They chose the former.[25] This left the Urban League with a full-time professional staff of one — the executive secretary.

A. L. Foster tried to carry on alone. He waged a letter campaign to secure employment for Negroes in the reviving beer industry and worked to combat discrimination during the Chicago World's Fair in 1933.[26] It was hoped that the League would be given the job of placing Negroes in white-collar and menial jobs at the Fair; but only a few were employed as white-collar workers, and the placement of menials was assigned to a commercial firm.[27] The executive secretary received some assistance in his efforts from the Illinois and Chicago Emergency Advisory Councils.[28] These bodies sent committees to protest discrimination by relief agencies and by firms operating under the codes of the National Recovery Administration. Representatives also conferred with officials in Washington on Negro

---

[24] Sutherland and Locke, *Twenty Thousand Homeless Men,* pp. 195-196. These authors gave good descriptions of the type of facilities provided and the activities of the men who used them.

[25] Albon L. Foster, "Twenty Years of Interracial Goodwill Through Social Service," in Chicago Urban League, *Two Decades of Service* (Chicago Urban League, 1936).

[26] *Chicago Defender,* Apr. 8, 1933.

[27] Annual Report of the Executive Secretary, 1932-33, Oct. 15, 1933, p. 2 (mimeo.); *Chicago Defender,* June 3, 1933.

[28] The National Urban League instituted the formation of Emergency Advisory Councils as a method of applying direct pressure on the administrators of New Deal recovery measures. Upper-class Negroes throughout the country were asked to form such Councils in order to provide an intelligent presenta-

participation in New Deal recovery projects.[29] Even so, without a staff, a formal program, and adequate financial support, the League was severely handicapped.

This situation did not indicate complete unawareness on the part of Chicago's leaders of the League's role in reducing tensions. Rather, it resulted primarily from the stringency of the charity dollar. Although many people had to reduce or discontinue their financial contributions, they continued their moral support. Interracial participation in League committee work and attendance at conferences and dinners remained good; and when special problems arose, League officials were asked to assist in their solution. It had been represented at the conference which formed the Governor's Commission on Unemployment; and when a type of activity was instituted in which the League could participate — the shelter program — it had received funds from this commission. Following the eviction riot, the executive secretary had been called back from vacation to take part in deliberations. The Commissioner of Public Welfare had tried to obtain additional funds from the city government to enlarge the League's shelter program, but available city funds were being used for more work-relief. The Chicago Council of Social Agencies, however, did secure enough money for a short period of shelter operation during the off-season.[30] Although these expressions of confidence were insufficient to stay the agency's decline, they did help it to maintain a semblance of activity until more adequate support could be provided.

By 1934, the most critical period of the depression had passed and things began to look better for social agencies. Unemployment remained high, but the combined forces of city, state, and federal governments worked to relieve hardship. With public agencies now bearing most of the relief burden, contributions for more varied programs became available to private institutions and organizations.

---

tion of the Negro's point of view and to inform the masses on the purposes and operations of governmental agencies. See Charles Radford Lawrence, "Negro Organizations in Crisis: Depression, New Deal, World War II" (unpublished Ph.D. dissertation, Columbia University, microfilmed, 1952), pp. 226-227; Arthur Paul Stokes, "The National Urban League: A Study in Race Relations" (unpublished Master's thesis, Ohio State University, 1937), pp. 35-36.

[29] *Chicago Defender,* Aug. 5, 1933; Aug. 12, 1933; Sept. 16, 1933; Dec. 2, 1933.

[30] *Annual Report, 1930-32,* pp. 24-25. Shelters were usually closed during the warm months. Consequently, they were not in operation in August, 1931 when the eviction riot occurred.

The Governor's Commission on Unemployment had developed into the Chicago Community Fund, and social welfare agencies could look to it for a percentage of their budgets.[31] Along with other agencies, the League's financial prospects began to improve. Between 1934 and 1940, income increased from about $10,000 to over $27,000, the Community Fund furnishing almost one-half of each year's budget.

Even so, rebuilding the League's financial structure was not an easy task. Annual budget estimates were subjected to close scrutiny by the Community Fund's budget analysts and reviewing committee. Any changes from one year to the next had to be fully justified. Then too, in order to receive its full allocation from the Fund, the agency had to raise its share of the budget.[32] This was a continuing problem for the Urban League. Contributions remained hard to come by, and a variety of fund-raising techniques had to be employed. Some were successful, others failed. Even so, the League's income was good by depression standards. Moreover, after 1934 the scope of the organization's work was not solely determined by budget size. For every staff member the League employed with its own money, additional workers were available through work-relief projects financed by the municipality, the Works Projects Administration, and the National Youth Administration. The N.Y.A. even furnished equipment for the use of some workers it assigned.

In 1934, progress began toward the resumption of activities in the League's traditional spheres of operation. A project in community organization was started in January. The area between Forty-seventh and Fifty-first Streets and from Cottage Grove Avenue to South Parkway was selected for an experiment. Through the formation of block clubs, the League began a demonstration of the effectiveness of community organization procedures in accomplishing neighborhood improvement.[33] But, it was in industrial relations that the first formal department was re-established. Early in June, Howard D. Gould — who had just completed a year of graduate study at the University of Pittsburgh on a National Urban League

[31] Unlike community chests in some other cities, the Chicago Community Fund has never tried to raise the entire budget requirements of its member agencies.

[32] Chicago Urban League Service Reports, 1934-40 (in the files of the Welfare Council of Metropolitan Chicago).

[33] Memorandum from Albon L. Foster to the Chicago Council of Social Agencies, Oct. 29, 1934 (in the files of the Welfare Council of Metropolitan Chicago).

Fellowship — was employed as industrial secretary.[34] Later in the year, an appeal was made to the Community Fund, based on the results obtained in the experimental project in neighborhood improvement, for a special grant to support more extensive work of this type. Specifically, the League wanted to hire two staff members to revive its department of civic improvement.[35] The grant was made and early in 1935, Frayser T. Lane returned to the League staff to reorganize this department. Lane had begun his Urban League career in Chicago under T. Arnold Hill, but he left to serve as executive secretary of the Kansas City (Missouri) Urban League.[36] By 1935, the League was well on its way toward recovery. Its staff was growing, and its program was expanding.

From the beginning Gould adjusted the industrial program to the realities of the new "social order." He realized that most Negroes with jobs were employed on work projects. So, the League's industrial program concentrated on creating new work opportunities under New Deal recovery measures; having Negroes and sympathetic whites appointed to policy-making and advisory groups; and securing equitable treatment for unskilled, semi-skilled, and skilled workers on projects sponsored by public agencies. In the meantime, efforts were made to establish contacts with private employers to assure future consideration for Negroes. Sometimes a few jobs were obtained, but it was not until the beginning of national defense production that primary emphasis was again placed on securing jobs in private industry.

Making jobs for the employment of Negro white-collar workers was among the first projects undertaken. The Federal Emergency Relief Administration had money available in 1934 for "make work" jobs to remove people from the relief rolls. Gould visited the administrators of this program to find out the types of projects acceptable and the procedures for having them approved. He became quite adept at preparing projects and guiding them to acceptance by relief authorities. Some of the research projects supervised by the League furnished valuable data for future programing, but the most important consideration from 1935 to 1940 was the number of people given work.[37] Approval was given for the first research

---

[34] *Chicago Defender,* June 9, 1934.

[35] Memorandum from Foster to Chicago Council of Social Agencies.

[36] *Chicago Defender,* Jan. 19, 1935; *Twentieth Annual Report, 1935,* Part I, p. 2.

[37] Interview, Chicago, June 27, 1961.

project initiated by the Urban League late in 1934. With a staff of twenty workers provided by F.E.R.A., "A Survey of Occupational Opportunities for Negroes in the Chicago Area" was begun.[38] Only half of the proposed project had been completed, however, when the F.E.R.A. work program was suspended. Undaunted, the League re-outlined the project and submitted it to the Works Progress Administration (W.P.A., later called Works Projects Administration). This agency approved the new plan and furnished a greatly enlarged staff for its execution.[39] Other research projects ranging from a survey to determine the best location for Negro Subsistence Homestead projects to a study of factors influencing the vocational choice of Negro youth were submitted to and approved by the W.P.A.[40]

Proposals for white-collar employment were not limited to research nor to work conducted under the supervision of the industrial department. In addition to helping other Negro agencies in formulating acceptable plans, cooperative projects were devised. The League's department of civic improvement in conjunction with the Y.M.C.A. and other established agencies used large numbers of workers in conducting community organization and recreation projects.[41] The introduction of adult education on the South Side was a pioneer League accomplishment. Foster boasted in 1936 that the adult education program then employed some 100 teachers and had a monthly payroll of $11,000.[42] Jobs were also sought outside the Negro community. The relief agencies were asked to use Negroes on their staffs and to place them on non-Negro supervised projects.[43] Teachers furnished by the N.Y.A. taught "brush-up" classes in various office procedures to help those who had "lost their skill" to prepare for clerical jobs.[44] Following the suggestion of the National Urban League, the Chicago branch encouraged Negro youth to take civil service examinations. Publicity was given to all examination announcements, and, when necessary, help was given those preparing for examinations.[45]

The great majority of Negroes, however, were not prepared for white-collar jobs. They were looking for work in unskilled, semi-

---

[38] *Chicago Defender,* Dec. 15, 1934.
[39] *Twentieth Annual Report, 1935,* Part III, pp. 6-7.
[40] *Ibid.,* p. 5; *Annual Report, 1937,* Part II, pp. 7-8.
[41] *Ibid.,* Part III, p. 5.
[42] Foster, in *Two Decades of Service.*
[43] *Twentieth Annual Report, 1935,* Part I, p. 10; Part III, p. 9.
[44] *Annual Report, 1937,* Part I, pp. 5-7.
[45] *Ibid.,* pp. 14-15; *Chicago Defender,* Oct. 2, 1937.

skilled, and skilled pursuits. The laboring masses, like the white-collar workers, were largely dependent upon governmental agencies for jobs, but there was a tendency to restrict the use of Negroes on work-relief and provide for their subsistence through doles. In order to obtain jobs for Negro workers, the League had to fight the discriminatory practices followed by local administrators and contractors on work-relief and Public Works Administration (P.W.A.) projects.

Organized labor also posed a problem. Unions in the construction trades were trying to secure as much of the available work as possible for their members and to maintain wage scales on relief projects at a level comparable to those on private jobs. They, therefore, sought restrictive practices which would assure that union members had the first choice of jobs. Since few Negroes belonged to unions at this time, because of lapsed memberships and exclusive policies, these demands resulted in few openings above the unskilled level for Negroes. Furthermore, relief administrators and contractors often used the racial policies of unions as a convenient excuse for their own discriminatory inclinations. Numerous complaints came from Negro workers that they were repeatedly turned away from construction sites while white workers were being employed.

The League's industrial department attempted to change this situation. The industrial secretary went to local P.W.A. officials but was told that "they were powerless" to alter conditions. He obtained a list of work projects underway in Cook County and visited each of these. Some contractors denied there was discrimination; but if they did admit its existence, they claimed inability to do anything about it. Failing to make any progress locally, the industrial secretary called upon Secretary of the Interior Harold L. Ickes for assistance. Ickes sent investigators who substantiated the League's allegations. An order from the Secretary of the Interior banning discrimination, however, did not materially alter conditions.

Blame for this continued discrimination was placed on the unions. The Urban League reported that:

> Throughout the Fall and Winter [1934-35], the Industrial Secretary met with various union officials . . . in an effort to persuade them to adopt a fairer attitude toward Negroes. In [the] spring of the year some unions began to do this, notably the plasterers and bricklayers. Accordingly, some Negroes went to work as skilled workers on PWA projects.[46]

[46] *Twentieth Annual Report, 1935,* Part III, p. 3.

In spite of these efforts, few skilled workers were employed. A *Defender* article said of the situation in early 1936:

> At present although there are many qualified Race workers who have had considerable experience as bricklayers, carpenters, painters, etc., only a very few of these men have been assigned to jobs. Although their work records qualify them for assignments as skilled workers at prevailing wage rates of $1 and more per hour the Race mechanics have been assigned as laborers at $55 per month.[47]

It was difficult, and often impossible, to determine who was actually responsible for restrictive policies. On one project, employing 1,000 Negroes and 200 white workers, it was found that Negroes — even those working in higher classifications — were paid the minimum wage, while over half of the white workers drew wages above this level. This situation was protested to the supervisor of W.P.A. projects in the Chicago Park District, who promised that "any instances of discrimination coming to his attention would be immediately rectified." Later it was found out that this supervisor had personally rejected recommendations from his subordinates for changes in job classifications.[48]

When it was learned that slum clearance and the construction of public housing would be undertaken by the P.W.A., the League was among the first organizations to start working for the equitable allocation of jobs to Negro workers. The industrial secretary took credit for suggesting to Secretary Ickes that contracts for public housing construction include quota clauses, prescribing the percentage of Negroes to be used on such projects.[49]

In late 1936 and early 1937, economic conditions seemed to warrant placing some emphasis on securing jobs in private industry. An assistant industrial secretary was employed, who spent considerable time interviewing officials in plants and businesses. Even menial jobs and positions in domestic service were welcomed. It was felt that every opportunity had to be seized; for the placement of Negroes in any capacity could lead to more and better jobs. The industrial department noted:

> Invariably when representatives of the League appear at conferences, at meetings, or contact individuals to urge better work opportunities for Negroes, the Industrial Department receives requests for domestic workers.

---

[47] *Chicago Defender,* Feb. 8, 1936.
[48] *Ibid.,* May 16, 1936; June 6, 1936.
[49] *Twentieth Annual Report, 1935,* Part III, p. 4; Interview, Chicago, June 27, 1961.

Naturally, we comply with these requests because an unfavorable reception on our part might be construed as an indication that Negroes are too particular about what work they will take, and really do not want to work at all.[50]

But, during the business recession in late 1937, the League returned to its fight against discrimination on public projects and began agitating for an increased quota of W.P.A. workers in Illinois.[51]

With the eruption of war in Europe, new adjustments were required. Concern in Washington shifted from depression to national defense. Funds previously used to make work for the unemployed were now being channeled into the production of war implements, and the wheels of industry began to turn at an accelerated pace.

The Chicago Urban League was now confronted with new problems. As governmental funds were diverted from relief to defense production, many work projects were discontinued and direct relief budgets were cut. The League lost its subsidized staff of W.P.A. and N.Y.A. workers. More important, however, was the fact that governmental agencies were releasing Negro laborers from work projects, and allocations to relief recipients for food and other necessities were being reduced. At the same time, the doors of reviving industries remained closed to them. In 1940, the League surveyed the situation and found that Chicago industries receiving defense contracts, in spite of National Defense Advisory Commission policies, were not employing Negroes. Some claimed that they were only recalling former employees; others maintained that Negroes lacked the training and experience for highly skilled and technical work; and a few frankly admitted that they just were not employing Negroes.[52]

Since the federal government was involved, League action on the national level seemed indicated. Chicago League President Earl B. Dickerson called upon the National Urban League to mobilize country-wide support behind a movement aimed at persuading President Roosevelt to issue an executive order requiring regular reports from all defense industries as to the racial identity of their employees and providing for equitable employment of Negro workers.[53] Howard Gould had already suggested to the National

[50] *Annual Report, 1937,* Part II, p. 2.
[51] Report of the Department of Industrial Relations and Research, Jan., 1938 (MS in the personal files of Howard D. Gould).
[52] *Chicago Defender,* Nov. 2, 1940; Dec. 7, 1940.
[53] *Ibid.,* Nov. 16, 1940.

League that it work for the appointment of "regional or field representatives" to coordinate the work of defense agencies in promoting effective utilization of Negro manpower.[54]

The seeming clarity of purpose and objectives motivating the League's industrial activities was misleading. Actually, serious ideological conflicts developed within the organization during the depression decade.

Generally, white friends of Negro causes saw the depression as a time for rededication to the principle of racial conciliation. They felt that a community of racial good feeling would grow out of the common suffering experienced by all groups. Harold L. Ickes expressed this sentiment in an address during the Chicago Urban League's twentieth anniversary celebration. Ickes felt that

> in a very real and fundamental sense, the Negro has probably profited more from this depression than any other class of our citizens.
>
> This benefit to the Negro has not consisted in the conferring upon him of material benefits, it has lain in the understanding and sympathy which have drawn him into closer bond with those of the white race. As the result of this better understanding and newer sympathy I am optimistic enough to believe that in the future there will not be the mistrust, the misunderstanding or the antipathy which has existed in the past between certain members of these two races. . . .[55]

But, the Negro masses were not satisfied with these "spiritual benefits." They also wanted to share in material benefits. They had become disillusioned with interracial conferences, persuasion, and education; such methods seemed too slow and uncertain to bring relief in the immediate crisis. Furthermore, the masses were losing confidence in the small Negro upper class of business and professional men, with their conflicting doctrines of salvation through Negro business and total integration into American life through conciliation. Widespread failures exploded the myth of Negro business, and the restless masses began looking for leaders with more direct approaches to the problems confronting them. It was widely felt that only through pressure could the Negro get a hearing on his grievances.

Actually, this was not just a localized sentiment. Throughout the country, there was a tendency toward placing greater reliance on pressure tactics. The National Urban League sensed this change

[54] Memorandum from Howard D. Gould to Lester B. Granger, Oct. 16, 1940, copy in Gould files.

[55] Text of the address was published in the *Chicago Defender,* Feb. 29, 1936.

in Negro opinion early in the depression. A report from the national organization on unemployment in 1931 warned that restlessness was evident from one end of the country to the other because Negroes were losing jobs which they would not regain when "normal times" returned. Furthermore, new jobs in public works were not adequate to meet their needs.[56] In 1936, Eugene K. Jones noted that "there had developed simultaneously with the depression the psychology that only by organized pressure could minorities and unpopular causes secure recognition."[57] It was evident that in order to maintain a position of influence among Negroes the League would have to make concessions to this protest psychology.

In its own program and for the guidance of its branches, the national organization tried to develop pressure techniques which were compatible with the movement's traditional social work methods. The first move in this direction was a "letter and telegram campaign." Through numerous appeals to the President, members of the Cabinet, and others in policy-making positions, the League hoped to "galvanize sentiment on behalf of Negroes."[58] The first attempt at organization for pressure purposes came with the formation of the Emergency Advisory Councils. The waning confidence of the Negro masses in the upper classes — who formed the membership of these Councils — limited the effectiveness of this project. Finally, the League decided to work directly with Negro workers. In March, 1934, a Workers Bureau was established, and later in the year, Lester B. Granger — who later succeeded Jones as national executive secretary — came to New York to direct its activities. Local branches were urged to organize Workers Councils to serve both as pressure groups and as mediums for educating Negroes in labor philosophy.[59] Appeals to the workers were made principally on the basis of the protest function. They were told:

> You must organize to compel the break-down of the discriminatory barriers that keep you out of unions, and, consequently, out of employment. You must organize to prevent the passing of legislation that will be

[56] National Urban League, Department of Industrial Relations, *How Unemployment Affects Negroes* (National Urban League, Mar., 1931), pp. 8-9. (Mimeo.)

[57] National Urban League, *A Quarter Century of Progress in the Field of Race Relations, 1910-1935: Twenty-fifth Anniversary Souvenir Booklet* (National Urban League, 1935). (Pages not numbered.)

[58] *Ibid.*

[59] Lawrence, "Negro Organizations in Crisis," pp. 259-269, 272-273.

a further aid to discrimination-practicing unions and employers. You must organize to demand, with other workers, a new deal for labor. . . .[60]

The decision, though, as to whether or not these and other national projects should be undertaken in League cities was made by the local branches.

The Chicago branch, while adopting many National League suggestions, developed its own methods of adjustment to new ideological conflicts. It was not until after 1934, when its financial situation improved, that the Chicago League was able to face the challenge to its leadership in the Negro community. Rather than attempting to integrate pressure tactics into its traditional methods, the Chicago League developed a sort of dualism. As some of its critics charged, it tried to face in two or more directions at the same time. Before its conservative white supporters, it placed the image of a social welfare organization using community organization, interracial cooperation, and education to better conditions within the Negro community and between the races. If pressure became necessary, it would be exercised through the time-sanctioned practices of petitioning. Among the restless Negro masses, on the other hand, the League wanted to be known as an organization in the forefront of the fight for racial advancement.

Yet, the aggressive protest–social work dualism was not altogether the result of conscious planning. It derived from several sources. A part of it entered the program through the ideological orientation of Negro board members and staff personnel. In addition, racial attitudes in Chicago caused some activities which began as social work projects later to take on protest features. In such cases, the League tried to restrict its role to stimulating others to take direct action. Then, there were also deliberate efforts made to create a protest image of the League in the Negro community.

Negro leaders within the Urban League engaged in a sort of pluralistic mode of thinking, which separated them on the one hand from the organization's white leaders and on the other from the Negro masses. Being a part of the Negro community, they shared the disillusionment of their group. They felt that strong positive action was needed to stay the forces which threatened the very

[60] Pronouncement addressed to the Negro workers, Apr., 1934, quoted in Eunice Joyner Jones, "A Study of the Urban League Movement in the United States" (unpublished Master's thesis, New York University, 1939), p. 19.

foundation of Negro life. Like the masses, these leaders had some doubt that traditional Urban League methods were equal to the situation. On October 9, 1930, A. L. Foster wrote to T. Arnold Hill: "The time has come for a more aggressive attitude on the part of Negroes. We of the Chicago Urban League realize that fact, and our future programs will be far more aggressive than they have been in the past."[61] Foster was never quite sure that social work was the answer to the big problem, employment. In an interview in 1961, he stated: "The *Whip* [boycott] campaign was successful. This was pressure not education. The Chicago Urban League was not getting the big job done."[62] One of the more moderate League staff members told a meeting in 1937 that "the so-called conservative elements of our population must use more spectacular methods of arousing active interest of Race citizens in the social, civic and economic affairs."[63] In a similar vein, Earl B. Dickerson, then a League vice president, was quoted as saying:

> We do not feel that we have made satisfactory progress in breaking down employment barriers in public utilities and such private industries as the dairies, bakeries and the large distributive industries whose products are used in such large amounts by Race citizens. By abolishing our placement service we shall be able to give much more time to the development of plans for group pressure.[64]

Generally, however, the Negro upper classes could not wholeheartedly commit themselves to the course dictated by the masses. Those in the League knew that the organization could not exist without white support. Furthermore, like their white counterparts, middle- and upper-class Negroes were rather contemptuous of the lower classes of both races. Still, they were bound to the Negro lower classes by the stigma attached to their race and by economic dependence upon them in their businesses and professions. The upper classes were willing to join such movements as the "Spend Your Money Where You Can Work Campaign," where they could simultaneously exercise leadership, fight racial prejudice, and strike a blow for Negro business. But, they usually disavowed more radical movements and those aimed at achieving working-class unity. Yet, it was difficult to keep these conflicting attitudes com-

---

[61] Quoted in Drake, *Churches and Voluntary Associations,* pp. 251-252.
[62] Interview with the author, 1961.
[63] *Chicago Defender,* Oct. 2, 1937.
[64] *Ibid.,* June 11, 1938.

partmentalized, especially in the operation of an organization like the Urban League.

The tendency of the social work and protest functions to combine was evident in the League's housing program. Beginning around 1933, the agency became involved in two types of housing activities. One purposed to promote self-improvement within the Negro community. The other sought outside assistance in providing better housing. While these started as separate types of activities, they were so closely related that it was difficult to keep them apart. Inevitably, the problem of improving housing and civic conditions led to the more fundamental problem of more and better facilities. But, some groups who reacted favorably to self-improvement among Negroes opposed any attempts to expand living facilities either through enlarging the "Black Belt" or the construction of new homes with governmental assistance.

Improving physical living conditions was a part of the League's broader program of civic improvement. When this work was reestablished in 1934, the expansion of Negro residential areas into neighboring white districts had been rigidly curtailed. The "Black Belt" had been hemmed in by a "veritable barrier" of restrictive covenants.[65] The League presented its civic program as being based on the realities of this situation. The staff said, in reporting the first year's operations, that:

> One of the first things we set out to do was to develop a common mind on the fact that for many years people are going to be living within this area and it is up to them to decide on the future value of their property and present moral conditions of the neighborhood, and the very fact that they are citizens, there is encumbered upon them a responsibililty to work for the improvement of their community.[66]

To accomplish these aims, the League proposed a program of education through block clubs and federations of these clubs. The educational work was designed to foster civic pride and, thereby, to improve "personal and group behavior."[67] Through bulletins, newspaper publicity, and personal contacts, the League waged a continuing campaign to arouse the citizens of the Negro community to

---

[65] For a discussion of the effects of restrictive covenants on Negro housing opportunities in Chicago, see Herman H. Long and Charles S. Johnson, *People vs. Property: Race Restrictive Covenants in Housing* (Nashville, Tenn.: Fisk University Press, 1947), pp. 12-15 *et passim.*

[66] *Twentieth Annual Report, 1935,* Part II, p. 1.

[67] Foster to Chicago Council of Social Agencies, Oct. 29, 1934.

greater efforts in improving their living conditions.[68] In 1937, the organization proclaimed:

> In two years' time, we have succeeded in making the city of Chicago realize that something must be done to improve this community, and individual residents and groups within the area have become more and more community conscious and are lending their support for improvement.
> A neglected and forgotten community has now been discovered. . . .[69]

The community organization project was designed to be a prime example of the League's social work approach to racial betterment. It was sanctioned by the Council of Social Agencies and given Community Fund support. It also provided numerous opportunities for using W.P.A. workers. Yet, landlords were reluctant to endorse this work. The lack of cooperation from "absentee landlords and their agents" was a constant source of disappointment to the League.[70] In 1938, however, a committee of South Side real-estate men did help in the educational program among tenants by joining in the distribution of cards urging greater care for rented property.[71] Landlords had vested interests in maintaining the status quo in the Negro community. They helped to build the barriers around the "Black Belt" in order to rent substandard buildings at exorbitant rates. Through political and economic influence, they were able to flout city ordinances pertaining to safety, zoning, and sanitation. Both outside interests and League officials knew that programs in community organization and adult education could not resolve the basic problems of overcrowding, high rentals, and substandard housing. The best that could be expected was an alleviation of the moral deterioration resulting from these conditions.

Concomitantly with its civic improvement program, the League was participating in efforts to have low-cost public housing constructed on the South Side. While the neighborhood improvement work brought some inconvenience to real-estate interests, resulting from agitation by block clubs for zoning laws, better police protection, and the enforcement of housing ordinances, they considered public housing a threat to the very foundation of their lucrative business. What the League, in cooperation with other groups, undertook as a routine effort to provide better housing and, at the

---

[68] *Twentieth Annual Report, 1935,* Part II, pp. 3-4; *Chicago Defender,* Nov. 5, 1938; May 13, 1939; June 3, 1939.
[69] *Annual Report, 1937,* Part III, p. 1.
[70] *Ibid.,* Part I, p. 14.
[71] *Chicago Defender,* Nov. 5, 1938.

same time, create construction jobs for Negroes, turned out to be a five-year struggle.

In November, 1933, A. L. Foster, who was on a municipally appointed commission on substandard housing, had assembled a small housing discussion group on the South Side. A permanent organization was formed and studies begun on the problems connected with low-cost housing projects. When public housing construction began under P.W.A., this group had a suggested location and information relative to property appraisal, taxes, assessments, and other pertinent questions. So, on February 11, 1934, final plans and a formal application — the first submitted from Chicago — for a low-cost housing project on the South Side was sent to Washington. In October, condemnation proceedings were filed to secure property but were later withdrawn.[72]

Delayed by litigation and technical problems, construction on the South Side, Ida B. Wells, housing project did not begin until August, 1939. When property acquisition began, in 1936, opposition was encountered from the adjacent covenant-protected white communities of Hyde Park, Kenwood, and Oakland. Taxpayers from these areas tried to stop condemnation proceedings by filing demurrers.[73] Businessmen's associations sent President Roosevelt a telegram protesting the site and deploring Harold Ickes' persistence in proceeding with the project. They pledged that "unless the project is abandoned, our group will continue their opposition to the acquisition of this proposed and disputed site and will use all the legal means within their power to prevent the acquisition of this much disputed site."[74] As soon as local objections had been overruled, a federal court decision in a Louisville (Kentucky) case questioned the legality of federal use of eminent domain to secure housing sites. In Chicago, the housing division turned from condemnation to the slower process of direct purchase from property owners.[75] Then, the enactment of the United States Housing Act in 1937 — which created the United States Housing Authority and placed responsibility for initiating projects on local authorities — brought new problems. Now, it was decided that low-cost projects would require state and city tax exemption in order to keep the

[72] *Ibid.,* Oct. 26, 1940.
[73] *Ibid.,* June 20, 1936.
[74] Published in *Ibid.,* June 27, 1936.
[75] Coleman Woodbury, "Housing," *Social Service Yearbook,* 1936, p. 89; *Chicago Defender,* July 11, 1936.

rental rates from being prohibitive. The City Council said that it lacked authority to grant such exemption and asked the state legislature for enabling legislation.[76] It was not until November, 1938 that the final barrier was removed. After action by the state legislature, the City Council passed an ordinance exempting the South Side project from taxation.[77] Finally, after more injunctions and restraining orders, contracts were awarded and construction was begun on August 2, 1939.

The Chicago Urban League was actively involved in the struggle for this project. It mobilized favorable opinion within and outside the Negro community, disseminated information on the status of the proceedings, and stepped up its campaign to dramatize the housing plight of Negroes. It held housing conferences to inform Negroes on the issues involved.[78] The civic department engaged in interpretative activities on Negro housing, and the department's director sought membership in groups of all types working in behalf of the project. League representatives appeared before the City Council and state legislature urging them to petition Washington for completion of this housing.[79] The delay in passing tax exemption legislation resulted in a League warning to Negroes that they would lose the project unless they took some "definite action," and the board of directors appointed a special committee to work with other groups to save the project.[80] Conferences were held with the mayor and the governor, and others were encouraged to approach these officials. When the housing bills reached the legislature, an interracial League delegation went to Springfield to join representatives from other organizations in lobbying for their passage. Supporters of the bills were unable to secure sufficient votes on their first attempt. So, Foster went to Governor Henry Horner, who pledged his assistance; and he called Chicago's mayor, who promised to call Chicago's leaders personally urging their support. Miss Amelia Sears, a white League vice president, remained in Springfield lobbying until the final passage of the bills.[81]

The League's concern did not end with the beginning of con-

---

[76] *Ibid.,* Mar. 26, 1938.
[77] Alex Elson, "Social Legislation," *Social Service Yearbook,* 1938, pp. 103-104; *Chicago Defender,* Nov. 5, 1938.
[78] *Ibid.,* Sept. 5, 1936.
[79] *Annual Report, 1937,* Part III, p. 8.
[80] *Chicago Defender,* Jan. 8, 1938.
[81] *Ibid.,* Mar. 26, 1938; June 11, 1938; July 2, 1938.

struction. Aside from its housing benefits, a principal reason for enthusiasm over the project was the prospects it offered for the employment of skilled Negro workers. Throughout the struggle, this objective had been kept before the Negro community. Under P.W.A., the League was relatively certain of its realization; Ickes had always been sympathetic to such proposals. But with the shifting of responsibility to the Housing Authority, uncertainty developed. At the first opportunity, Foster brought the question to the attention of Housing Administrator Nathan Straus. Straus saw no reason why Negro technical and skilled workers could not be used. He instructed Administrative Assistant Robert Weaver to handle the situation with the Chicago Housing Authority. Foster and his delegation left the interview confident that Negroes would be employed.[82] Several months later, however, the Chicago Housing Authority was being charged with duplicity. Negro architects and engineers had been passed over in favor of a firm headed by the former chairman of the Housing Authority, whom Negroes considered unsympathetic to them.[83]

While the controversy raged over the South Side project, three P.W.A. projects in other sections of the city were started and completed. The Jane Addams Houses, Julia Lathrop Homes, and Trumbull Park Homes were ready for occupancy before the end of 1937. The construction of these projects, while the South Side project was being delayed, led Negroes to the conclusion that "malignant forces" — principally real-estate interests — were blocking this project in order to keep out even this minor threat to their wanton exploitation. Although it was pointed out that the completed homes were constructed principally on vacant sites, the Jane Addams Houses, largest of the three, did entail condemnation of property.[84]

The completed projects inspired a League campaign for racially integrated public housing. In late 1936, as the Jane Addams and Trumbull Park Homes approached completion, the League urged Negroes in the vicinity to apply for occupancy.[85] Many did, and it was revealed that personnel in the renting offices were discouraging Negroes from applying and insisting that they make application to the proposed South Side project. The League asked Washington officials to alter this practice. According to Foster, they "wrote to

---

[82] *Ibid.,* July 30, 1938.
[83] *Ibid.,* Sept. 10, 1938; Sept. 24, 1938.
[84] Elizabeth A. Hughes, "Housing," *Social Service Yearbook,* 1937, p. 80.
[85] *Chicago Defender,* Nov. 28, 1936.

Secretary of the Interior Harold Ickes, requesting that he take steps to assure Race members of the chance to live in projects outside the so-called 'black belt.' We were told by the secretary that the matter would be thoroughly considered. We knew the secretary's policy in regard to residential and other types of segregation and we felt certain that he would see to it that Race members were included."[86] Ickes sent Dewey R. Jones, a special assistant on Negro affairs, to investigate the Chicago controversy. After Jones was in the city several days, the *Defender* announced that fears that the Jane Addams project would be " 'lily-white' may now be dispelled."[87]

It was soon announced that several Negro tenants had been selected, but a plan for racial segregation was also revealed. The project manager said that one building with thirty apartments would be reserved for Negro tenants. This caused a new rash of activity in the Negro community. Protests were made both to Ickes and Housing Administrator Straus, and the Urban League board endorsed its housing committee's decision to accept no compromise on the question of discrimination in projects.[88] League staff members met with persons whose applications had been rejected to hear their grievances and to gather information. In February, 1938, Dewey R. Jones returned to Chicago and received the Housing Authority's assurance that the same criteria were used in considering all applications.[89] Shortly after he returned to Washington, it was reported that "no change in the attitude of the Authority has been noticed as a result of Mr. Jones' visit."[90] Now, the demand began for Negro representation on the Housing Authority. "The answer," said the *Defender's* editor, "lies in the appointment of a Race representative to the Chicago Housing Authority. There is nothing radical or presumptive about that suggestion. It is being done in other cities where a clearer conception of Americanism holds forth — Philadelphia, for example. . . . Should an example nearer home be desired, Maj. R. A. Byrd is treasurer of the Springfield authority. . . ."[91]

After much agitation by Negro organizations, Robert R. Taylor became the first Negro appointed to the Housing Authority. In the meantime, occupancy of the housing projects had begun on a segre-

[86] Quoted in *Ibid.,* Sept. 18, 1937.
[87] *Ibid.*
[88] *Chicago Defender,* Jan. 29, 1939; Feb. 5, 1938.
[89] *Ibid.,* Feb. 19, 1938.
[90] *Ibid.,* Feb. 26, 1938.
[91] *Ibid.,* Feb. 12, 1938.

gated basis. Several Negro families had been admitted to the Jane Addams Houses, but they were all restricted to one area. Upon the insistence of Taylor, the Authority decided in the summer of 1939 to end all discriminatory practices at this project. Five days after the first earth was turned at the South Side project site, the first Negro family moved into a nonsegregated area of the Jane Addams project. When the family moved in on August 7, white tenants threatened to move, held mass meetings, and hurled bricks through the windows of the new family's apartment. Three days of disturbances ensued.[92] Thus began a long and bitter chapter in Chicago's history and that of Negro organizations — the violent struggle to integrate the city's public housing.

While the pressures exerted by the League in housing generally conformed to social work procedures and were sanctioned by the board, staff members engaged in other protest activities which they tried to keep disassociated from the agency's formal program. It was these activities which evidenced the organization's dualism and the declining confidence of its staff in social work methods. Since employment was the greatest concern of the Negro community, aggressive movements were most common in this field. League personnel worked as individuals and provided leadership in organizations agitating for Negro employment. Although League officials conducted some of these organizations as adjuncts to the Urban League, they were independent organizations. If it became necessary, the League could always disclaim responsibility for their actions. Nevertheless, it was realized that many Negroes would not make the fine distinction between the private activities of staff members and their work as League employees. Therefore, any militant leadership given by League personnel would help create an aggressive image of the organization among Negroes.

League staff members participated in the founding of three major groups — the Chicago Council of Negro Organizations, the Negro Chamber of Commerce, and the Negro Labor Relations League — and several lesser ones.

The Chicago Council was oldest of the three. Formed around 1935, as a means of "marshalling the forces" of the Negro community for united action, it was the moderates' answer to left-wing activity. The Council was an attempt by conservative leaders to

[92] *Ibid.*, Aug. 12, 1939.

"steal a little of the radical's thunder."[93] This was a confederation of Negro clubs, social agencies, and betterment groups. Beginning with forty member organizations, by 1937 the Council claimed a membership of sixty-five. From its founding to 1939, the League's executive secretary, A. L. Foster, served as Council president. Yet, the League disclaimed any control over the Council's policies and activities, beyond its role as a member organization. In 1937, however, the League's annual report said that while the Council was not "an Urban League subsidiary, our contribution to its success is so substantial and its assistance to us so potent that we feel justified in mentioning a few of its accomplishments. Our office has been the headquarters for this Council since it was first organized and our own clerical force has handled the stenographic details. The Executive Secretary . . . has served as its president and has devoted much time and attention to the development of its many activities."[94]

The Negro Chamber of Commerce was founded in 1937. Its primary purpose was to help in solving unique problems — securing credit, finding suitable locations, and purchasing in wholesale lots — faced by Negro businessmen. Moreover, it was to serve a racial protest function. Foster served as chairman of the committee which drew up the Chamber's constitution,[95] and after it was formally organized, he became executive vice president.[96]

A campaign — in which the League's industrial secretary played an active role — to secure promotions for a group of newspaper carriers led to the organization of the Negro Labor Relations League. In 1937, Joseph Jefferson, a Y.M.C.A. employee, and Howard Gould represented *Herald and Examiner* carriers before company officials to secure their elevation to branch managers. The success of this campaign motivated a group of young men to form an organization to press for jobs which had been "held tightly against" Negroes. The Labor Relations League had the support of N. George Davenport, editor of a militant Negro paper with anti-Semitic overtones. The Labor Relations League, however, did not ascribe to the editor's anti-Semitism.[97]

---

[93] See Drake and Cayton, *Black Metropolis,* pp. 736-739.
[94] *Annual Report, 1937,* Part I, pp. 4-5.
[95] *Chicago Defender,* Apr. 17, 1937.
[96] *Annual Report, 1937,* Part I, p. 5.
[97] See Drake, *Churches and Voluntary Associations,* pp. 252-253.

Of the three organizations, the Labor Relations League was the most aggressive. Both it and the Chamber of Commerce were member organizations of the Chicago Council of Negro Organizations. Many of the more militant projects began with the Labor League and were then endorsed by the Council. This organization also continued several projects which became too controversial for the Council.

The upsurge of militant protest among conservative groups became most pronounced in 1938. By this time, "it had become respectable to support a demonstration or a boycott in the struggle for Negro rights."[98] Up to this time, the Chicago Council's activities had been rather innocuous. It had held "monster" mass meetings, staged "mammoth" parades, and passed resolutions.[99] These served more as a catharsis for the participants than as means of changing the conditions protested. In 1936, however, after the Urban League's industrial secretary had personally instigated the picketing of South Side motion picture theaters to force the employment of more Negro projectionists,[100] the Council assumed sponsorship of the project.[101] But it withdrew when the undertaking threatened to become embarrassing to the Urban League. Then, in 1938, the Council instituted a campaign against the dairies, aimed at forcing the employment of Negro milk wagon drivers. "Milkless days" were proclaimed, during which Negroes were asked to boycott white drivers and stores selling products from "Jim Crow dairies."[102] Meanwhile, the Negro Chamber of Commerce revived the fight for jobs with the Chicago traction companies.[103] The Negro Labor Relations League resumed picketing the theaters, took over the fight for milk drivers when the Council faltered, and began urging Negroes to remove their telephones to back up the demand for Negro operators.[104]

This militant ferment on the South Side became embarrassing to the Urban League when it began to acquire distinct tinges of anti-

[98] Drake and Cayton, *Black Metropolis,* p. 738.
[99] *Chicago Defender,* Oct. 3, 1936; Nov. 28, 1936; Oct. 2, 1937; Nov. 20, 1937.
[100] Interview, Chicago, June 27, 1961.
[101] *Chicago Defender,* Nov. 28, 1936.
[102] See *Ibid.,* Oct. 8, 1938; Sept. 24, 1938; (editorial), Oct. 15, 1938.
[103] *Ibid.,* Sept. 24, 1938.
[104] Drake, *Churches and Voluntary Associations,* pp. 235-254; *Chicago Defender,* Aug. 27, 1938; Sept. 3, 1938; Oct. 1, 1938; Oct. 15, 1938; Nov. 5, 1938; Nov. 12, 1938.

Semitism. This manifestation of intolerance, however, stemmed more from anti-white sentiment and economic competition than from religious beliefs. The masses of Negroes probably made little distinction between Jewish and non-Jewish white merchants. They picketed and boycotted stores because the owners were white and did not employ Negroes. Since the great majority of white businesses in the Negro community were owned and operated by Jews, it was probably inevitable that the employment drives would take on anti-Jewish connotations. On the other hand, many Negro businessmen were quite conscious of Jewish competition for the Negro market. In addition, they believed that there was a Jewish conspiracy to monopolize the best business locations on the cross streets of the community.[105] This was one of the problems which motivated the founding of the Negro Chamber of Commerce. According to the Urban League, it was "almost impossible for Negro businesses to be established on the main arteries, especially if they are likely to be in competition with white businesses. This condition forces Negro business into basements in residential districts."[106] Yet, Negro League officials certainly did not intend for their fight against what they considered to be racial prejudice against Negro businessmen to be construed as anti-Semitism on their part.

The most repugnant aspect of this matter was the attempt by a few unscrupulous Negro leaders to capitalize on it in order to discredit other leaders and organizations. Several "secret groups" distributed circulars and pamphlets urging that the Jews be driven from the South Side. The names of League staff members and leaders of member organizations of the Chicago Council of Negro Organizations were sometimes illegally listed as sponsors. It was suspected that a Negro labor leader of questionable reputation, who was said to have been involved in underworld activities, was largely responsible for this vicious propaganda. His principal concern was to discredit and silence his critics, many of whom were League staff members and leaders of Chicago Council member organizations.[107]

The Chicago Urban League could not ignore this situation. In the first place, these attacks were inconsistent with fundamental League philosophy. Then, too, many of the League's active board

---

[105] Interview, Chicago, June 26, 1961; Drake and Cayton, *Black Metropolis*, pp. 437-453.

[106] *Annual Report, 1937*, Part I, p. 5.

[107] Interviews, Chicago, June 26, 1961; July 29, 1961; *Chicago Defender*, Oct. 1, 1938; Feb. 25, 1939.

members and most consistent contributors were Jews. Although individual Jews probably shared the general white sentiment against Negroes, other individuals and groups formed the nucleus of most interracial movements. With persecutions going on in Nazi Germany, the Chicago Jewish community was quite sensitive to the South Side outbreak. In June, 1938, the League's board named a five-man committee "to make a thorough study of conditions responsible for the situation." The Committee asked individuals and organizations to submit any information they had on the question.[108] In approaching this problem, the League sought to separate the questions of attacks on religious and racial groups and the Negro's struggle for economic justice on the South Side. It took the position that the organization opposed any campaign attacking a specific group of people; but, at the same time, it "recognized the fact that some business persons engaged in unfair and overreaching practices which cause community indignation."[109] The committee said that it was concerned with "the method, and not the purpose of these attacks." It suggested that "in publishing articles relative to economic conditions of the south side, reference should be made to individuals, without emphasizing race affiliations."[110] The League made its major contribution in curbing this outbreak through publicity in the Negro press, conferences with merchants, and a series of sermons and discussions.[111]

In 1939, the League began a gradual withdrawal from active affiliation with other Negro organizations. Some of their activities were bringing the League adverse publicity and thus complicating its relations with some of its white supporters and with organized labor. But Chicago was becoming more receptive to Negro protest activities, and the League had the financial support to undertake a bolder program on its own, though not as aggressive as those of all-Negro organizations. The first indication of this withdrawal came in 1939 when the executive secretary relinquished the presidency of the Chicago Council of Negro Organizations in order to devote more time to his League duties. In any case, the beginning

---

[108] *Ibid.*, June 18, 1938. The Committee consisted of a white and two Negro attorneys, a rabbi, and a white social worker.
[109] *Ibid.*, July 2, 1938.
[110] *Ibid.*, Oct. 1, 1938.
[111] Adena M. Rich, "Protective Services," *Social Service Yearbook*, 1938, p. 94.

of defense production and then World War II were about to change the nature of Negro protest.

Two rather distinct periods marked the League's development during the depression years. The first encompassed the "Hoover Phase" and the first year of the New Deal, extending roughly from 1930 to 1934. These were "lean" years for the League. The bulk of the available private philanthropy was needed to provide relief for the more severe cases of hardship. It was difficult for the League to secure enough money to remain in operation, and by 1933, only the executive secretary and a clerical worker were left on the agency's staff. Forces were at work, however, which changed this situation. Agitation by radical groups, especially the Communists, and the enactment of New Deal legislation caused a shift in the responsibility for relief. From around 1933 to the end of the depression, governmental bodies carried most of the relief burden formerly left to private agencies. After 1934, the League received a larger share of the charity dollar. It then began activities designed to help Negroes adjust to depression conditions and to assure them equitable participation in relief activities. But, as the League's financial situation began to improve, it was faced with challenges to its leadership. The Negro masses lost faith in education and persuasion as methods of racial advancement. They demanded overt action and militant protest. Had not the League and other established organizations furnished the type of leadership desired, other groups, particularly the Communists, would have filled the void. Yet, the League could not fully accede to the demands of its Negro constituency and, at the same time, retain the confidence of its white supporters. Concessions had to be made to both groups, giving the organization a sort of dual personality and planting the seeds of future internal discord.

6

INTERNAL DISSENSION, 1941-47

The Chicago Urban League's board of directors, following a meeting on July 29, 1946, summarily dismissed A. L. Foster and two of the three department heads. Rumors had circulated for several months that the League was having internal problems, but the public had no indication that the trouble was so deep rooted as to require firing the organization's top executives. On the contrary, articles in the Negro press, League reports on program and staff expansion, and evaluations by the Council of Social Agencies gave the impression that the period 1941 to 1945 was one of unparalleled growth and vigor. Nevertheless, the 1946 upheaval was not the result of impulsive or abrupt board action; rather, it was the culmination of a complex of internal problems. In spite of these problems, however, the League actually had made important contributions during the war years.

The department of industrial relations was especially active. From late in 1940 to 1942, this department concentrated primarily on opening new employment opportunities for Negro women. A special project was made possible through a grant of $2,500 and the cooperation of the National Youth Administration. The NYA paid over half of the salaries of three young women and provided clerical help. These three workers interviewed women seeking work and visited employers in search of jobs for them. After nine months of operation, this project had resulted in an extensive survey of work opportunities for Negro women, the opening of new jobs in twenty-five companies, the upgrading of workers in several plants, and the employment of additional workers in twenty-four firms. During this period, approximately 3,000 persons received employment as a result of this campaign.[1] Probably the least successful phase of this project was the effort to secure jobs in Loop department stores. One of the workers felt that their visits to these stores "amounted pretty much to a softening up process."[2] When the NYA withdrew its support, the League had to resort to using other organizations and volunteers for the continuation of this special campaign.[3]

In 1942, the work of the industrial department became more diversified. As the labor supply diminished, the League received numerous requests for assistance from governmental agencies, defense employers, and employers in nonessential fields. With the United States Employment Service concentrating on placements in defense industries, the League resumed its placement work in service fields. It advised governmental agencies and defense industries on the "practical steps" involved in using Negro workers for the first time and worked with employers on behavior problems. Negroes were encouraged to take advantage of the training classes provided to teach essential skills and to refer problems of discrimination to the President's Committee on Fair Employment Practices.[4] By 1943, there was no problem in finding jobs. In fact, the League's placement service was having difficulty in finding people willing to accept jobs as domestics and in other service fields. The staff devoted most of its time to counseling employers on problems within plants, trying to obtain a distribution of workers throughout Chicago industries, and to combating segregation in plants. Attempts were still being made, however, to breach the color bar in Loop stores.[5]

By the end of 1943, the industrial department was planning to broaden the labor relations services offered to employers. In December, A. L. Foster asked the Community Fund for a budgetary supplement of $5,500 for three additional workers. The League planned to work more closely with management and labor in adjusting problems which tended "to retard the ready acceptance of

---

[1] Chicago Urban League Service Report, Aug., 1941 (in the files of the Welfare Council of Metropolitan Chicago).

[2] Interview, Chicago, July 20, 1961.

[3] *Chicago Defender,* Feb. 7, 1942; Dec. 19, 1942.

[4] Chicago Urban League Service Report, Oct., 1942.

[5] Report of staff members of the industrial relations department, 1943 (in the personal files of Howard D. Gould); Report of Department of Industrial Relations, Sept., 1943 (in the Gould files).

Negroes in industry."[6] The new staff members went into industrial plants in Chicago and neighboring towns to handle complaints by employers and employees.[7] During 1944, in addition to its counseling work, the department started to prepare for postwar problems. In filling requests for workers "emphasis was placed upon the spread of Negroes throughout Chicago's industry. The reason for this is that Negroes will be in many industries, instead of a few, so that large groups of them will not be so seriously affected in a period of unemployment. This plan also tends to further social integration, since it prevents working in concentrated groups."[8] In 1945, two more staff members were added to work with returning servicemen.[9]

With so much concern being placed on economic developments, the League was slower in adjusting its program to social problems. But, the impact of the war on social relations was as profound as on economic conditions. Chicago being an area of short labor supply, it became a focal point of wartime migration. The lure of jobs attracted an estimated 65,000 Negro migrants. These newcomers — many of whom came from rural areas of the South — crowded into existing Negro neighborhoods, where housing, schools, and recreational facilities were already inadequate. Such neighborhoods became breeding grounds for antisocial behavior. The combination of racial conflicts in employment, unsatisfactory living conditions, and a large unadjusted rural group led to increased racial tensions.[10] The Urban League was aware of these problems, but it lacked the staff to work effectively. So, up to 1944, only small gestures were made toward improving social conditions. There was, however, a program of civic improvement, basically a propaganda campaign. Messages on public conduct, work habits, and morality were publicized with cartoons on posters, by "trailers" at motion picture theaters, and through churches and other organizations.[11]

---

[6] Albon L. Foster to Pierce Atwater, Dec. 24, 1943 (copy in Welfare Council files).
[7] Notes of Industrial Relations Committee Meeting, Sept. 25, 1944 (in Gould files).
[8] Chicago Urban League Service Report, Feb., 1945.
[9] *Chicago Defender,* Sept. 15, 1945.
[10] See Robert C. Weaver, "Racial Tensions in Chicago," *Social Service Yearbook, 1943* (Chicago Council of Social Agencies, 1944), pp. 1-8.
[11] Odessa Cave (Evans) to Lottie Mornye Thomas, Mar. 10, 1943, copy in Lottie Mornye Thomas, "An Historical Evaluation of the Place the Chicago Urban League Holds in the Community," (unpublished Master's thesis, School of Social Work, Atlanta University, 1943), pp. 50-51.

It was not until 1945 that a definite plan of expansion was instituted for the civic department. In February, a proposal for a community service project was submitted to the Community Fund. The purpose of the new program was to work with the large Negro population within the areas bounded by Twenty-sixth Street, Sixty-third Street, State Street, and Cottage Grove Avenue. It was to be educational in nature and was designed to help migrants from rural areas adjust to urban life. Staff requirements, in addition to the director of the department, were an assistant director and five field workers. The Community Fund made a special allocation to help initiate this project.[12] As a publicity gimmick and probably in an effort to prolong the duration of the program, it was labeled the five-year plan. A press release, in describing the program, said:

> Each of the five years allotted for completing the program will be devoted to some specific aspect of Negro life in Chicago. The program for the first year consists of helping the Negroes to help themselves. In the second year, an analysis will be made of the basic causes of the problems of the Negro.
>
> Household management, home furnishings, training of children, and education of [*sic*] civic responsibilities will be studied the third year. In the fourth year, according to present plans, seven centers for Negroes will have been established in various parts of the city, for daily classes on all phases of Negro life.
>
> During the fifth year the league plans to utilize and coordinate all existing agencies, settlements, social centers, case workers, recreational agencies, and juvenile delinquency prevention agencies. However, during the first year, all phases of the program will be included.[13]

In essence, the five-year plan was just a revival of the League's old program of self-improvement for the Negro community. Like the earlier project, it approached the social problems confronting the community through block clubs. It placed emphasis on the symptoms of community disorganization, rather than the basic causes. While the project's objectives had merit, it was largely a superficial approach to grave problems.

As a result of the growing concern over increased racial tensions, the Urban League, in 1944, established a department of public relations. This concern developed after the Detroit riot on June 20, 1943. It was realized that many of the same conditions which were basic to the violence in Detroit were present in Chicago and that a

---

[12] Special Report on the Operation of the Community Service Project by Mary A. Young, in Chicago Urban League Service Report, Feb., 1945.

[13] *Chicago Defender,* Apr. 21, 1945.

minor incident could cause a similar occurrence there.[14] The Chicago Urban League appointed a committee consisting of Louis Wirth, a University of Chicago professor; Hugo B. Law, an advertising executive; and Horace Cayton, a Negro author. This committee studied the overall situation and recommended the development of a program of public education. The Community Fund approved the proposal and allotted about $18,000 a year for its execution.[15] In the summer of 1944, a year after the Detroit riot, the League launched its new department. The investigator for the Council of Social Agencies described the role and methods of the department as follows:

> The function of this new department is to develop attitudes of racial understanding through interpretation of the Negro to the White groups and vice versa. Although the department utilizes publicity methods to a large degree, it is not primarily a publicity department. All departments of the League channel much of its [*sic*] interpretation through Public Relations. . . .
>
> The Public Relations Department is also developing a Speaker's Bureau which will provide speakers on race relations to interested civic groups. They also utilize the channels of the press and radio.[16]

Offices on North Wabash Avenue, in the Loop, were secured for this work, and Miss Sara Drucker was employed as director. This marked two significant changes in the League's organizational structure. A whole department was now housed in quarters other than the headquarters and separate from the other departments. In addition, the staff now became integrated, making the Chicago League one of the first to break the tradition of an interracial board and Negro staff. These changes were destined to contribute to future conflict.

At least two important factors influenced the scope and effectiveness of League programs during the war years. In the first place, the organization worked in the shadow of governmental agencies, especially in employment services. Second, the League's financial support did not keep pace with the growing prosperity of wartime.

During the war, the federal government assumed much of the responsibility for securing full utilization of the nation's manpower. In areas of labor tightness, such as Chicago, particular attention was

[14] See National Urban League, *Racial Conflict, a Home Front Danger: Lessons of the Detroit Riot* (New York: National Urban League, 1943).
[15] Interview, Chicago, July 19, 1961.
[16] Chicago Urban League Service Report, Feb., 1945.

given to the effective use of minority groups. President Roosevelt issued Executive Order 8802, on June 25, 1941, which reaffirmed a policy of nondiscrimination in defense production and created the President's Committee on Fair Employment Practices (FEPC). When Executive Order 9346 was issued, in May, 1943, strengthening the FEPC and providing for its decentralization, a regional office was established in Chicago.[17] The United States Employment Service (USES) concentrated on placements in defense industries and cooperated with the FEPC and other groups in combating discriminatory practices. One report stated:

The USES . . . made every effort to secure the most effective use of available manpower by urging employers to hire persons belonging to minority groups and by attempting to effect a change of attitude. Procedures were developed for handling situations where employers were adamant in their refusal to employ minority groups. Special visits were made by representatives of the Employment Service to the employer, particular orders with discriminatory specification were not accepted, and employers who persisted in their refusal to hire minority groups were cited to the War Manpower Commission for further action in order to remove such discriminatory practices.[18]

The official bodies motivated changes which private groups, such as the League, could not have obtained. The government's entrance into this work, however, was not altogether voluntary. It took considerable pressure from Negro organizations to get the President to act, and continuing pressure had to be exerted on the various bodies responsible for implementing federal policies.[19] Nevertheless, once this governmental machinery was set up, the League and other such organizations were forced into marginal fields of operation. They could prod the governmental groups, collect information on discrimination, and make placements in the less desirable jobs; but they were overshadowed by the official agencies.

Probably the greatest blow to the Chicago League's total program came with the formation of the Mayor's Committee on Race Relations (now the Chicago Commission on Human Relations). This was the city's official response to the Detroit race riot. The Chicago

[17] See Robert C. Weaver, *Negro Labor: A National Problem* (New York: Harcourt, Brace and Company, 1946), pp. 135-143.

[18] "Employment and Vocational Services," *Social Service Yearbook, 1942,* p. 34.

[19] Weaver, *Negro Labor,* pp. 134-135; John Hope Franklin, *From Slavery to Freedom: A History of American Negroes* (New York: Alfred A. Knopf, Inc., 1948), pp. 561-564, 573-580.

Committee, appointed by Mayor Edward J. Kelly in July, 1943, was the first municipal committee of its type. The Mayor's Committee worked for changes in many of the areas in which the League had held a virtual monopoly — law enforcement, employment, housing, public schools, health and recreation, and community organizations.[20] Naturally, the League resented this new body. One director expressed the opinion that "there was a strong feeling at that time that race relations was the private domain of Urban Leagues and that injecting another organization somewhat parallel and with governmental support [was] getting into our racket."[21] It was felt by some leaders that the Committee was established as a move to forestall demands for basic changes. Earl B. Dickerson, president of the Urban League, termed some of the appointments to the Committee unfortunate. He also said that: "The Mayor's almost complete failure to recognize the Chicago Urban League in his appointments . . . appears very strange to anyone who understands the present situation." Dickerson continued:

> The Mayor should be urged by all those who have the real good of this important project at heart, to select further members whose experience qualifies them beyond any question — men who have shown by their records that they are true believers in democracy, and who are completely free to act without bias.
>
> I'm sure that I speak for all those who want action, and not mere words, when I urge the Mayor to make further appointment of men who can be counted on to do the sort of job that is so desperately needed.[22]

Some felt that Dickerson may have been the reason why the League was ignored. His stand on Negro rights was far too aggressive for many white leaders. Then, too, he was not in good favor with the regular democratic organization. Negro "machine politicians," led by Congressman William L. Dawson, supported the Mayor.[23] With the controversy taking on political overtones, A. L. Foster issued a statement pledging the League's full cooperation with the Committee on Race Relations.[24] Nevertheless, since there was no clear-cut distinction between the spheres of operation of the two groups, the League lost stature in competing with an official agency.

---

[20] Mayor's Committee on Race Relations, *Race Relations in Chicago* (Chicago, December, 1944), pp. 5-23.

[21] Interview, Chicago, July 19, 1961.

[22] *Chicago Defender,* July, 17, 1943.

[23] *Ibid.,* July 24, 1943.

[24] *Ibid.,* Aug. 7, 1943.

The Urban League's financial situation reflected a lack of strong community response to the agency's program. But, there was evidence of continued Community Fund confidence. The League's income did not keep pace with the rapid expansion in the economy between 1941 and 1943. In 1941, the approved budget totaled $27,639, with the agency scheduled to raise $14,451 of this amount. It actually raised $14,097.[25] Income increased about $2,000 in 1942 and $3,000 the following year. Only in 1943, however, did the agency receive contributions equal to the estimate in its approved budget.[26] Since during this period, the Community Fund required agencies to raise their own income for salary increases, for instituting special projects, and to meet the rising cost of materials due to inflation,[27] the League was unable to expand its work fast enough to respond immediately to new needs. Relief came after changes in Fund policies in 1942 and 1943. In 1942, the Fund began financing part of the increased cost caused by war. Then, the next year, it began making supplementary grants for special projects.[28] These changes enabled the League to start expanding its work. The Urban League received special allocations for enlarged programs in industrial relations and civic education and for the new department of public relations. Since plans for each project had to be approved by the Council of Social Agencies and the Fund, these grants indicated continued confidence in the League's work. In 1946, the organization's budget exceeded $90,000, and in spite of adverse publicity, it raised $39,899 of the $47,719 which it was scheduled to raise.[29]

Even though external forces had profound effects on the agency's wartime operations, the upheaval of 1946 came principally from internal causes. The first indication that there was discord within the League was a curt announcement that the staff had rejected, by a vote of 20 to 11, an effort to organize a chapter of the United Office and Professional Workers of America (UOPWA), a CIO union. It was also reported that some workers charged that they had been intimidated before the election.[30] The union called upon

---

[25] Reports of Budget Analyst to Reviewing Committee of the Community Fund, Aug. 4, 1941 and Feb. 2, 1943 (in the Welfare Council files).

[26] Reports of Budget Analyst, Feb. 2, 1943 and Feb. 10, 1944.

[27] Linn Brandenburg, "Central Joint Financing of Private Health and Welfare Services in Chicago," *Social Service Yearbook, 1944,* pp. 10-11.

[28] *Ibid.*

[29] Report of Budget Analyst, Jan. 29, 1947.

[30] *Chicago Defender,* Nov. 3, 1945.

the board of directors to investigate activities of some staff members which constituted "unfair labor practices."[31] Then, in December, Foster notified two members of the industrial department staff that they would be released at the end of the month. Labor members of the board and Willard S. Townsend, head of the United Transport Service Employees of America (Red Caps) and a National League vice president, came to the defense of the employees. Other labor groups joined the protest and openly accused Foster of antilabor practices.[32] Foster maintained that the men had been employed with the understanding that they were assured work for only one year. He denied, however, that he had dismissed them. "I am the sole employing and discharging officer of this organization," Foster was quoted as saying, "and I want to make it emphatically clear that I have not discharged either [John] Sloan or [Ralph] Amerson and have no intention of doing so."[33]

In the meantime, he had dismissed Howard Gould, director of the department of industrial relations. Gould appealed his dismissal to the board of directors, which appointed a committee to investigate the matter. The committee reported that the firing was warranted but felt that Foster had not "proceeded in the proper manner in discharging Mr. Gould." It therefore recommended that Gould be reinstated, but placed on probation for six months.[34] In its December, 1945 meeting, the board adopted the committee's report and passed a resolution reaffirming its approval of unionization for its employees. Also, a previously appointed committee on labor practices was instructed to proceed with hearings and investigations of charges "of improper action by any person or persons connected with the league."[35] Gould's original firing was generally ascribed to his support for unionization of the League's employees. At least this was the interpretation placed on it by labor men on the board.

The board, in its meeting on February 6, 1946, empowered Foster to dismiss Gould as of July 1 and set up a committee to review the industrial secretary's work during the interim. The committee could, if it saw fit, dispense with his services before July 1. During

---

[31] *Ibid.,* Nov. 17, 1945.
[32] *Ibid.,* Dec. 15, 1945; Dec. 22, 1945.
[33] *Ibid.,* Dec. 22, 1945.
[34] Wayne McMillen, "A Survey of the Administrative and Personnel Practices of the Chicago Urban League," July, 1946 (unpublished study in the files of the Chicago Urban League), pp. 31-33.
[35] *Chicago Defender,* Dec. 29, 1945.

this meeting, two labor men resigned from the board. They said that their decision was actuated by the action of the board in rescinding its December decision in regard to the Gould-Foster controversy. In their letter of resignation, John L. Yancey and Michael Mann asserted:

> The action of the board on February 6, indicates that the executive director will have a free hand in dealing with union matters concerning his staff which according to knowledge we have gained has been subtly unfair as regards the particular union seeking recognition. As representatives of labor and members of the executive board we cannot conscientiously justify ourselves by remaining in an untenable position.
>
> In our judgment the executive board has yielded its authority to the executive director and we cannot support a move which places such an important program and a program of such magnitude in the hands of one individual who is subject to error . . . and whose actions in the instant [Gould] case clearly indicate that his personal desires create an obsession which closes his eyes to the needs of the cause which he serves.[36]

On March 4, eight members of Labor's Council for Community Action wrote to Dickerson. They asked for an opportunity to appear before the board to voice their opinions. A report from a subcommittee of their organization was enclosed which accused Foster of hypocrisy and of using "all kinds of threats and intimidations to keep his workers from joining the union."[37]

In spite of the publicity being given this conflict, little was known by the public of its actual nature. Dickerson told the press that it was chiefly a matter of "personality clashes," which was true in a sense, but he also announced an impending "shake-up" of the agency's administration.[38] Foster banned discussion of internal problems by the staff both with outsiders and among themselves.[39] Editorially the *Defender* called upon League officials to institute a "vigorous and honest investigation" and give the public all the facts, since they had failed to resolve the controversy while keeping the "public in the dark."[40] Actually, as the editor of the *Defender* knew quite well, an investigation had been underway for several months. The board of directors had commissioned Wayne McMillen

---

[36] John L. Yancey and Michael Mann to Earl B. Dickerson, Feb. 11, 1946 (copy in Gould files). (Mimeo.)

[37] Willoughby Abner and others to Earl B. Dickerson, Mar. 4, 1946 (copy in Gould files). (Mimeo.)

[38] *Chicago Defender,* Mar. 2, 1946.

[39] *Ibid.,* Mar. 30, 1946.

[40] *Ibid.,* Apr. 6, 1946.

of the University of Chicago to study the administrative and personnel practices of the League.

Meanwhile, the UOPWA won its fight for recognition. The labor policy committee of the League's board had reported that the employees favored unionization. So, the board recognized the UOPWA as the sole bargaining agent for its employees, and during the first week in June, started negotiating a contract with this union.

But, when Gould's probationary period ended, Foster exercised his authority to dismiss him. The board upheld Foster's action, but Gould promised to fight the decision. The Urban League chapter of the UOPWA entered the controversy. William Prince, president of the chapter and a member of Gould's department, said that the union would appeal the firing.[41] A decision on this appeal was delayed, however, pending board consideration of the forthcoming McMillen report.[42]

On July 29, the McMillen report was acted on by the board. McMillen made three "primary" recommendations. He said that: "The most important of all of the needs of the Chicago Urban League is the reform of the governing board." A procedure was suggested for effecting this reform. All members would submit their resignations, but no action would be taken on these until a subsequent meeting. The president would appoint a committee to screen board personnel. Those who could actively participate in the affairs of the organization would withdraw their resignations. Others would be accepted. If only a few members remained, this group would institute a "conservative policy of recruiting board members" and would add members "on the basis of clear advance explanation of the obligations involved in board membership." It was also thought desirable to reduce the size of the board to around twenty-five directors. Second, McMillen stated: "Changes in staff are needed in the Chicago Urban League." And, he designated the particular changes he thought necessary.

In the interest of restoring harmony and efficiency promptly in the Chicago Urban League, it would be particularly helpful if resignations were submitted by:

1. The Executive Director
2. Director of the Department of Industrial Relations
3. Director of the Department of Public Relations

But, the report continued,

---

[41] *Ibid.*, July 13, 1946.
[42] *Ibid.*, July 20, 1946.

If at least the three resignations mentioned above are not forthcoming at once, the governing board should dismiss these three persons. . . .

Third, it was recommended that program and staff be reduced to a size consonant with the equipment and space available to the agency.[43] The League's board of directors adopted the report and, consequently, the recommendations. Foster, Gould, and Miss Drucker were notified of their immediate dismissal, and steps were taken to implement the recommendation on board reform.

McMillen's "primary" recommendations, along with sixty-four "secondary" recommendations, were based on the investigation of three aspects of the League's organizational structure. Except in illustrations and passing references, no consideration was given to program. The areas included were board policies and procedures, personnel practices and personnel administration, and executive-staff relations. McMillen was quite critical of the League's operations in respect to the activities studied. He found that the constitution, which had not been changed since 1916, was outdated and largely ignored in operating the agency. The constitution was too specific on operational matters and, therefore, rather inflexible, and it contained inadequate definitions of powers and duties. In the relationship between the board and management, the distinction between policy-making and administration had been obliterated. There was mutual infringement on each other's prerogatives between the board and management. Much of the League's difficulty was charged to a lack of dynamic leadership on Foster's part. He was unable to get the board actively involved in policy-making and fund raising, and the supervision and direction of programs were uninspired. Conflict within the staff, McMillen felt, sprang from several causes. There was no clear statement of personnel practices, personnel records were incomplete, and no uniform system of evaluation was used. Moreover, since no job descriptions existed, it was virtually impossible to make a fair evaluation of staff performances. In addition, equipment and space were far from adequate. Some employees had no place to work and nothing to work with. The report placed the brunt of the responsibility for these conditions on the executive director.[44]

---

[43] McMillen, "A Survey of the Administrative and Personnel Practices of the Chicago Urban League," pp. 74-78.

[44] Summarized from McMillen, "A Survey of the Administrative and Personnel Practices of the Chicago Urban League."

Actually, the McMillen report was primarily a camouflage. League officials hoped to avoid publicity on what they thought were the real problems. Both the published issues and those which were not disclosed, however, were more effects than causes. Many of the board's actions were motivated by these effects. The directors knew that the internal situation was growing more intolerable; yet, they were afraid to dismiss Foster. In his many years with the League, he had made many friends. "There was great danger," said one director, "that if the board fired him, they would ruin the whole organization." By employing McMillen, who they knew would make a respectable study, the board hoped to gain support for their predetermined course of action.[45] To a large extent, the results of the study were a foregone conclusion.

As far as the unionization issue was concerned, it was a result of staff unrest, rather than a cause. Labor representatives on the board made no attempt to encourage unionization. In fact, they were quite conservative on labor matters and had little enthusiasm for the UOPWA, which they considered kind of "pinkish" or Communist infiltrated. But, when the employees decided that a union was in their best interest, the labor men had no alternative but to support the principle of unionization. The basic problem was the growing feeling of insecurity on the part of some staff members. Methods of staff administration used in the 1930's were inadequate for the 1940's. Among only five employees, or thereabout, close interpersonal relationships could develop. There was little need for elaborate formal procedures. But, in the late 1940's, with as many as thirty-one people on the staff, administration could not be conducted on a strictly personal level. As the staff grew, the employees with long tenure became a group apart from the new personnel. Each group developed its cliques, which tended to look upon each other with suspicion. Since the group with longer service had closer relations with the executive, the new people felt that they were discriminated against in wage increases, promotions, and other administrative actions. As a first resort, they looked to their department heads to intercede for them. Then, as conflicts began to develop among department heads, with the executive taking sides, the group which felt threatened turned to unionization as a means of having standardized procedures established.[46]

---

[45] Interviews, Chicago, July 19, 1961; Aug. 8, 1961; July 29, 1961.
[46] *Ibid.*, Chicago, June 27, 1961; July 20, 1961.

Since this problem became more acute in 1944, with the establishment of the department of public relations, officials were hesitant to discuss this part of the conflict. They felt that it would reflect on the organization's experiment in staff integration. They failed to take into consideration, however, that expansion was taking place in all departments and that the problem was more basic than the personalities involved. Had not the problems involved in establishing the public relations department brought the latent hostilities to the surface, something else probably would have. In any case, with so much attention being given to getting the new department started, people in the other departments, especially industrial relations, became wary of the new department's powers. This was aggravated by the fact that the public relations staff, in its Loop offices, was separated from the other employees. In launching the new program, many concessions were made to the director of public relations. Some thought that she was exercising undue influence on the executive director and, thereby, negating the influence of their own department heads. This group, composed mainly of new employees, charged the older group with abetting the situation and, later, with helping the executive to block their efforts at unionization.[47]

The Gould-Foster controversy was also tied into this situation. But, it too was more basic than unionization or even staff unrest. To a great extent it was a legacy from the depression. During the depression, the board of directors abrogated many of its powers to the executive; for, there was little need for policy-making. Throughout the 1930's, investigators of the Council of Social Agencies described the League's board as being largely advisory in nature. The authors of a 1936 study wrote:

> A reading of the minutes corroborates the statement of the executive secretary that the Board is more advisory in character than directing, although whenever any matter of policy in the agency comes up, it is always brought to the attention of the Board for a decision rather than the executive and staff deciding what should be done.[48]

Board meetings were poorly attended, and the few active members became a self-perpetuating body. The constitution provided for the

---

[47] *Ibid.*

[48] Dorothy Counse, Louise Gilbert, and Agnes Van Driel, "The Chicago Urban League," June, 1936 (unpublished study in the Welfare Council files), p. 27.

election of board members during annual meetings,[49] but these meetings lost their business character and became annual dinners.

Through the years, Gould gradually became a threat to Foster's supremacy over the board. Gould had come at a low point in program operations and started making contacts with businessmen and labor leaders. He made friends among the more conservative Negro unionists and gained the respect of industrialists. Many of these people came onto the League's board, and others accepted membership on the industrial relations advisory committee. They also became important contributors to the agency's budget.[50] The board, and to some extent League constituents, divided into two groups, the followers of Gould and the followers of Foster. Gould was able to build his department into virtually a separate agency. He had a strong advisory committee, which went beyond its proper functions and formed policies, and strong support on the board to back him in his periodic disputes with Foster. This was an untenable situation for the executive director, since he was head of the organization.[51] Yet, he was afraid to fire Gould on his own authority, and he could not get the board to do it for him. Then, after 1943 as the fortunes of the League improved, the board wanted to regain some of its lost authority. Several directors thought the League should be more aggressive in its activities and felt that Foster was too committed to the old way of doing things.

Into this confused situation came the department of public relations. Jealous of his independence, Gould balked at changing some of his procedures to facilitate the incorporation of the public relations department into the agency's total program. He and the director of public relations were frequently at odds, with the executive director supporting the latter. When the union issue arose, Gould had little choice but to support his union friends, and he knew that unionization would be a blow to the executive. As the conflict grew more bitter and rumors began to circulate in the city, some members of the board, led by the president, concluded that the situation required drastic action. Thus came the debacle of July 29.

The decision to adopt the McMillen report was only the begin-

---

[49] Constitution (1916), arts. III and VI.

[50] Interview, Chicago, June 27, 1961.

[51] McMillen, "A Survey of the Administrative and Personnel Practices of the Chicago Urban League," p. 20; Interviews, Aug. 8, 1961; June 27, 1961; July 19, 1961; July 29, 1961.

ning. Since the League was not a membership controlled organization, a strife ridden board of directors had to try to reform itself. In addition, Foster would not quit without a struggle, and his friends made persistent efforts to have him reinstated. It was six months after the July 29 meeting before conditions returned to a semblance of normality.

A number of Foster's Negro friends rallied to his support. They formed the Citizens' Committee for the Advancement of the Urban League. This group termed the board meeting which adopted the McMillen report a "star chamber" session and termed Foster's firing a "civic lynching." They called for public disclosure of the McMillen report's contents, a "complete" reorganization of the League, and the reinstatement of Foster. During a pro-Foster mass meeting, a resolution was passed asking for a general membership meeting to review the board's action. President Dickerson denied these requests and pointed out that the membership could make no decisions which would be binding on the board. He charged, moreover, that the pro-Foster forces were disrupting reorganization proceedings.[52]

On August 16, Foster issued his reply to the McMillen report. He said that unethical procedures had been used in "engineering" his dismissal. Since the common practice was to submit the final draft of a study to the executive of an agency so that he could check it for mistakes, he felt that in the case of the McMillen study,

> with the content of the report so unprecedentedly uprooting . . . it would seem more important than usual for a careful re-check and for the parties concerned to have ample time to evaluate and discuss it. Neither the board members or [*sic*] the three paid officials whose resignations were recommended had a chance to give proper consideration to the report and the haste with which action on the report was forced, made it impossible for either to exercise mature judgment.[53]

Furthermore, he charged that Dr. McMillen admitted revising the original draft of his report at the insistence of the advisory committee for the study — a committee whose membership composition was open to question. The nature of the revisions was not stated, but Foster charged the members of the advisory committee with bias. He rightfully questioned the propriety of having representatives of the Community Fund and the Chicago Association of Commerce and Industry serving on the advisory committee. "It is

---

[52] *Chicago Defender,* Aug. 3, 1946; Aug. 10, 1946.

[53] Memorandum from Albon L. Foster, Aug. 16, 1946 (copy in Gould files). (Mimeo.)

quite likely," Foster wrote, "that members of the board who voted on the report were somewhat influenced by the fact that members of the advisory committee concurred in the recommendations." He continued:

It was probably felt, at least by some, that this concurrence carried the official endorsement of the Community Fund and the Association of Commerce and the financial support from the former and endorsement by the latter might be withheld if all of the recommendations contained in the report were not accepted. Because this seemingly improper participation may become a precedent, it is of vital importance to the member-agencies of the Council of Social Agencies and should become the subject of serious discussion. . . .[54]

These words were more prophetic than Mr. Foster probably knew. The findings of the McMillen study were to haunt the Chicago Urban League for a number of years to come.

Foster's rebuttal also pointed out another serious weakness of the report. Since program activities were not covered, the impression was given that the League had "no real assets." The report failed to show what effects the antiquated administrative and personnel practices had on the work of the agency. In making a villain of the executive director, the report failed to consider his work during the greater part of his twenty-one-year tenure. By limiting consideration to the last years of the war, it overlooked the yeoman service rendered during the period 1925-43. Furthermore, it did not take into consideration the debilitating effects the depression had on the organization and on the thinking of its leaders. As Foster pointed out:

It is probable that the Chicago Urban League expanded too rapidly — spread itself out too thin due to the ever-increasing demands upon our services — demands which could not be ignored. Perhaps it is true that the staff — and most members of the board too — have considered it far more important that the League has rendered services to thousands of individuals and has accomplished much of its purpose of improving race relations and raising the social and economic status of the Negro population than that it has "failed to purchase a new typewriter or adopted a new report form. . . ."[55]

But, what effects did the activities of Foster and his friends have on the reorganization?

Several people denied that the pro-Foster agitation had any sig-

[54] *Ibid.*
[55] *Ibid.*

nificant effects.[56] Yet, the reorganization procedures were changed in several respects after the initial decisions were made. Following the meeting of July 29, Dickerson sent letters of outright dismissal to the staff members concerned; appointed a committee, with himself as chairman, to screen the board of directors; named Frayser T. Lane as acting executive director; and filled the vacancies in public relations and industrial relations with two other staff members.[57] Subsequently, Dickerson turned over the chairmanship of the membership screening committee to former League President M. O. Bousfield; and during a September meeting, the board reviewed its action on the McMillen report. A motion was turned down which called for reconsidering the adoption of the report, but another which asked for "blanket approval of Dickerson's action" was also lost. The board reaffirmed its action of July 29, and the president agreed to modify his dismissal procedures. Dickerson withdrew his letters of dismissal, with the understanding that Foster would be considered on leave as of the date he was dismissed.[58]

These developments gave Foster and his supporters new hope. Although the pro-Foster campaign had accomplished about all it could, Foster still expected one or more of several organizations — the Chicago Council of Social Agencies, the Community Fund, the Chicago Chapter of the American Association of Social Workers, and the National Urban League — to question the unorthodox manner of his firing.[59] It finally became evident that little could be expected from these organizations. So, in January, 1947, Foster wrote his partisans: "I am satisfied that any continued efforts in my behalf will serve no good purpose. . . . I respectfully request that your two committees discontinue those activities which may be construed as seeking my re-instatement."[60]

The period of internal conflict from 1944 to 1947 was tragic in several respects. The public was unwilling to support wholeheartedly an organization in constant turmoil. Consequently, at a time when its services were badly needed, the League was operating largely on a month-to-month basis, both financially and in its programs. A service report said of the situation:

---

[56] Interview, Chicago, July 19, 1961; *Chicago Defender,* Sept. 28, 1946.
[57] *Ibid.,* Aug. 3, 1946; Aug. 10, 1946.
[58] *Ibid.,* Oct. 5, 1946.
[59] *Ibid.,* Sept. 28, 1946; Oct. 5, 1946; Oct. 19, 1946.
[60] *Ibid.,* Jan. 11, 1947.

> The entire period involved in the Administrative Study of the organization and the reorganization resulting from the recommendations has had a derogatory effect upon staff and consequently upon program. Many staff members have felt insecure and the programs have suffered because of readjustments in leadership.[61]

Probably more tragic than the effect on the organization was that on individuals. The whole affair was conducted largely on a personal basis. The integrity of respected and able men was questioned and their reputations placed in jeopardy for rather dubious reasons. Out of all of this bitterness and assassination of character came only one concrete result. In February, 1947, the board employed a new executive. The irony of it all was that after two years of conflict the basic ideological and organizational problems remained unsolved.

---

[61] Chicago Urban League Service Report, Jan., 1947.

7

TIME OF TROUBLES, 1947-55

Continuing internal discord and external pressures marked the period 1947 to 1955 as a time of troubles for the Chicago Urban League. Administration, executive direction, and programing had, by 1955, reached advanced stages of deterioration. This condition resulted mainly from two sets of circumstances. In the first place, it was a legacy from the reorganization of 1947, which changed the executive leadership of the League but did not reorganize the staff, reform the board of directors, or redefine the organization's basic policies. During a period of racial peace, these internal problems probably would have had little effect on the League's relations with other groups. But these were not years of peace. After 1945, Chicago became a "seething caldron," with the city coming closer to general race war than it had since 1919. Employment and housing, two perennial problems, loomed large among the causes of racial friction. This circumstance of prolonged racial conflict had profound effects on the course of development of the Chicago Urban League.

The character of the employment problem changed somewhat after World War II. The exigency of a short labor supply combined with the work of the President's Committee on Fair Employment Practices, the Chicago Urban League, and other organizations brought a dispersal of Negro workers throughout Chicago's industrial establishments. This tended to stabilize the employment of Negroes and other minority groups. Nonwhite workers were employed and upgraded both in the thousands of small plants, which provide diversity and stability to Chicago's industries, and in the large basic industries — steel, farm machinery, and food manufacturing. In addition, the number of nonwhites in service pursuits, other than domestic service, increased greatly. In all of these fields, most plants either already had trade unions or organized them during the war. Through collective bargaining contracts, minority group workers achieved seniority rights and, thereby, a measure of job security. This was especially true in small industries which continued to make their peacetime products during the war and had no problems of reconversion after V-J Day. Of the situation in these industries, the Commission on Human Relations said: "With these workers from minority groups solidly set in these plants, their seniority guaranteed and protected under the collective bargaining agreements, and with a limited number of workers returning with seniority rights, these stable situations represent a new factor in the employment situation in Chicago."[1]

Nevertheless, the end of the war was accompanied by a rise in discriminatory practices. Employment agencies began receiving a large number of job orders specifying white workers only; and although layoffs in manufacturing plants occurred in equitable proportions, nonwhite workers were not re-employed or added to the work force after normal operations were resumed. In spite of the broader occupational distribution of Negro workers, the great majority remained in lower level unskilled and semi-skilled jobs and in service pursuits. The war had, however, fostered a greater acceptance of Negro workers and broadened the range of employment opportunities open to them.[2] Although efforts were still being made by the Urban League and other organizations to secure positions as clerks in department stores, as telephone operators, and in other restricted jobs, they began to place primary emphasis on the broader area of fair employment practices. After the war, responsibility for safeguarding minority rights again devolved on local agencies. The President's Committee on Fair Employment Practices suspended operations when the war ended, returning the fortunes of minority group workers to the hands of private employers. In 1945, the Chicago City Council passed a FEP ordinance, but it was largely a statement of policy. Most groups interested in minority employ-

[1] Mayor's Commission on Human Relations, *Race Relations in Chicago: Report for 1945* (Chicago, 1945), p. 3.

[2] Mayor's Commission on Human Relations, *Human Relations in Chicago: Report for Year 1946* (Chicago, 1946), pp. 11-13.

ment felt that in the absence of legislation by the Congress, state action was needed. The Mayor's Commission asserted:

> A sound realistic personnel policy and practice on the part of management and labor is needed if Chicago's industrial establishments are to achieve the full utilization of all workers without regard to their race, color, or national origin. For industrial peace and prosperity there must be complete elimination of discriminatory practices in the hiring and upgrading of workers, technicians, and professional men and women.
>
> Apparently these things cannot be achieved by business and trade unions acting on voluntary good will alone. Therefore, progressive and fair-minded citizens must press for the statement and enforcement of public policy in a State Fair Employment Practice Statute.[3]

Beginning in 1947, FEP proposals were introduced in each session of the Illinois Legislature until a bill was finally passed in 1961.[4] Most civic groups had no objection to the "general principle" of fair employment practices, but the great majority of businessmen strongly opposed legislation to achieve this objective. Any agency dependent upon business groups or organizations dominated by such groups for support had to be quite circumspect in advocating FEP legislation. The early campaigns generated considerable controversy.

Housing, however, was the major cause of racial conflict. To a large degree, it was a matter of simple arithmetic. The Negro community simply could not accommodate the ever increasing population. Between 1940 and 1960, there was a tremendous increase both in the number of Negroes in Chicago and in the percentage they comprised of the total population. Chicago's Negro population numbered 277,731 in 1940. Ten years later, it had grown to 492,265; and by 1960, it had jumped to 812,637. In 1940, only 8.2 per cent of the total population were Negroes. This proportion rose to 13.6 per cent in 1950 and to 22.9 per cent in 1960.[5] During the war, the Negro community absorbed the greater portion of these newcomers, but there was a limit to the number of people existing Negro neighborhoods could accommodate. As early as 1939, the main Negro area had a density of 75,000 persons and over per square mile. By

---

[3] *Ibid.*, p. 19.

[4] See Chicago Urban League, "Leadership Conference for Fair Employment Practices," Feb. 25, 1961 (mimeo. program). FEP bills were passed by the Illinois House of Representatives in 1947, 1949, 1951, 1953, 1955, 1957, and 1959; but it was not until 1961 that the measure passed the Senate.

[5] From data compiled by the research department of the Chicago Urban League, July, 1961.

1945, an estimated 300,000 people were crowded into territory described by the Chicago Plan Commission as suitable for a maximum of 225,000.[6]

Furthermore, the housing supply was actually diminishing. After 1948, an average of 2,800 families and 860 individual occupants were displaced each year to make way for expressway routes, low-rent public housing, and private redevelopment projects.[7] Those displaced from clearance sites were, in many cases, ineligible for accommodations in new facilities constructed on these sites. This was particularly true of public housing. A majority of the families dislocated had income in excess of the legal limit allowed low-rent housing tenants. Private builders were doing nothing to relieve the situation; and the construction of public housing was delayed by lack of relocation housing, opposition from real-estate interests, and political maneuvering.

White neighborhoods, moreover, were determined to bar entrance to Negroes. Restrictive covenants, neighborhood associations, political influence, and, in the final analysis, violence were employed to keep them out. Nevertheless, as the housing shortage became more critical and after covenants were declared unenforceable by the United States Supreme Court, Negroes began to break out of the ghetto in larger numbers. Neighborhoods adjacent to the "Black Belt" remained in a state of seige. In 1946, the people of Chicago were warned that the "lack of housing lies at the base of the most dangerous and serious problems in human relations in our city. Unless more homes are provided, no one, regardless of good will or police power, can check the social conflicts which are inherent in this situation. No words strong enough can be found to arouse Chicago to the need for facing this problem and solving it."[8] As the barriers around the ghetto crumbled, hysteria seemed to pervade white communities. Even the rumor of a Negro move-in occasioned the gathering of mobs and wanton attacks on persons and property. The Commission on Human Relations, reporting on conditions between 1947 and 1951, said:

While the overall shortage of housing was extreme, for Negroes it

[6] *Race Relations in Chicago, 1945,* pp. 25-26.
[7] Chicago Department of City Planning, *Rehousing Residents Displaced from Public Housing Clearance Sites in Chicago, 1957-1958* (Chicago: City of Chicago, Oct., 1960), p. 7.
[8] *Human Relations in Chicago,* 1946, p. 80.

seemed a crisis within a crisis, exaggerated by the artificial restriction upon the movement of Negroes out of the ghetto. Many short sighted people were determined to seal the lid on this boiling kettle until its contents exploded, and all chances of an orderly, natural dispersal of the nonwhite population might be lost. Years of agitation to maintain segregation had magnified the fears of white property owners. Each incident, no matter how small, carried the seeds of possible explosion.[9]

Fortunately, the big explosion did not occur, but there were many smaller disturbances. And, the threat of a major conflagration was always present.

The pattern of violence went from isolated attacks by a few individuals and gangs to prolonged and organized mob action. Immediately after the war, in 1945 and 1946, there were incidents of arson on buildings occupied and owned by Negroes. Clashes occurred between gangs of young people in parks and other recreational facilities, and Negro and interracial groups were attacked on the streets.[10] A more virulent type of disturbances began in November, 1946. These were motivated by the efforts of the Chicago Housing Authority to implement its policy of nondiscrimination in selecting tenants for veterans' emergency housing projects. The construction of these projects was a joint municipal-federal program to provide temporary homes for returning veterans. Knowing the Housing Authority's policy on open occupancy, many communities in which sites were obtained for temporary housing objected to its construction. Rumors circulated that various projects would be burned. Then, on November 16, a Negro veteran and his family moved into Airport Homes, a project in southwest Chicago at Sixtieth Street and Karlov Avenue. In spite of preparatory activities by the Commission on Human Relations, this move-in occasioned an outburst of violence. For over a month disorder prevailed. Crowds gathered around the project. They overturned automobiles, threw stones at buildings and passing cars, and attacked policemen on guard duty. The Negro family, representatives of the Mayor's Commission, Housing Authority officials, and other visitors needed police escorts to get in and out of the project.[11] In early 1947, the two

[9] Chicago Commission on Human Relations, *The People of Chicago: Five Year Report, 1947-1951* (Chicago, 1952), p. 7.

[10] *Race Relations in Chicago, 1945,* pp. 40-41; *Human Relations in Chicago, 1946,* pp. 119-149.

[11] Memorandum on Airport Homes in *Human Relations in Chicago, 1946,* pp. 119-149.

Negro families living in Airport Homes were still having trouble getting such services as milk and ice deliveries.[12]

The next serious incident occurred when Negro tenants moved into the Fernwood Park project, also in southwest Chicago. When the first families arrived on August 12, 1947, milling crowds gathered in the area. That night a mob surged toward the homes, setting fires on vacant land and throwing rocks at policemen. Thwarted in its attempt to reach the project, the mob went onto the main streets of the area and stoned passing Negro motorists. For two nights, roaming gangs assaulted any Negro found in a square-mile area around the project. Feelings rose in the Negro community, and retaliatory attacks were made against white people in and near Negro areas. It took over 1,000 policemen to bring the situation under control. But, in the meantime, more fuel had been added to the smoldering fires of racial hatred. According to the Commission on Human Relations: "Few Chicagoans know how close to the disaster of unrestrained rioting the city stood during those trying nights."[13]

Between 1945 and 1954, there were at least nine major riots in Chicago. Several were not even reported in the Chicago press.[14] From 1948 to 1951, there were 217 reported attacks against property.[15] Attacks against persons probably exceeded this figure. The most vicious assaults on both persons and property took place during the Peoria Street riot, the Cicero riot, and the Trumbull Park disturbances.

The Peoria Street trouble began as a protest against Negro guests in a home in the neighborhood. Aaron Bindman, an organizer for the Warehouse and Distribution Workers' Union, had a meeting of shop stewards in his home on November 8, 1949. Eight of the guests were Negroes. The rumor was circulated that Negroes were about to move into the building. A small crowd assembled protesting the presence of the Negroes. The police escorted the guests out but did not heed a warning to disperse the crowd. Two nights later, it had been learned that the owner of the house was Jewish. Now swelled to about 400 people, the crowd moved toward the house shouting epithets at the owner and threatening to burn the building. With

[12] *The People of Chicago, 1947-1951*, pp. 7-8.
[13] *Ibid.*, pp. 9-10.
[14] Charles Abrams, *Forbidden Neighbors: A Study of Prejudice in Housing* (New York: Harper and Brothers, 1955), p. 106.
[15] *The People of Chicago, 1947-1951*, p. 12.

reinforcements, the police were able to keep the mob back; but gangs roamed the street attacking Jews, Negroes, and strangers, especially students from the University of Chicago. It was not until the mob swelled to some 2,000 milling people and after five days of violence that the police decided to employ dispersal as a method of preventing further mob activity.[16]

In June, 1951, Harvey E. Clark, Jr., a Negro veteran, tried to move into an apartment in Cicero, a city which joins Chicago on the northwest. The owner of the building was warned by city officials that they would not be responsible for what happened if a Negro moved in. When Clark arrived with his furniture, police halted the van and warned him to get out or he would be arrested. Later in the evening, the chief of police came with about twenty officers, beat Clark up and ran him out of town. On June 26, a federal judge issued an injunction enjoining the city of Cicero from "shooting, beating or otherwise harassing Clark." After Clark moved in, however, mob action began. On July 11, a crowd of 4,000 gathered with only sixty policemen assigned to the area. Nothing was done to maintain order. Policemen moved out of the way or joined the mob as it surged into the building, setting fires and breaking windows. Governor Adlai Stevenson declared martial law in Cicero on July 12 and sent the state militia in to restore order. On January 18, 1952, a Cook County grand jury indicted the N.A.A.C.P. attorney who had represented Clark, the owner of the building, her lawyer, and her rental agent. They were charged with conspiracy to injure property. No member of the mob was indicted. Following a storm of protests, these indictments were dropped, and federal indictments were brought in against various Cicero officials. The police chief and two policemen were later fined for their part in the riot.[17]

Chicago's largest, costliest, and most prolonged racial disturbances took place at the Trumbull Park Homes. These disturbances began in August, 1953 and continued beyond the period under consideration in this chapter. They were occasioned by the leasing of an apartment in Trumbull Park Homes to a Negro family. This was one of the first three low-cost public projects constructed by the Public Works Administration and later turned over to the Chicago Housing Authority. The Negro family — Donald Howard, his wife,

---

[16] *Ibid.*, pp. 18-19; Abrams, *Forbidden Neighbors*, pp. 106-107.
[17] See *Ibid.*, pp. 103-106.

and two small children — moved into their apartment on July 30, 1953. Several days later, sporadic acts of violence began. Soon these developed into an organized campaign of terror and intimidation. The *Chicago Daily News* reported, on April 10, 1954, that:

The disturbances at the Trumbull Park Housing Project are not spontaneous but are being fostered by two small organizations.

The campaign of police harassment, window smashing, rock tossing and barn burning that began last August can be traced, at least in part, to them.

The *Daily News* looked into the background of the violence at Trumbull Park. It found:

— The campaign appears to be organized.

— A group advocating extreme racial measures, although having only a tiny membership, lends its support to the campaign.

— Peaceful citizens unwilling to participate in the violence may find their property afire. City authorities believe others "go along" out of fear.

The two organizations in the background of the disturbances are:

1. The South Deering Improvement Association.
2. The National Citizens Protective Association, a small group founded in St. Louis, Missouri. Its national organizer, John W. Hamilton, was once a Lieutenant of Gerald L. K. Smith, rabblerouser.

The article also stated that: "Weaving in and out of both groups is Joseph Beauharnais, leader of the almost defunct White Circle League, another race supremacy group."[18] After undergoing nine months of harassment, the Howard family moved out in May, 1954; but in the meantime, other Negroes had moved in. In May, 1955, there were twenty-nine Negro families in the project, and a large police detail was still required to maintain a semblance of order.[19]

How could a city like Chicago allow conditions of severe racial friction to continue unabated for over a decade? Charles Abrams made an incisive summary of the underlying factors behind this "continuing wave of explosions in Cook County." These underlying factors were, to quote Abrams:

1. The in-migration of Negroes and other minorities to take jobs.
2. A shortage of housing.
3. Their inevitable movement into white areas to compete for existing housing.
4. Failure of the citizenry to insist upon a solution of the problem and bring pressure upon their public officials.

---

[18] Quoted in Chicago Commission on Human Relations, *The Trumbull Park Homes Disturbances: A Chronological Report August 4, 1953 to June 30, 1955* (Chicago, 1955), p. 39.

[19] *Ibid.*, p. 58.

5. Creating fears of loss of property values and fears of Negroes as neighbors.
6. The fanning of tensions by troublemaking groups.
7. The hostility or apathy of public officials and police.[20]

It is against this background of racial strife and apathy on the part of city officials and social and civic leaders that the problems of the Chicago Urban League between 1947 and 1955 must be viewed.

A new executive secretary took over the Chicago League in February, 1947. He was Sidney Williams, who left the Cleveland League to take the Chicago position. Williams had been in the League movement since the 1930's, except for a period when he served as a club director with the American Red Cross.[21] He was best known, perhaps, for his work in the late 1930's as industrial secretary of the St. Louis Urban League, where he earned a reputation for aggressive leadership among Negro workers.[22] In Chicago, Williams almost immediately became a militant exponent of controversial causes. But he gave little attention to resolving the grave internal problems confronting the Chicago League.

Williams effected no significant improvement in personnel administration. In fact, staff problems became more acute after 1947. The new executive secretary lacked the temperament required for dealing with routine administrative details. A personnel practices manual was formulated, but its provisions were not adhered to and were allowed to become outdated.[23] Many of the executive's actions on staff problems only aggravated a bad situation. Soon after taking office, he was accused of casting aspersions "indiscriminately on staff competence and qualifications." "The charges," said a National League official, "came back to staff and angered it because they violated professional ethics, and because they were based upon snap judgment not upon firm knowledge of staff function and performance."[24]

Early in 1947, Williams began having trouble with the employees'

---

[20] Abrams, *Forbidden Neighbors,* p. 108.

[21] *Chicago Defender,* Feb. 8, 1947; Mar. 22, 1947.

[22] Horace R. Cayton and George S. Mitchell, *Black Workers and the New Unions* (Chapel Hill: University of North Carolina Press, 1939), pp. 410-411.

[23] Nelson C. Jackson, "An Evaluation of the Chicago Urban League," May, 1955 (unpublished study in the files of the Chicago Urban League), pp. 65-67.

[24] W. R. Valentine, Jr., "Report of Field Trip, Chicago Urban League, June 5-July 3, 1947," quoted in *ibid.,* p. 71.

union. In March, he dismissed William Prince — a field worker in the industrial department and chairman of the union — for allegedly failing to give notice of his intention to take a short leave of absence. Williams charged Prince with "gross misconduct." Prince said that he did communicate with the office before taking his leave, and the union claimed that Williams' action was an attempt at "union-busting" and was a "threat to job security." Following discussion by the personnel practices committee of the board of directors, the dispute was settled by conditionally reinstating Prince.[25] Soon, however, Williams was in disagreement with the union again. He did not know, after over a month in office, that the League had a receptionist. He suggested that one be employed. Learning that there was already a receptionist, who had been with the agency for two years, he decided that she was not qualified for the position, and since the receptionist did some interviewing, a person with a master's degree should be employed. The union's grievance committee asked to discuss the situation with him. A member of the committee reported that Williams "couldn't see why we would insist that the girl hold her job, while admitting she was doing a good job. He blew up. It was this type of thinking that we were up against."[26]

In 1949, the executive decided that the head of the community organization department (formerly the department of civic improvement) was not qualified for his position. Williams wanted to transfer this man to another job and to bring in a "new top-notch person" to head the community organization department. The union objected to passing over people in the department, in violation of the union contract, and bringing in someone from outside. The executive said that the person in line for the position did not meet the qualifications he desired.[27] An outside person was finally employed and another blow was dealt to staff morale.

Later in the year, the union took exception to the methods used in curtailing operations, necessitated by decreased income. Five instances of contract violation were cited to the board of directors.[28] There was little, however, that the union could do. With the financial problems the agency was having, there was no assurance that any staff member could long be retained in his position or, even if he held his job, that he could be paid for his services.

---

[25] *Chicago Defender,* Mar. 22, 1947; Mar. 29, 1947.
[26] Interview, Chicago, July 20, 1961.
[27] Minutes of the Board of Directors, Jan. 12, 1949.
[28] *Ibid.,* Sept. 16, 1949.

Payless paydays were a major staff grievance. In 1950, the staff was still trying to collect salaries due since 1947. The board submitted this matter and a dispute over some employee dismissals to a board of arbitration. It was decided to make this debt a part of the budget for 1951.[29] Many staff members, however, were more concerned about collecting current salary. Payments were seldom made on time, and garnishments were made on a number of employees for failure to meet obligations to their creditors. The policy followed in making salary payments was to pay clerical workers first and then professional staff members, if there was any money left. Several persons suffered embarrassment and "loss of items purchased because of the inability to pay their debts." The reason for this situation was explained by a member of the administrative staff.

> In an agency of this kind where all of our funds are on a voluntary basis, it is very difficult to know the exact amount from day to day that is coming in. We have no possible way of knowing whether we will be able to meet, on the 2nd and 16th, the complete or any part of the payroll. As far as the Community Fund is concerned, there is no exact date to expect their monthly allocation. From time to time we have notified staff that there will be a delay in the issuance of checks, but this has not been done consistently.[30]

These conditions furnished infertile soil for the development of a strong labor union. The United Office and Professional Workers of America was replaced briefly, in the 1950's, by a chapter of the United Transport Service Employees of America. This union did not long survive the frequent changes in League personnel.

Staff turnover was the principal characteristic of personnel administration between 1947 and 1955. In the operating departments — industrial relations, community organization, public education, and the West Side branch office — there were twenty-three employees in 1947. By 1950, the number had been reduced to twelve. Of these, seven remained from the 1947 staff, but only five were in the same departments in which they worked in 1947. There were thirteen staff members in 1951 — six remained from 1950 and four of the six had been with the agency since 1947.[31] Nelson Jackson counted twenty resignations between 1950 and 1954, with eleven occurring in 1954.[32] This continuing exodus of employees evidenced

[29] *Ibid.*, June 2, 1950; June 30, 1950.
[30] Quoted in Jackson, "An Evaluation of the Chicago Urban League," p. 67.
[31] *Thirty-first Annual Report, 1947*; Chicago Urban League Staff, Mar., 1950 and Mar., 1951 (lists in the League files).
[32] Jackson, "An Evaluation of the Chicago Urban League," p. 67.

poor administrative practices and extremely low staff morale. Under these conditions, effective programing was virtually impossible.

These years were a period of program stagnation. The community organization department continued the five-year plan inaugurated in 1945. It also sponsored "block beautiful" contests and conducted guided tours of the South Side.[33] The department of public relations, renamed public education, had neither the personnel nor the resources to perform its stated function of intergroup interpretation. Its principal activities were disseminating League propaganda and conducting fund-raising drives. The public education department took over responsibility for guided tours in 1948 and, two years later, began publishing a League bulletin.[34]

There were also few important changes in the industrial relations program. In spite of an agreement with the Welfare Council of Metropolitan Chicago (formerly Chicago Council of Social Agencies), this department engaged in mass referral and placement services. Some League officials felt that the Illinois State Employment Service did not adequately safeguard the interests of Negro workers.[35] The welfare of workers, however, was only one consideration involved in the League's reluctance to abandon making mass placements. The agency did not wish to discontinue the main activity engaged in by its industrial department. Also, it was realized that numerous contracts with employers would be lost. In 1953, the board approved a one-dollar fee for registration and placement services. This fee brought in an average of twenty dollars a day. Such a practice violated traditional Urban League policy, but the hard-pressed Chicago League needed the money.[36] A pilot placement project was proposed in 1949 "to secure employment for specially qualified Negro workers in professional, technical and allied occupations." Although this plan received the approval of the Welfare Council, the League could not raise the necessary funds for its implementation.[37] Five years later, the agency was still debating the

[33] *Thirty-first Annual Report, 1947*; Community Organization Department's Proposed 1952 Program (MS in the League files); *Chicago Defender,* July 5, 1952; Sept. 18, 1954.

[34] Jackson, "An Evaluation of the Chicago Urban League," pp. 80-96; Minutes of the Board of Directors, May 12, 1950.

[35] *Ibid.,* Feb. 9, 1949.

[36] Jackson, "An Evaluation of the Chicago Urban League," p. 150.

[37] Proposed Pilot Placement Project, Mar. 17, 1949; Special Report from Mary A. Young to Reviewing Committee on Specialized Services of the Welfare Council of Metropolitan Chicago, May 10, 1949 (MS in the League files).

issue of mass placement, with board members lining up on both sides. At this time the executive secretary favored curtailing placement services as an economy measure. The board decided to "concur in the recommendation of the Executive to eliminate the current practice of accepting mass applications for and referrals to unskilled jobs and in its place substitute an industrial service that would include a more select screening of better qualified applicants for the exceptional jobs; that the principle of requesting contributions for all select referrals to exceptional jobs be adopted."[38] Throughout the period, the campaign to secure jobs in Loop stores was continued, and banks were added to the firms covered.[39] By this time, however, numerous other organizations — including the Commission on Human Relations and the Friends Service Committee — were working in the same field. One barrier of long standing did fall. The Illinois Bell Telephone Company employed its first Negro operators in 1947.[40]

One rather significant change did take place in the industrial department. Vocational guidance services were expanded and strengthened. A special grant from the Community Fund enabled the League to establish a separate department of vocational guidance. The first director took over in July, 1953. He resigned a year later, and a new director, Donald H. Moos, was employed.[41] In spite of financial hardship — between October, 1954 and April, 1955 the department spent only $364.50 — this program remained one of the more progressive features of the League's work.

Another new program development was the establishment of a housing department. This was short-lived. The staff called upon the board in 1948 to employ a full-time staff person to serve as housing secretary. Such a department was created in that year, but a shortage of funds necessitated abolishing the position of housing secretary before the end of the year.[42] Further activities in this field were left to the executive secretary and to the board of directors.

The League's housing work after 1948, though not extensive, created considerable ill will toward the agency. As early as 1947,

[38] Minutes of the Board of Directors, Oct. 28, 1954.
[39] *Chicago Defender,* Mar. 6, 1948; Apr. 28, 1951; Minutes of the Board of Directors, Jan. 9, 1953.
[40] *Chicago Defender,* Oct. 4, 1947.
[41] Jackson, "An Evaluation of the Chicago Urban League," pp. 170-173; Minutes of the Board of Directors, Feb. 6, 1953; Apr. 10, 1953; Sept. 21, 1953; *Chicago Defender,* July 2, 1953.
[42] Jackson, "An Evaluation of the Chicago Urban League," p. 121.

the rumor was spread that the League was responsible for Negroes' moving into white neighborhoods. When the first Negro family occupied temporary veterans' housing, it was said that the League was furnishing them financial support.[43] During the Cicero riot, the agency was accused of moving the Clarks to Cicero. At about the same time, the *Chicago Daily News* reported that the League was to administer a defense fund being raised by the Dearborn Real Estate Board to help Negro families "facing problems in new areas." The League's board denied all of these charges and asked the *Daily News* to correct its statement. The executive secretary said that his activities in connection with the Cicero affair had been limited to keeping the National League informed, working through the N.A.A.C.P. and the Council Against Racial Discrimination, and commending the Governor for calling out the militia.[44]

During the Trumbull Park disturbances, the League remained largely on the sidelines. Its activities were restricted to consultation with other organizations working to curb this violence. Still, rumors about the agency became more prevalent.[45] The League did, however, become involved in controversies related to Trumbull Park. The executive secretary of the Chicago Housing Authority, Miss Elizabeth Wood, came under fire for her insistence on carrying out the Authority's policy of open occupancy. Ironically, John Yancey, the only Negro member of the Housing Authority, led in the movement to curtail Miss Wood's powers. Yancey — who had formerly been a member of the League's board — had received Urban League endorsement, although he was ranked third among the three men recommended, for the position he held.[46] Miss Wood's demotion and subsequent resignation were viewed nationally as a serious blow to the principle of open occupancy. League President Dickerson and Executive Secretary Williams both made strong statements, seemingly without any board discussion on the matter, denouncing Yancey and supporting Miss Wood. Nelson Jackson questioned the authority of "these two officers to involve the Urban League in an internal conflict between the Housing Authority Director and the

[43] *Chicago Defender,* Nov. 1, 1947.
[44] Minutes of the Board of Directors, Sept. 26, 1951.
[45] Executive Secretary's Report to the Board of Directors, Sept. 21, 1953.
[46] Minutes of the Housing Committee of the Chicago Urban League, Oct. 3, 1950, copy in Jackson, "An Evaluation of the Chicago Urban League," appendix, p. 256.

Housing Authority Commissioners without giving the board an opportunity to debate and vote on the issue."[47]

On one occasion, Sidney Williams drew the editorial ire of the *Chicago Defender* with one of his housing pronouncements. This occurred during the 1951 National Housing Policy Conference in St. Louis. Roy Wilkins of the N.A.A.C.P. initiated a move to substitute a statement recommending a policy of "integrated and nonsegregated housing for all American citizens" to replace the vague resolution brought in by the resolutions committee. Several northern delegates spoke in support of Wilkins' motion. In seconding the motion and in subsequent comments, Williams succeeded in creating considerable confusion. Some northern delegates seemed willing to support the measure so long as it was viewed as an implicit condemnation of the South. Williams interjected the issue of northern segregation and, in doing so, was complimentary of southern conditions. Even though there may have been much truth in his contentions, Williams' remarks showed poor judgment and bad tactics. A southern delegate took advantage of the situation and proclaimed: "This is a fostered attempt to cloud the issues and make them fully unacceptable." On this delegate's motion, the Wilkins substitute was tabled.[48] The *Defender* blamed Williams for this action. ". . . Sidney Williams of the Chicago Urban League elected to make a grandstand, rabble rousing speech which left the resolution open to misinterpretation. Mr. Williams found himself in the position of the salesman who wins a customer over and before the sale is completed, he brings up matters that lead the customer to change his mind."[49]

Throughout this period, the League was having a housing problem of its own. It was evident by 1949 that something would have to be done about providing better office facilities for the agency. After over thirty years as League headquarters, the old Frederick Douglass Center building — which was described as "leaning against the building next door" — was becoming increasingly dilapidated. A fire in 1949 made it even more unsuitable for further use. The question of a new home for the League was complicated by lack of agreement on relocation. A few directors favored renovating the old headquarters. Another group thought that the agency should

---

[47] Jackson, "An Evaluation of the Chicago Urban League," pp. 125-126.

[48] National Housing Policy Conference, *A Report to the Nation* (St. Louis, 1951), pp. 74-78.

[49] *Chicago Defender,* Mar. 31, 1951.

move, but that it should remain on the South Side. The executive secretary contended for moving the headquarters to the Loop.

In compliance with the recommendations of the McMillen report, efforts had been made in 1946 to improve the South Side building. Major repairs were effected, including a new roof and cleaning and redecoration. The Loop office, which had housed the department of public relations, was closed and its furnishings brought to the South Side headquarters.[50]

Williams, from the beginning of his administration, tried to convince the board of directors that the main office should move to the Loop. The board approved the plan in 1947 and appointed a committee to investigate suitable Loop sites.[51] The matter remained in abeyance, however, until after the 1949 fire, when the executive renewed his campaign. He presented his plans to the committee on location and argued his case before the board. During the board meeting, one staff member took strong exception to the Loop relocation plan, and several board members seemed skeptical about the claims made in its support. The board dodged the issue by deciding: "That the League stay in its present location until such time as it seems feasible to move."[52]

Yet, the fact remained that something had to be done about rehousing the agency. Three years later, the board was still debating the question. It was decided that the problem of location would be turned over to a broker, and in the meantime, the agency would get Community Fund approval for conducting a capital fund campaign to raise $100,000.[53] The Fund approved a League building fund drive to be conducted during the period November, 1952 to August, 1953.[54] But, in spite of the executive secretary's continued insistence, the board would not face the problem of location. It was decided to defer a decision until the results of the campaign were known.[55]

Although successive building fund campaigns failed to raise the desired $100,000, they were more successful than drives to raise operating expenses. The first campaign began with a dinner com-

---

[50] Chicago Urban League Service Report, Jan., 1947 (in the files of the Welfare Council of Metropolitan Chicago).
[51] *Chicago Defender,* Apr. 5, 1947.
[52] Minutes of the Board of Directors, Mar. 2, 1949.
[53] *Ibid.,* Mar. 7, 1952; Apr. 4, 1952.
[54] *Ibid.,* July 2, 1952.
[55] *Ibid.,* June 6, 1952.

memorating the 125th anniversary of the Negro press. This affair brought in over $3,000.[56] By 1955, the amount raised had reached almost $20,000. Considering the facts that the building fund campaign was conducted only during periods when it would not conflict with other drives and that financial support of the League was quite haphazard, the amount raised was rather substantial. The relative success in raising building fund money was credited to good techniques. Earl B. Dickerson was especially active in bringing together individuals who were potential donors and motivating them to make pledges. Many people who would not contribute to the regular budget gave to the building fund.[57]

The Chicago Land Clearance Commission settled the issue as to whether or not the League would remain in its old building. The League was notified in 1954 that the area in which it was located had been designated for redevelopment. The following year, the Land Clearance Commission purchased the League's South Side property for $17,000. The agency was allowed to remain in the building until it found new quarters or until the area was scheduled for demolition.[58] Now the board was confronted with the problem of whether to try to rebuild in the redevelopment area or move to another section of the city.

In the meantime, the executive secretary had come up with another housing proposal. He suggested that the League merge with the Parkway Community House, a settlement. This institution owned several buildings, but it was burdened with debts. The board suspected that the executive secretary was probably more anxious for this merger than Parkway's officials. Board members questioned the propriety of using building fund money to settle Parkway's debts, and some doubts were expressed as to the advisability of merging with an institution with denominational affiliations.[59] In mid-1955, there was over $30,000 in the building fund, including the proceeds from the sale of the South Wabash Avenue property; but no progress had been made toward solving the housing problem. In fact, throughout these years, other problems overshadowed the housing need. By 1955, a new home was one of the least of the League's problems.

---

[56] *Chicago Defender,* Nov. 22, 1952; Minutes of the Board of Directors, Jan. 9, 1953.
[57] Interviews, Chicago, July 17, 1961; July 19, 1961.
[58] Minutes of the Board of Directors, May 4, 1955; May 20, 1955.
[59] *Ibid.,* Nov. 19, 1954.

The executive secretary's penchant for becoming involved in controversial causes kept the agency in turmoil and alienated many of its influential friends. Early in his career in Chicago, Williams became active in the campaign for FEP legislation. Even though the board had made no policy statement on the matter — it could be assumed that the League directors supported the principle of merit employment — or the procedures the organization would follow, the annual report for 1947 carried a statement on why the League supported FEP legislation.[60] The National Urban League took the position, at this time, that FEP was outside the League's field of operation. It was realized that a local executive who pushed this issue would make himself unpopular with businessmen and, to a large extent, with his own board.[61] Nevertheless, by 1949, Williams was playing a leading role in city-wide movements working for a state FEP statute. He delivered speeches in Chicago and other sections of the state and helped with fund raising. In March, 1949, the executive committee decided that the board should make a statement of policy on FEP. Oddly enough, this decision was not motivated by the merits of the legislation, but by the fear that "failure of the League to make a forthright stand on FEPC might be reflected in contributions" from the Negro community. Even so, the executive committee's only action was a motion "that the Executive Committee recommend to the Board that the League go on record as supporting the FEPC Bill and the Board be polled by telephone or letter in order to get the majority vote."[62]

Probably the executive secretary's most controversial project was the Committee to End Mob Violence. This organization was an outgrowth of the Peoria Street riot. One participant said that "a hush-hush policy was very much in force, and the city as a whole didn't know too much about it [the riot]. But, naturally the Negro community was very exercised, and this so-called Committee to End Mob Violence, I think, has to be characterized to begin with as a completely normal, spontaneous action largely by Negroes, but it did involve some white people. . . . It was an informal group at first, which, I think, very rapidly became a protest group and . . . a wholesome one."[63] Executive Secretary Williams told the League's

[60] *Thirty-first Annual Report, 1947.*
[61] Interview, Chicago, July 19, 1961.
[62] Minutes of the Executive Committee, Mar. 7, 1949.
[63] Interview, Chicago, July 19, 1961.

board that he had felt that no organization "primarily concerned with the welfare of Negro citizens" was doing anything to stem the rising tide of mob violence. He, therefore, took the initiative in calling together a group of Negro leaders "for the purpose of discussing, planning and perhaps some action to unify the community leadership around a remedial program." The first meeting was held on November 16, 1949, and the group present agreed to hold a second meeting involving more people. Williams became chairman of a committee to draw up an agenda. Invitations to the next meeting went out on Urban League stationary, over Williams' signature. In these sessions, the Committee to End Mob Violence in Chicago was born.[64]

The Committee quickly became a controversial organization. In the first place, it became known as a Communist-inspired movement. Participants admitted that "the commies were really in there," but they denied that Communists either inspired or controlled the Committee. Several members of the Urban League board contended that "whereas there may have been some 'left wing' groups in attendance at the meetings, on the whole the meetings represented a very broad cross section of the community; and that some of the action taken at the meeting [on November 19] was responsible for the Mayor's recent statement [against mob violence]."[65] In any case, the Committee was stigmatized with a Communist label.

Moreover, powerful political and religious groups took umbrage at some of its proceedings. During one meeting, Mayor Martin H. Kennelly was castigated for his vacillation in the face of continued racial friction. The police department was criticized for failure to disperse crowds, fraternization of policemen with members of mobs, and indiscriminate arrests of Negroes. One speaker demanded the impeachment of both the mayor and the chief of police. It was also brought out that considerable evidence substantiated the contention that the leaders of the Peoria Street mob used Catholic facilities as their headquarters. This charge and the fact that the city officials whose impeachments were demanded were Catholics aroused considerable resentment among Catholic groups.[66] The Catholic members of the Urban League board resigned. In a 1955 study, Nelson Jackson stated: "Community interviews with former board mem-

---

[64] Minutes of the Board of Directors, Dec. 2, 1949.
[65] *Ibid.*
[66] Interviews, Chicago, July 19, 1961; July 21, 1961.

bers who were strong Catholic adherents revealed that they could not go along with the organization because of the activities of the Executive. They accused him of 'associating with communist groups,' or 'left-wing elements.' They transferred their allegiance to the Catholic Interracial Council."[67]

Williams committed two grave errors in connection with the Committee to End Mob Violence. First, he got the League involved in this movement — by using Urban League facilities and working with the Committee in his role as executive secretary of the League — without first obtaining the sanction of the board of directors. Second, he disregarded the sound advice of several board members not to accept the chairmanship of the Committee. It was felt that leadership of such a movement was untenable for an Urban League executive secretary, even an aggressive one.[68]

These activities, along with his choice of associates — some of whom were alleged to be Communists — his work in behalf of FEP, and his speeches and public pronouncements, brought Williams and, consequently, the League into disrepute with influential groups. Serious questions were raised as to his fitness to head a social work organization. Many groups resolved to withhold their support from the League so long as he remained in office.[69]

The organization had begun experiencing fund-raising difficulties in 1947. It had deficits in both 1947 and 1948.[70] The situation became acute in 1949. The executive secretary told the board in June that he had suggested to department heads "that they begin thinking about the reorganization of their work minus the service of one professional worker." The board established a special committee "to adopt and carry out a program of retrenchment."[71] This special committee decided: "That one professional worker each from the Industrial Relations and Community Organization Department[s] be eliminated; because of the acute clerical shortage, one clerical worker be added to the staff to serve the two departments, i.e., Community Organization and Industrial; that the clerical vacancy in Public Education be filled. . . ." By these and other reductions in

---

[67] Jackson, "An Evaluation of the Chicago Urban League," p. 47.
[68] Minutes of the Board of Directors, Dec. 2, 1949; Interviews, Chicago, July 19, 1961; July 21, 1961.
[69] Jackson, "An Evaluation of the Chicago Urban League," pp. 72-73.
[70] *Thirty-first Annual Report, 1947;* Minutes of the Board of Directors, Jan. 12, 1949.
[71] *Ibid.*, June 3, 1949.

operating costs, it was hoped that expenses would be reduced by $3,700.[72]

Then, in 1950, largely as an aftermath of the Committee to End Mob Violence, the League's entire budget was placed in jeopardy. The Community Fund threatened to drop the League as a member agency. In addition, the Chicago Association of Commerce and Industry temporarily withheld its endorsement, without which the League could expect little success in its fund-raising campaign.

In early February, a letter was received from Jesse Jacobs, secretary of the Association of Commerce and Industry's Subscription and Investigating Committee. Jacobs notified the agency that its endorsement for 1950 was being held up, "pending additional information in connection with the Board's compliance with the McMillen Report." A committee from the League was invited to meet with Association representatives — one of whom was Wayne McMillen, author of the 1946 report — to discuss the matter. This meeting was held on February 8, but nothing was accomplished.[73]

Two days later, the Reviewing Committee of the Community Fund held its hearing on the League's 1950 budget. The Reviewing Committee was informed that the Association of Commerce had withheld its endorsement of the League. A Community Fund staff member voiced the opinion that the League "had no case to present to the Association of Commerce." Several days later, the League was informed that the Reviewing Committee had voted to give it a terminal grant of $35,000 for 1950. If at the end of the year, the League could satisfy the Committee that it had "met certain conditions," an application for 1951 would be considered.[74] The amount of the proposed terminal grant was later reduced to $30,000 and then to $29,370.[75]

On February 23, Jesse Jacobs wrote that the Subscriptions Investigating Committee had decided to endorse the League "with reservations." The letter reaffirmed the Investigating Committee's belief that Chicago needed an effective Urban League and offered several recommendations for the board's consideration.

It was the opinion of our Committee that the League needs to give serious attention during the next few months to:

[72] *Ibid.,* Sept. 16, 1949.
[73] *Ibid.,* Feb. 23, 1950.
[74] *Ibid.*
[75] Report of Budget Analyst to Members of Reviewing Committee, Dec. 7, 1950 (in the files of the Welfare Council of Metropolitan Chicago).

a) the development of an interested and representative Board of Directors which will meet regularly and which will be responsible for the development of policy and for playing a dominant part in fund raising;
b) the improvement of administrative and personnel practices so that routine administrative matters are handled efficiently and that administrative practices are under constant review by the Board;
c) the development of a few important elements of a program to the extent where some real contribution to the community is evident. . . .[76]

The Community Fund also relented. It decided not to make the League's allocation in the form of a terminal grant, but it also submitted recommendations for improving League operations.[77] In June, the League learned that its 1950 budget had been approved and that it would be permitted to present a budget for 1951.[78]

In the meantime, however, the League had lost another source of income. The treasurer reported in March that two packing companies, Armour and Swift, had not made their usual contributions of $1,500 each. A vice president of one of the companies had reported by telephone that they were still considering whether or not a contribution would be made.[79] A member of the board of directors went out to talk with Swift officials, since it was felt that the other companies "pretty much followed Swift's lead." The official contacted had compiled a voluminous file on the League's executive secretary. He said that Williams was suspect and implied that his company would not support the kind of beliefs which Williams espoused.[80]

The League's financial troubles did not end in 1950. The board became increasingly disassociated from fund-raising activities. These tasks devolved largely upon the executive secretary and the staff. Most of the board's time was spent in discussing proposals for fund raising submitted by the executive and in trying to answer criticisms coming from the Community Fund. As contributions from individuals declined, the League became increasingly dependent upon the Community Fund; but, at the same time, the Fund was claiming that its support of the League was causing it to lose contributors.

[76] Jesse A. Jacobs to Elbridge B. Pierce, Feb. 21, 1951, copy appended to Minutes of Executive Committee, Feb. 23, 1950.
[77] Minutes of the Board of Directors, Apr. 14, 1950.
[78] *Ibid.,* June 30, 1950.
[79] *Ibid.,* Mar. 3, 1950.
[80] Interview, Chicago, July 19, 1961.

Each year the League's fund-raising efforts grew more disappointing. In 1951, the executive spent considerable time sending out appeal letters to a "selected group of persons," but the "tangible results were none-too-favorable." One State Street merchant consented to sign an appeal letter if other merchants could be found who would sign with him. Not one other merchant would allow his name to be used. This letter finally had to go out over the League executive's signature.[81] Even in the Negro community, it was difficult to find dedicated workers. The 1951 fund-raising chairman lamented: "I am sure we could reach our goal of $50,000 if we could get more workers interested. The harvest is great, but the laborers are few, and many of the workers who have committed themselves are not bringing in reports."[82] The 1951 campaign raised only $3,200 among Negroes. In spite of desperate appeals and large contributions added at the beginning of the drives to serve as stimulants, by 1954 Negro contributions had only increased to $7,495.[83] In 1953 — a year in which the agency was scheduled to raise $53,000 — the League raised $40,532. Of this amount $26,273 came from white contributors, foundations, trusts, and firms; and $14,158 came from all sources in the Negro community. Benefits — concerts, parties, etc. — which accounted for $5,000, represented, by far, the largest single source of income from Negroes.[84]

Meanwhile, it was becoming increasingly difficult to get budgets approved by the Community Fund. Each year the League requested that the Fund finance 50 per cent or over of its budget. This was the case in 1951 when the organization submitted an $80,000 budget. The budget analyst, however, recommended a smaller budget, with a Fund contribution of $29,370 and a League responsibility of $48,155. After much board protesting, the Fund allocation was raised slightly.[85] In the light of the League's fund-raising difficulties, the agency's budgets throughout this period were unrealistic. For instance, after failing to meet an $89,100 budget in 1952, the agency presented one for $105,967 in 1953. Then, after falling far short of the proposed 1953 budget and ending the year with a deficit, the

[81] Minutes of the Board of Directors, Sept. 26, 1951.
[82] *Chicago Defender,* June 2, 1951.
[83] Jackson, "An Evaluation of the Chicago Urban League," p. 108; *Chicago Defender,* Apr. 19, 1952; June 19, 1954; Dec. 25, 1954.
[84] Minutes of the Board of Directors, Feb. 4, 1954.
[85] *Ibid.,* Jan. 5, 1951; Mar. 9, 1951.

board decided to submit a $130,000 budget for 1954.[86] By this time, it was apparent that drastic action was needed if the League were to survive.

What brought the organization to this impasse? The most obvious answer is the executive secretary's actions. The executive, however, was only an employee who could not have held his position without the sanction, or at least the acquiescence, of the board of directors. Yet, Williams remained in office for over seven years — years during which he was attacked from within by board members and staff personnel and from without by both extremist groups and influential Chicago leaders. Williams, in large measure, became the personification of a more fundamental dissatisfaction with League operations. In the final analysis, it was the board of directors which was primarily responsible for the deterioration of the Chicago Urban League.

The board was never able to reform itself. Its members became roughly divided into two groups. One group believed in the traditional role of the Urban League. They felt that the organization should hold fast to its social work functions and limit its methods to education and persuasion. Furthermore, they urged that the agency restrict its activities to a few well-defined fields. For convenience, those who advocated a distinctly social work–oriented League may be called conservatives. Opposed to them were a group of directors who favored an aggressive organization. This group interpreted League philosophy and purposes broadly. In their opinion, there were few, if any, problems confronting the Negro which were outside the purview of the Urban League. Although they may not have always agreed with the executive secretary's methods, they were usually in sympathy with the causes he espoused. And, lest repudiation of method be interpreted as repudiation of cause, they upheld the executive, albeit sometimes with a mild reprimand for indiscretions. This group, again only for convenience, will be called progressives. Naturally, as is true of any general classification, it would be difficult to fit any given board member neatly into either of these categories. Furthermore, this is not to imply that the Chicago Urban League board was divided into two warring factions.

The ideological divisions resulted more often in stalemate and indecision than in continued strife. The conservatives took on the

[86] Reports of Budget Analysts, Jan. 22, 1953; Nov. 15, 1954; Minutes of the Board of Directors, Nov. 16, 1953.

character of a loyal opposition. Many conservatives were inactive, and others, such as the Catholic directors, showed their displeasure by resigning. But, the views of the conservative group conformed closely to what the majority opinion in Chicago thought the League should be. Their criticisms of procedures agreed, in most cases, with those of the Association of Commerce, the Welfare Council, and the Community Fund. Largely by default, however, leadership in the League fell to the progressives. They formed a majority of the active members. Although the progressives could not override the conservatives and public opinion, they could forestall any drastic actions designed to reshape the League in a conservative image. The stalemate between these groups was reflected in the difficulty experienced in finding people willing to be elected president, in the inability of the League to attract a representative group of directors, and in the indecisive actions taken by the board of directors.

Following the acrimony of the 1947 reorganizations, Earl Dickerson, who had been president since 1939, wanted to relinquish this office. When election time came, however, there was no obvious candidate for president. Several directors hurriedly started looking around and came up with the name of a "right-wing" CIO leader. Both the incumbent president and the executive secretary strongly opposed this recommendation. To maintain peace, the board elected Rabbi Louis Binstock.[87] Although it was announced that Rabbi Binstock was elected for a three-year term, he gave up the office after one year. None of the progressives would take the presidency. They knew that they would have difficulty in dealing with the Community Fund and other outside groups. At the same time, qualified conservatives seemed unwilling to mix in the "real struggles of the day."[88] Elbridge Bancroft Pierce, former president and elder statesman of the Chicago Urban League, consented to take the office. Pierce served until 1950, when he resigned to go into semi-retirement in Michigan.[89]

Caught without an acceptable conservative candidate, the board again turned to Earl Dickerson.[90] Dickerson was not anxious to go back into office. He knew that political and business groups considered him a controversial figure. Hence, he thought of himself as

[87] Interview, Chicago, July 19, 1961.
[88] *Ibid.*, Chicago, Aug. 12, 1961.
[89] Minutes of the Board of Directors, Mar. 3, 1950.
[90] *Ibid.*

a "caretaker" who would hold the office until a man "untouched by past forces" could be found.[91] It was most difficult to find such a man. Dickerson was re-elected in 1951 and again in 1952. Finally in 1953, he decided to resign from both the presidency and from the board of directors. His letter of resignation stated:

There is a danger to the growth and development of a charitable organization like the League when persons hold on to the same position too long; that officers and board members of the League should rotate office every two or three years; after two or three years in a particular office of this kind the incumbent has about used up all of his ideas and new approaches to the tasks and assignments of this office. What follows thereafter is merely repetition to the point almost where the organization might well become static.

He went on to outline accomplishments of his administrations to which he pointed with pride.[92] "After considerable discussion," according to the board minutes, "it was agreed both collectively and individually that Mr. Dickerson's resignation could not be accepted. The following motion by Dean [Curtis] Reese, duly supported, was passed; that the Board request Mr. Dickerson to withdraw his resignation and reconsider continuing as a member of the Board. This he agreed to do."[93]

In 1954, as the League's problems grew increasingly severe, the conservatives began to stir. Dickerson was still determined to give up the position, but the conservatives could not agree on a candidate. One member of the nominating committee suggested that they "go outside the Board and find another person whose name and good reputation is city-wide." The committee urged this member, a public relations executive, to take the job; but he would not even agree to serve "until the kind of person needed could be located." The committee therefore asked Dickerson to continue in office "until a suitable successor" could be named. Dickerson refused to keep the office on a month-to-month basis. He was elected for a one-year term. The conservatives again missed the opportunity to name a president.[94] Their trouble was the conception they held of who was a "suitable" person. They wanted a "big name" white businessman from downtown. Although the progressives would go along with electing a conservative who was already on the board, they would

---

[91] Interview, Chicago, Aug. 12, 1961.
[92] Minutes of the Board of Directors, Sept. 21, 1953.
[93] *Ibid.*
[94] *Ibid.*, Mar. 15, 1954.

not agree to bring in an outsider just to be president. Nevertheless, following the 1954 election, at least one conservative continued his quest for a "prestige" person. He took the problem to a State Street banker and to an official of the Association of Commerce. The banker said that he was willing to ask the mayor to call together several "outstanding citizens," one of whom might accept the League presidency. The Association of Commerce official favored a meeting of some fifty "outstanding citizens," evidently for selecting both a president and new directors. A majority of the board opposed these plans. One member stated that "he would be willing to have the Nominating Committee screen anyone recommended, but that these recommendations must be submitted in writing to the Board and must be fully discussed so as to know the nominees' positions on various matters of policy; and then a decision should be made as to limitation of time on the Board before taking over the presidency."[95] The nominating committee was instructed to stop looking for an outsider to head the League and to concentrate on filling board vacancies.[96]

It was almost as difficult to fill vacancies as it was to find a president. Because of numerous resignations, the board lost its representative character. Many influential groups — such as Catholics, the CIO, and downtown businessmen — were not represented.[97] In spite of frantic and persistent efforts, little success was achieved in recruiting members from among these and other groups. By 1954, resignations and failure to find "suitable" replacements had decimated the affluent and influential members of the board.

The inability of the Urban League board to take decisive action was best exemplified in attempting to deal with crises. The first major crisis was the threat to drop the League from the Community Fund in 1950. It was apparent to all concerned that this trouble stemmed from opposition to the executive secretary and his activities. The main objective being sought by those bringing pressure to bear was the removal of Sidney Williams. In order to regain the confidence of civic, business, and political leaders, there were possibly two sources of direct action open to the board. It could have sacrificed its executive secretary and employed another whom these groups approved; or it could have formulated a clear and definitive

[95] *Ibid.*, Apr. 21, 1954.
[96] *Ibid.*
[97] Jackson, "An Evaluation of the Chicago Urban League," pp. 45-48.

statement of policies and methods and placed Williams under strict discipline to work in conformity with this statement. The progressives were unwilling to abandon the executive, and some conservatives who disagreed with Williams' methods were in sympathy with the principles motivating his actions. As to the second alternative, the board could not agree on the limitations which should be placed on program activities and methods of operation. Then too, without a reformation of the board, it is doubtful that either of these alternatives would have, in the long run, solved the League's problems. Williams' removal may have, however, made it easier to recruit representative board members. In dealing with this situation, the board made some concessions to its critics and took temporary expedients, but it ignored the basic problems.

Between 1950 and 1955, the situation grew progressively worse. A continuing barrage of anti-League propaganda, to the effect that the League was buying property in white neighborhoods and moving Negroes in, caused both the League and the Community Fund to lose contributors. The League's board was at a loss as to how to combat this propaganda, and the Community Fund felt that an official denial from the Fund would only help to spread the rumors.[98] By mid-1954, the Community Fund could no longer ignore the situation. It appointed a special committee to deal with the League problem and called upon the agency to help stop the attacks by reforming itself. In a meeting between this committee and League representatives on July 12, it was suggested that the Urban League voluntarily withdraw from the Community Fund. It was claimed that the Fund was losing an estimated $300,000 a year because of League participation. The League's board took the position that it was the Fund's job to combat the rumors and that the agency would not yield to pressure and withdraw from the Fund. One director voiced the majority sentiment when he said that

> since the Fund is under attack, it must first get itself right on the charge; that to this end we submit ourselves to examination and, if not guilty, then it is the Fund's duty to commit itself to a clear cut public statement of its findings. We categorically deny the charge and place the responsibility for making this denial to the public upon the Community Fund which has the resources available for the purpose. The League has no answer to this problem any more than the Fund. . . .
>
> . . . This problem of rumors about the League is part and parcel of

[98] Interview, Chicago, July 19, 1961; Minutes of the Board of Directors, Nov. 6, 1953.

the problem affecting Negro people as a minority in our whole city. It is a planned and promoted affair. Witness: Trumbull Park. Much of the rumor springs from communities like Trumbull Park. . . .[99]

With racial tensions running so high, the Community Fund did not want to undergo the embarrassment of expelling the League. The only course left was to force the agency to reform and make itself acceptable to important dissident groups. In October, 1954, the Fund's special committee approached the League concerning the possibility of having a thorough study made of League operations. The League suggested that the proposed investigation cover the whole race relations picture in Chicago. The Fund, however, made it clear that it wanted a study limited to the "philosophy, purpose and function of the Chicago Urban League."[100] A letter from Mrs. Linn Brandenburg, associate executive director of the Fund, made this point clear.

The Committee on the Urban League, which is a sub-committee of the Board of Directors of the Community Fund, is in agreement that a study should be made of the Urban League's function to the end that it could more carefully define its work and that the League could be more effective in action. In other words, the Committee is interested in a study that would set forth not only what an Urban League program should be in theory but what should be the function of the Urban League in Chicago and the reasons why the Urban League should be performing certain functions in Chicago. There is no question that various members of the Committee are very much interested in having defined appropriate present and future areas of the League's activity. The Committee continues its interest in a study that would lead to a strengthening of the administration and the board of the League.[101]

This demand was punctuated with a decision by the Fund's Reviewing Committee to withhold approval of the League's budget.[102] The Urban League board had no choice but to follow the dictates of the Community Fund.[103] On October 29, the Fund was told that the League would accept the proposed study. Since it had the choice of who would make the investigation, the League's board asked that the study be made by the National Urban League. The National League sent three staff members under the direction of Nelson C. Jackson, its director of community services, to make the

[99] *Ibid.,* July 21, 1954.
[100] *Ibid.,* Oct. 28, 1954.
[101] Quoted in Jackson, "An Evaluation of the Chicago Urban League," p. ii.
[102] Report of Budget Analyst, Nov. 15, 1954.
[103] Minutes of the Board of Directors, Oct. 28, 1954.

Chicago study.[104] This was the first step toward a complete reorganization of the Chicago League.

To sum up, between 1947 and 1955, the Chicago Urban League was an organization in trouble in a troubled city. A lack of agreement among members of the board of directors as to the proper functions and methods of the League in dealing with the critical race relations situation in Chicago led to confusion in policy and procedures. The nature of League activities was largely determined by the executive secretary, whose militant philosophy and aggressive actions caused conflicts with those upon whom the League was dependent for support. Influential individuals and groups reacted by withholding their services and financial support, resulting in progressive weakening of the board of directors and recurrent financial crises. Financial insecurity and poor administrative practices caused low staff morale and frequent personnel turnovers. In addition, programing became stagnant. In his attempts to keep the League before the public, the executive secretary only aggravated the internal problems of board disorganization and staff morale and drew increased pressure from outside groups. When lack of confidence in the League began to have serious effects on the efforts of the Community Fund to raise money, the Fund used its control over the League's budget to force reform.

---

[104] Jackson, "An Evaluation of the Chicago Urban League," p. iii.

8

REORGANIZATION AND THE "NEW" URBAN LEAGUE, 1955-59

After the Community Fund's emphatic directive of October, 1954, there was no doubt that a reorganization of the Chicago Urban League would take place. Only its character was left to be determined. This question was settled when the conservative members of the Urban League board gained the ascendency. This group favored a complete and thorough reformation. To accomplish this goal, the League was shut down on July 15, 1955. Six months later, the "new" Urban League commenced operations. The interim had been spent in redefining policy, "selling" the idea of a revitalized agency to various interest groups, and recruiting a new executive and new staff personnel. After these preliminary steps had been taken, the job of building the "new" Urban League could begin. If the new agency was not to founder on the same shoals of unresolved problems that had undone the reorganization of 1946, basic issues had to be faced and resolved. Over the next four years, the board of directors and the executive director undertook the fundamental and interrelated functions of establishing a sound financial structure, instituting a dynamic program in keeping with the statement of policy, and recruiting a representative and influential board of directors.

The reorganization actually began in late 1954. In November, the conservatives made their first moves toward taking over the presidency. A conservative-dominated nominating committee was able to get three important recommendations accepted by the board of directors. The committee asked that nominations for officers be delayed, that future nominations be first cleared with the board, and that Howard Mayer be empowered to approach downtown interests for help in strengthening the League's board. In accepting these recommendations, the board of directors reiterated its decision not to accept a hand-picked president from downtown.[1] Nevertheless, the conservatives gained time to rally and organize their forces.

Two men came forward to provide leadership for the conservative group. They were Nathaniel O. Calloway, a Negro physician, and Hugo B. Law, an advertising executive. There seems to have been an agreement between them that they would undertake to guide the reorganization to an acceptable conclusion. Calloway handled the internal problems, and Law mobilized public opinion behind the new leadership. On March 2, 1955, the nominating committee submitted Dr. Calloway's name to the board for election to the presidency and recommended that other officers be continued in office for one month. The committee's report was approved, and Calloway was unanimously elected.[2] The conservatives had finally found a president from among their ranks on the board. The following month other officers, except for several inactive members, were retained in office.[3] At this point, it was not too important who held the other offices; and since a majority of board members would have to support reorganization plans, drastic changes would have been unwise.

Constitutional revision was the first step in organizational reform. President Calloway, through the executive committee, submitted a number of proposed constitutional changes to the board of directors. Many of these, dealing for example with the size of standing committees, were minor; but others were designed to clarify and enlarge the powers of the board.[4] When the time came to act on the proposed changes, some question arose as to the authority of the board of directors to amend the constitution. This power was vested in the membership. Article VI of the constitution clearly stated that amendments required "a two-thirds vote of the members present at any Annual Meeting or any special meeting of members called for that purpose." It was pointed out, however, that the laws of Illinois made no distinction between constitutions

[1] Minutes of the Board of Directors, Nov. 19, 1954.
[2] *Ibid.,* Mar. 2, 1955.
[3] *Ibid.,* Apr. 13, 1955.
[4] *Ibid.,* May 4, 1955.

and by-laws. Since the board could amend the by-laws, why not redesignate the constitution as by-laws? In that way, the board could arbitrarily rule article VI as being of no effect and proceed to make any changes it desired. The board, therefore, ruled "that all articles in the constitution become by-laws." The by-laws were then amended in several important respects. Naturally, article VI was eliminated. The president was made a full, rather than ex-officio, member of the board; it was made explicit that the board, not the membership, was to elect officers; and the board's authority to fill its own vacancies and to call special meetings of the membership was clarified. In addition, to provide more supervision over finances, a committee on budget and expenditure was authorized.[5] The amendments to clarify powers were probably designed to forestall demands, such as were experienced in 1947, for membership participation in the reorganization.

The new Urban League leadership seemed determined to avoid acrimony. They proceeded slowly, and their moves were well planned. It must not be forgotten, however, that they had the full sanction of the Community Fund and the Welfare Council of Metropolitan Chicago for their work. The most delicate problem anticipated was getting rid of Sidney Williams. Williams' militant activities had attracted a considerable following, especially among Negroes. Consequently, until a plan could be devised for raising personnel changes above the personality level, no official mention was made of this matter. But private efforts were made to get Williams to resign. When Nelson Jackson and his staff from the National League came to Chicago, they had a private talk with Williams. Jackson strongly urged him to get out before the study was completed. Williams refused and reportedly said that if he was fired he would take the matter to the public.[6] This was not a threat to be taken lightly. Although he could not have won, a conflict over ideology would have greatly disrupted the reorganization. In the prevailing climate of race relations, it would not have been well for the League to have been publicly accused of yielding to pressure from business and political groups. Urban League leaders wanted the reorganization to appear largely as an internal effort to revitalize a defunct organization.[7]

---

[5] *Ibid.,* June 8, 1955.
[6] Interview, Chicago, July 19, 1961.
[7] See, for example, *Chicago Defender,* July 16, 1955.

Although it had an important function, the Jackson report played a far less significant role in the actual reorganization than the McMillen report had done in 1947. The causes of the 1955 upheaval were apparent to all concerned; there was no need for a cover-up study. Jackson's job was to document what everybody already knew and to provide a medium for gathering opinions from the supporters and officials of the Community Fund and from other influential groups. The report certainly did not, and probably could not, accomplish its stated purpose of setting forth "what should be the function of the Urban League in Chicago." Actually, this had to be determined by the local leaders who controlled the destiny of the agency. During the course of his study, however, Jackson did make important suggestions on needed changes. Many of these recommendations, such as for constitutional amendments, were modified and put into effect before the study was completed. It was President Calloway, rather than Jackson, who served as the chief theorist of the 1955 reorganization.

The president reported to the board, in June, 1955, that he had received a copy of the summary and conclusions of the Jackson study. He was authorized by the board to secure sufficient copies of the complete report for each member of the board to have one. It was also decided to refer the report to the executive committee for study and recommendations.[8]

In the meantime, Calloway began working on his own reorganization plans. On July 1, he sent to board members his appraisal of the Urban League situation. In a lengthy report, he recommended plans for immediate action and for future development.[9] The board met on July 13 to act on the president's recommendations and to discuss the Jackson report. Budget commitments had also been received from the Community Fund. In opening the meeting, Calloway tried to set the temper for deliberations. He announced that they "were to deal with the problems of the Chicago Urban League as indicated in the Jackson report to the Special Advisory Committee. He stated that we were to deal with the basic facts of the situation and not give the impression to anyone that we are yielding to pressure from either the conservative right or the left."[10] The board heeded this admonition and proceeded to act in accordance

[8] Minutes of the Board of Directors, June 8, 1955.
[9] Nathaniel O. Calloway, "Plans for the Chicago Urban League," July 1, 1955 (MS in the files of the Chicago Urban League).
[10] Minutes of the Board of Directors, July 13, 1955.

with the president's plan for reorganization. His recommendations were formed into seven motions, all of which passed unanimously. The minutes stated:

It is moved that the Board of the Chicago Urban League in special meeting assembled this day take the following action:

(1) That as of July 15, 1955 the Board commence its plan of reorganization of the activities and program of the League; that such reorganization in contemplation should ripen into reality not later than January 1, 1956.

(2) That because of this pending plan of reorganization the Board hereby suspends all of the League's regular activities as of July 15, 1955.

(3) That such suspension of activities render unnecessary the further employment of the regular staff of the League beyond said date, July 15, 1955.

(4) That the Board hereby directs its President, Dr. N. O. Calloway, to notify forthwith each member of the staff of the order herein taken.[11]

Other motions made provisions for staff separation and interim housekeeping operations and approved the basic plan for rebuilding the League. These provided:

That the Chicago Urban League Board hire Mr. Frazier [Frayser] Lane and Mrs. Odessa Cave Evans to operate the League until such time as the League has been reorganized. . . .

That a sub-committee of the Executive Committee be appointed to distribute approximately $8,000 as severance pay to all employees, except Mr. Williams, Mr. Lane, and Mrs. Evans, taking into consideration the length of service rendered the League. . . .

That the budget of $23,783.00 coupled with our obligation to raise $5,000 be accepted. . . .

That the President appoint a committee of volunteers to carry on the Block Beautiful Contest. . . .

That the Executive Committee be authorized and directed to start a search for a new director. . . .

That the President be empowered and directed to appoint a Citizens' Committee, with the approval of the Board, to assist in the reorganization of the League. . . .[12]

After making its reorganization decisions, the board invited Sidney Williams into the meeting and informed him of its action. He was allowed to make a statement and was then given a "rising vote of appreciation."[13] Thus ended the "old" Urban League and began the job of building the "new" League.

[11] *Ibid.*

[12] *Ibid.*

[13] *Ibid.*

Why was the unique and drastic method of shutting down the agency employed? There were several reasons for this procedure. It made the problem of personnel screening much easier. Releasing the entire staff removed the necessity for making individual evaluations and thereby hazarding prolonged conflict. Some staff members still felt that their dismissal implied incompetence. In reply, Calloway said:

> The only thing the board could do was to consider the possible alternatives and make the best possible choice. With the sharp drop in our income, we couldn't have kept more than half of the staff, at best. That would have called for numerous outright firings and very serious damage to the professional reputation of those selected to be fired.
>
> Furthermore, if we were going to bring in a new executive, we could put him in a better position to handle a very tough situation by giving him a free hand to build a new, fresh organization.
>
> The method we chose, considering all these points, was the fairest and least harmful way for all concerned. . . .
>
> I suppose it is only natural that newspaper reports on this matter all refer to the staff releases as firings. . . .
>
> The fact is, nobody was fired. We acted in such a way as to avoid singling out and really hurting numerous individuals. . . .[14]

A second reason for suspending operations, frequently cited by board members, was to shorten the time required for reorganization. It was the opinion of League officials that a process of gradual reform, while continuing program activities, would have taken years. They did not feel that the League had this much time.[15]

Probably the most basic consideration was the need for an interval during which confidence in the League could be restored. The shutdown served two purposes in accomplishing this objective. In the first place, it was heralded as marking a "clean break with the past." The "past" in this instance really meant the previous eight years. Since the League theoretically no longer existed, groups which had opposed the agency could now be invited to help build a new organization in conformity with their conceptions of what an Urban League should be. Second, the interim provided time to recruit and organize influential and representative supporters. Time was needed to convince these people that the policies and programs of the planned organization actually would be different. Also, careful consideration could be given to the selection of a new executive and staff and to building a better financial structure.

---

[14] Quoted in *Chicago Defender,* July 30, 1955.
[15] Interview, Chicago, June 28, 1961.

There were some doubts, though, as to the efficacy of this plan. Destroying the organization was not considered too difficult, but trying to rebuild it was another matter. According to Dr. Calloway:

> One of the big fears that everyone had in Chicago when I first approached them with the idea that we should completely reorganize the League was "how are you ever going to get the thing started again?" It took a little effort, but not a great deal to sell the idea, not only to our friends, but to our enemies . . . and it was soon found out that our friends all thought we could improve it and our enemies all thought — my God, let's get rid of what exists now and see what happens! Nothing could be any worse. . . .[16]

In the final analysis, the real test of the plan was in its execution. As it turned out, Calloway and Law — the architects of the "new" Urban League — along with some other board members, provided forceful and deliberate leadership.

Following the board meeting of July 13, the president began immediately to carry out his mandate. All programs ceased on July 15, except for the token activities carried on by the temporary skelton staff; and the executive committee soon had a scheme for distributing severance pay.[17] It had already been decided to pay the former executive his salary for six months, and the Community Fund agreed to furnish one-half of this amount.[18] By July 28, the president was able to make a favorable progress report. All bills, salaries, and severance allowances had been paid to that date. The reorganization was attracting little adverse publicity, and efforts to precipitate fights within the board had failed. Only one board directive — that the Block Beautiful contest be continued with volunteers — could not be carried out. It had been assumed by participants that the project would be discontinued, and it was impossible to get them reactivated.[19]

The president suggested that the board of directors begin concentrating on executing the plan for rebuilding the League. This plan had three main features. Basic to the entire operation was the recruiting and effective use of a citizens' advisory committee.

---

[16] Nathaniel O. Calloway, "Administration of an Urban League; from a Board Member's View Point," Sept. 5, 1956 (speech delivered before the 1956 Annual Conference of the National Urban League, Cincinnati, Ohio).

[17] Report of Sub-committee of the Executive Committee on Severance Pay, July 28, 1955 (in the League files).

[18] Minutes of the Board of Directors, July 13, 1955.

[19] Nathaniel O. Calloway to Members of the Board of Directors, July 28, 1955 (in the League files).

The advisory committee would consist of representatives from influential business, religious, political, labor, and civic groups. These representatives would assist in defining the League's proper area of service, in the selection of representative people to serve on the board of directors, in securing adequate financial support, and in finding a suitable executive director. Prerequisite to the success of these functions was the ability of the members of the citizens' committee to "sell" the concept of a reorganized Urban League to their respective groups and to the general public. Simultaneously with the formation of the advisory committee and in conjunction with it, the board had to redefine the policies of the League and to employ an executive director who would launch a program within the limits set by the new policy statement.

Efforts to find people willing to serve on the advisory committee began soon after League operations ceased. In late July, the president expressed the hope that formation of the advisory committee would be completed by the first week in August.[20] But these hopes were too optimistic. Some difficulty was experienced at the beginning in getting people to serve. By mid-September, letters had gone out to thirty "top-flight business, religious, labor and social service leaders," but they were slow in responding. Nevertheless, one important figure had been recruited. Mayor Richard Daley had consented to allow the use of his name as Honorary Chairman or "in any other capacity the committee may so desire."[21] Later in the month, of forty-two people who had been invited to serve, fifteen had accepted and thirteen had refused. There was hope that many of those who had not replied would give favorable answers. Even so, board members and officials of the Community Fund were urged to submit additional names of potential committee members.[22] The situation had changed by October. So many acceptances began to come in that the advisory committee became larger than had been planned.[23] Business groups underwent a change of heart and almost overloaded the committee with their representatives. One board member said that the primary motive behind the participation of businessmen was "to get some people down there to see that we behave ourselves."[24] In any case, an advisory committee of thirty-

[20] *Ibid.*
[21] Minutes of the Board of Directors, Sept. 14, 1955.
[22] Minutes of the Executive Committee, Sept. 26, 1955.
[23] Minutes of the Board of Directors, Oct. 17, 1955.
[24] Interview, Chicago, July 19, 1961.

four members was finally formed. It met in late October, formed a steering committee, and became quite actively involved in the reorganization.[25]

The initial reluctance of some people to accept advisory committee appointments probably resulted from their uncertainty about the nature of the reorganized League. In addition, when the recruiting of members began, the League's board had not clearly defined the role and functions of the committee. These shortcomings were soon rectified. In fact, from the beginning, the League's leaders had emphasized their determination to reshape the agency into a distinctly social work organization whose activities would be limited to certain well-defined spheres of operation. Even so, those the League wished to attract as supporters had to be convinced that the announced aims were actually the goals sought. With a good public relations program, spearheaded by H. B. Law, the League was able to create favorable sentiment toward the reorganization. So effective was the propaganda campaign that many people who were actually anti-Negro were persuaded to lend their assistance. Some of them probably thought that they were helping to establish a placement service for domestic servants.[26] At the same time, the board of directors was clarifying the role of the committee. Although it was agreed that the group would be "purely advisory," it was also emphasized that the committee would have considerable influence on policy formation, the composition of the board of directors, and the selection of an executive director.[27]

In spite of the work accomplished by the board of directors and the advisory committee, the eventual effectiveness of the reorganized League would depend largely upon the executive director. The board and advisory committee could establish guides for programing, but the executive director would have to translate policies into programs. Therefore, the selection of an executive was a key part of the reorganization process. Certain procedures for executive recruitment already existed. In the first place, a League the size of that in Chicago and with its problems could not go outside the Urban League movement and hire an inexperienced person. The

[25] Chicago Urban League Service Report, Dec., 1955 (in the files of the Welfare Council of Metropolitan Chicago).
[26] Interview, Chicago, June 28, 1961.
[27] Minutes of the Executive Committee, Sept. 26, 1955; Oct. 3, 1955; Oct. 19, 1955; Minutes of the Board of Directors, Oct. 17, 1955; Calloway, "Administration of an Urban League."

search could be limited to men in local branches comparable to Chicago. A list of such men, who might consider changing positions, was supplied by the National League. Yet, Urban League executives were as different as the conditions in the various cities in which they worked. The problem was to find just the right man to tackle the job in Chicago. Some felt that the "right" man might hesitate before risking his career in trying to rebuild a defunct branch — especially in a city which the press called the "graveyard of Urban League executives."

The big question was: what qualifications should the right man have? There seems to have been general agreement on the type of executive desired. The board wanted a man who could differentiate between policy-making and administration, who was a competent administrator, and who had demonstrated effectiveness in public relations and fund raising. Beyond these points, however, the board and the advisory committee were probably somewhat at variance. Many members of the advisory committee had in mind a "moderate" executive who would run a rather innocuous agency. When the Urban League conservatives characterized the organization as a social work agency, however, they were usually thinking in terms of method. They referred to the use of education, persuasion, community organization, and public relations as opposed to picketing, boycotts, and legal action, which they considered the methods of direct action organizations. It was not the intent of the board that the executive avoid controversial fields. Rather, as one director said: "We definitely felt that we wanted someone who would be able to carry on a very forward looking type program and not lag behind the times, but to be able to do it without constantly getting himself in dutch."[28]

Surprisingly, the list of candidates was rather impressive. Lester Granger, of the National League, submitted a list of ten possible candidates, and numerous unsolicited applications came in. The task of screening so many applications grew too large for the entire board; it was then turned over to the executive committee.[29] Much of the work involved in the preliminary screening fell to the president. The choice was finally narrowed to four men — the executives in Baltimore, Pittsburgh, Portland (Oregon), and St. Louis. One of these was eliminated because his salary demand was $2,000 above

[28] Interview, Chicago, July 19, 1961.

[29] Minutes of the Board of Directors, Sept. 14, 1955.

the maximum figure budgeted, and another asked that his name be withdrawn from consideration. In choosing between the two remaining candidates, there was a choice between a man who used the traditional approach of working quietly but effectively, without too much fanfare, and one who was an aggressive but skillful and articulate executive.[30] On October 19, the executive committee voted unanimously to offer the position to Edwin C. Berry of Portland.[31]

The last item on the reorganization agenda was the formulation of a statement of policy. It was generally agreed that some practical limitations on scope and methods were needed as guides for both the board and the executive in launching the new program. Writing such a statement was probably the most difficult part of the reorganization. A statement was wanted which would be definite and specific as to fields and methods, yet which would not be stultifying and which would be broad enough to synthesize the conceptions of an Urban League held by widely diversified groups.

In November, the board authorized a joint advisory committee–board of directors committee "to draw up basic policies by which the League and the new Secretary shall operate." Berry was invited to participate, and he and the committee set to work drafting a statement. Their finished product failed, however, to meet the approval of the Welfare Council. This body considered it "too inclusive as to fields covered and not specific enough as to action."[32] Nevertheless, the committee had done about the best it could do. It defined Urban League methods as being "fact finding, negotiation, education and cooperation," and it listed the League's fields of service as "research, employment, vocational guidance, housing, health, family welfare and education."[33] Actually, this was only a restatement of traditional Urban League methods and program areas. In the final analysis, the character of program activities was left to be determined by the executive director and the staff he recruited.

Consequently, when the "new" Chicago Urban League began

---

[30] Minutes of the Executive Committee, Oct. 3, 1955; Oct. 17, 1955; Interview, Chicago, July 19, 1961.

[31] Minutes of the Executive Committee, Oct. 19, 1955.

[32] *Ibid.,* Nov. 4, 1955; Minutes of the Board of Directors, Dec. 14, 1955.

[33] Chicago Urban League, *Statement of Policies and Areas of Service* (undated pamphlet); Chicago Urban League Service Report, Dec., 1955.

operations in 1956, the central figure in launching the new agency was Edwin Carlos Berry. Berry received his education at Oberlin College, Duquesne University, and the schools of social work at Western Reserve University and the University of Pittsburgh. His career with the Urban League began in 1937 in Pittsburgh, where he remained until 1945 when he left to become executive director of the new Portland, Oregon Urban League. Berry helped to establish the Portland League and served as its director for ten years. This branch was a product of World War II, when thousands of Negroes, many from the South, had been drawn into the city to work in the shipbuilding industry. In a short period of time, Portland's Negro population more than doubled, and the city suffered the usual traumas associated with Negro migration. The Portland Urban League was founded in 1945 to help resolve the resulting problems. Ten years later, this agency was being heralded as a "model organization," Portland had been cited as "America's most improved city in race relations," and "Bill" Berry had established himself as a leader in race relations in Oregon.[34]

Yet, Berry left this rather secure position in January, 1956 to undertake what some considered to be the impossible job of building an effective Urban League in Chicago — a city reputed to be resistant to reforms and reformers of all types. In November, 1955 when a reporter asked Berry about his motives for coming to Chicago, the new executive director indicated his awareness of the problems he faced. Nevertheless, "Chicago," Berry said, "presents a great challenge"; and as the "Crossroads of America," he considered Chicago "the most important city in race relations in the world."[35] This was a rather unusual attitude for an established Urban League executive, especially in 1955. Even some of the more "moderate" executives were finding it difficult to defend their agencies against racist attacks which came in the wake of the Supreme Court's school desegregation decisions. Such men were not thinking in terms of challenges but were trying to maintain the status quo in financial support and program. Several of the candidates who cited inadequate salary as their reason for ending negotiations with the Chicago board of directors were probably as

[34] *Chicago Defender,* Nov. 26, 1955; Lerone Bennett, Jr., "North's Hottest Fight for Integration," *Ebony,* XVII (March, 1962), 31; Biographical Sketch of Edwin C. Berry, 1959 (in the League files).
[35] *Chicago Defender,* Nov. 26, 1955.

much concerned about the prospects for failure. In some instances, the salary offered was considerably more than they were then receiving.[36]

"Bill" Berry, however, was not the usual type of Urban League executive. His conception of program administration, although essentially consonant with traditional methods, marked him as one of a new breed of League executives. The Chicago League's statement of policy, as one board member pointed out, could be administered on any one of three or four levels of moderation or aggressiveness. What the majority of the board of directors wanted, as opposed to the advisory committee, was an aggressive director, who, at the same time, was articulate, skillful, and diplomatic.[37] Their new executive director was such a man. Berry outlined his rather unconventional concept of Urban League programing in a speech delivered at the 1959 annual conference of the National Urban League. In this speech, he analyzed the implications for Urban League programing of growing urban complexity — from metropolis to megalopolis — and the increased tensions in race relations which accompanied it. Much of what he said was based on the four years he had spent in Chicago. In some of his specific elements of program, however, he was in advance of several Chicago board members and many League supporters, but on others there was little disagreement. For instance, Berry's first program element, the need for a change in approach, had been generally avowed by the Chicago board of directors from the beginning of the reorganization. They realized that it was time for the League to abandon trying to solve the problems faced by individual Negroes through the "old handmaiden approach" — case work, mass placement, and block organization — and to work on causes instead of effects. It was also generally agreed that dynamic community organization should replace the old approach and that research was fundamental to any efforts at community organization. In essence this was simply a change in emphasis on traditional program elements.

Berry, however, seemed less concerned about the traditional image of the Urban League than about the new climate being created by the Montgomery bus boycott and the school crisis in Little Rock. He called for a program that would "take cognizance of the time

[36] The author reached this conclusion from a review of the correspondence with the various candidates.

[37] Interview, Chicago, July 19, 1961.

and condition under which it works." He continued: "This is the last half of the 20th century, *the age of sputniks as well as the age of Urban Sprawl.* Negroes have emerged from two and one-half world wars, with a new dimension of personal significance. They are no longer willing to be half slave and half free. They are at war with the status quo, and will no longer accept the leadership of any agency or organization that does not know this and will not act on it forthrightly. . . ."[38] Berry was, in fact, calling for a radical change in image. He chided his fellow Urban League officials, men traditionally considered to be accommodating or "safe" leaders, to be daring — without being "silly or reckless or irresponsible." He warned that "Uncle Tom's day is over and Uncle Thomas' days are numbered. (Uncle Thomas is an Uncle Tom with a College Degree and a Brooks Brothers suit.) Intelligent whites know this and for the unenlightened who do not know and understand, it is our job to help them to higher ground. . . ."[39] The new breed League official would set forth a program that would utilize the technique of "testing the line" to see how far change could be pushed in any given area. "We have in the past," Berry stated, "played it so safe that we were well behind the safety zone." Another implication of this new age, which Berry found it necessary to reiterate to his own board from time to time, was the fact that the Urban League had to *"inspire the confidence of the Negro in the community before it can be useful or respected by the total community."*[40] It was the program philosophy set forth in this speech that the new Chicago League executive tried to follow up to 1959 and would follow in greater measure after 1960.

Even more basic to the rebuilding process than the hiring of an effective executive director was the reformation of the board of directors. This had been the great failure of the 1946 reorganization — the board never became broadly representative. Hugo B. Law, N. O. Calloway, and other board-member architects of the "new" League, as well as the Welfare Council, the Community Fund, and interested outside groups, were determined that this mistake would not be repeated in 1956. Moreover, the composition of the board

[38] Edwin C. Berry, *Urban Sprawl: Its Impact on Urban League Programming* (Chicago: Chicago Urban League, Public Relations Department, 1960), p. 9.
[39] *Ibid.*
[40] *Ibid.*, p. 8.

would determine the agency's financial potential and, consequently the nature and extent of its program.

In spite of the better climate of acceptance created during the reorganization interim, the job of recruiting suitable board personnel was not easy. First, there needed to be some determination as to what the often-used term "balanced board" meant. It was generally agreed that there should be representatives from the three major religious groups — Protestants, Catholics, and Jews — from business and industry, from labor, and from politics. Also, under Urban League regulations and long tradition, the board had to be interracial. It would have been bad policy to try and establish quotas from any group. A policy in this area, therefore, could not be openly proclaimed. The steering committee of the advisory committee expressed concern "about clergy and big business representation on the board, and the racial distribution," but they could not determine what would constitute a "balanced board." The Urban League board could only agree that "it would not be wise to have a policy statement on racial distribution."[41] Several board members seemingly envisioned a board dominated by business and industrial interests.

Finally, leadership in recruiting was turned over to an *ad hoc* nominating committee under the chairmanship of long-time board member William E. Hill, a race relations adviser to the Public Housing Administration. The business-dominated advisory committee named Hale Nelson, an Illinois Bell Telephone executive, as the advisory committee representative. When the committee was appointed in December, 1955, President Calloway instructed it to "(1) review the names of present members whose terms expire in 1956, and recommend nominations from among them for re-election; (2) screen the names of persons who would be qualified to fill the existing board vacancies; (3) recommend a slate of officers for nomination and re-election to the board at the next annual meeting."[42]

The committee began work immediately. By February, 1956 it had formulated its conception of a "balanced board" and qualifications for board membership. The committee stated that its job was "to select a panel of nominees in which there would be representation from top industrial leadership of the community, as well as

---

[41] Minutes of the Board of Directors, Jan. 11, 1956.
[42] *Ibid.*, Feb. 8, 1956.

representation from top business and commercial leadership of the Central South Side of Chicago. The panel was also expected to include leadership from the South Side church community. The qualifications of these persons are that they be willing to serve, take a part in the formulation of policy for, and add prestige and influence to the Urban League."[43] At the same time that new members were being sought, the committee was reviewing the records of present board members. The resignations of several inactive members, who agreed to withdraw, were readily accepted. Other inactive members who met the committee's qualifications for membership — such as Marshall Korshak, an attorney and state senator, Leo Rose, a State Street clothier, and Theodore Jones, a Supreme Life Insurance Company executive — were urged to remain on the board and become active. In at least one case, the individual consented only after given time to see if he could ascribe to the new policy statement and the new program.

Individual members of the nominating committee approached prospective nominees who met the stated criteria for board membership. Hale Nelson canvassed Campbell Soup Company, Sears, Roebuck and Company, Inland Steel, Western Electric, and similar firms in search of candidates. Charles Thompson, a Negro dentist, contacted South Side prospects, and other board members sought religious and labor representation. This flurry of activity began to bring results. In March, 1956 eight new members were added to the board. These were George Bynum of the AFL-CIO; Attorney William R. Ming; William H. Harvey, alderman of the second ward; Publisher John H. Johnson; C. V. Martin of Carson Pirie Scott and Company; William Caples of Inland Steel; Ernest H. Reed of International Harvester; and James C. Worthy of Sears, Roebuck and Company. To facilitate the recruiting of additional men of "prestige and influence," the board amended the by-laws to increase board membership from twenty-five to thirty-six members.[44] Recruiting became less difficult after these initial successes. During the period 1957 to 1958, other business and religious leaders accepted board membership. The accretion of new members and resignations by both new and old members soon resulted in a radical change in board composition. Although men like N. O. Calloway and Hugo B. Law remained active leaders, by the end of this period

[43] *Ibid.*

[44] *Ibid.*, Mar. 14, 1956.

probably a majority of the board had been elected since reorganization. This new board was, in many respects, more conservative than the old board, but it was also less parochial. Men accustomed to large-scale business operations were not reluctant to approve expanded budgets, involved fund-raising schemes, and elaborate programs, when they could be convinced of the soundness of such activities.

By 1958 the board had plans for policing itself and was trying to make recruiting more systematic. Early in 1957 the nominating committee asked for instructions concerning the renomination of "nonproductive board members." A committee was authorized by the board and appointed by the president to formulate a policy on standards for board membership. It was suggested that the new policies be applied "prior to 1958 election to total board regardless of expiration of terms." The board was not yet ready to go this far, but the board standards committee was empowered to confer with each member concerning attendance and participation.[45] Nevertheless, before the committee completed its work, the board had become rather broadly representative, with the exception that "strong representation" from labor had not been obtained. In January, 1958 the nominating committee, now a regular standing committee, asked board approval for procedural changes which would facilitate the implementation of the forthcoming board standards report and provide closer screening of nominees for board membership. Thereafter, all prospective board members would be considered in accordance with the approved policy on board standards. The names of candidates would be presented to the board for approval before initial contact with them by the committee; then, after an interview, the names would be resubmitted for election.[46] The adoption of this complex procedure evidenced increased facility in filling board vacancies. Later in the year, the nominating committee had a backlog of suitable candidates.[47]

The long-awaited board standards report came to the board in February, 1958. By this time, board members felt in a better position to impose stringent measures. The report recommended amending the by-laws to empower the board "to declare vacant the position of any Director who has not fulfilled the Standards of Board

[45] *Ibid.,* Feb. 20, 1957.
[46] *Ibid.,* Jan. 15, 1958; Feb. 19, 1958.
[47] *Ibid.,* May 21, 1958.

Membership as prescribed by the Board." In addition, the committee devised a service chart providing for evaluation in six areas—attendance at regular meetings, special meetings, and committee meetings, participation in agency and agency-related conferences, "special contributions for good of the agency," and fund raising. The board standards committee became a standing committee and was ordered to prepare and circulate service charts for each board member. At semiannual intervals, the committee would analyze these charts and report its findings and recommendations to the board.[48] In 1959 the functions of the nominating and board standards committee were combined in one committee. The internal policing procedures were accepted by board members in good spirit, and the Chicago board was frequently described as the most active and hard-working board in the Urban League movement.

The real test of the reformed board, however, was its ability to help resolve the problems confronting the agency. Suitable office space, adequate finances, and a program relevant to the times could not wait until board reform was completed.

Although the "old" Urban League bequeathed the new agency a housing problem, it also left the beginning of a building fund. At the end of 1956, the agency had the $10,423 left from capital fund drives and the $16,981 paid by the Chicago Land Clearance Commission for the Wabash Avenue building, but it had no offices. Location posed a difficult problem. Should the League be near the people it was trying to influence, downtown businessmen, or the people it served, the Negro community? Then too, the financial situation made buying and renovating a building out of the question.[49] Something of a compromise was reached when the building at 2400 Michigan Avenue became available. The Illinois Automobile Club wanted to sell the building, but space was rented to the League temporarily. The location was considered ideal; for it was fifteen minutes from both downtown and the heart of the South Side Negro community.[50] In 1958, however, John Sengstacke, publisher of the *Chicago Defender,* bought the building to house his newspaper. He offered to continue to make space available to the

---

[48] See The Board Standards Committee Report to Chicago Urban League Board of Directors, Feb. 14, 1958; Minutes of the Board of Directors, Feb. 19, 1958; Mar. 19, 1958.

[49] Interview, Chicago, June 28, 1961.

[50] Chicago Urban League Service Report, Nov., 1956; Minutes of the Board of Directors, Oct. 4, 1955; Feb. 8, 1956; Interview, Chicago, June 28, 1961.

League at an increased rental, but a conference between a special board committee and Sengstacke resulted in a reduced rental and more space. It was understood, however, that the League would move by July 1, 1959.[51] In the meantime, the building fund had been converted into a revolving fund to be drawn on and replaced during "periods of famine and plenty."[52] The agency expanded so fast that the periods of plenty never compensated for the periods of famine, and by 1959 the building fund was depleted. In late 1959, arrangements were made for an extended lease with Sengstacke, and the League's executive director ostensibly was convinced that "it would be advantageous to remain here until a permanent location is acquired."[53] It would take several more years for the agency to find a final solution to its housing problem.

During the reorganization in 1955, there was no clear indication as to what the League needed or could expect in financial support for 1956. President Calloway planned for a very modest beginning. In his suggestions for long range program, he estimated that the first year's budget should not exceed $60,000. His suggested itemized budget totaled only $47,600, but after talking to Berry, he realized that the League could not be rebuilt on this budget.[54] The earlier estimate had gone to the Community Fund, however, and Calloway now had to convince the Fund that a larger amount was required. When a new request for an $80,000 budget was sent to the Community Fund, the League was asked to justify this increased asking. Calloway admitted that his earlier figures were "only a guess." "Anticipating, however," he added, "that our department heads will have to be paid in the neighborhood of $8,000 each to get men that are adequate to cope with the problems in Chicago, as I am sure you would be interested in us doing, it would be necessary for us to have a larger budget."[55] Even so, the League was not able to commit itself to raising any substantial portion of this amount. As yet the League's board was uncertain about the agency's fund-raising potential, and the Fund's budget analyst shared this uncertainty. He doubted the League could raise $40,000 and suggested

[51] Minutes of the Board of Directors, Nov. 19, 1958; Dec. 17, 1958.
[52] *Ibid.,* Jan. 16, 1957.
[53] *Ibid.,* Nov. 18, 1959.
[54] Calloway's budget estimates and itemized budget were included in his "Plans for the Chicago Urban League."
[55] N. O. Calloway to Frank J. Arendt, Community Fund Budget Analyst, Nov. 29, 1955 (in the files of the Welfare Council of Metropolitan Chicago).

that the reviewing committee require League representatives "to fully discuss their projected fund-raising program."[56]

The League's board of directors proceeded to plan on the basis of an $80,000 budget. In January, 1956 President Calloway reported that the Fund had been requested to provide 70 per cent of the budget and, in addition, to release an allotment early in the year to support the agency until its own fund raising could get underway. The board empowered its executive committee to receive and act upon a budget "not to exceed $80,000" to be presented by the executive director. The final budget submitted to the Fund, however, was set at $100,526, with the League scheduled to raise $55,391. At the same time that the final 1956 budget was submitted, a preliminary budget of $165,000 was presented for 1957. When the year ended, the League's income had exceeded $90,000, and a small surplus existed.[57]

Some of the uncertainty about fund raising during the reorganization period resulted from League participation in the Joint Negro Appeal. Although J.N.A. had a worthy objective, several Urban League officials felt that it had come along about twenty-five years too late. The idea behind J.N.A. was to end the numerous uncoordinated fund-raising campaigns in the Negro community. Since the Community Fund provided only a portion of its member agencies' budgets, each agency had to go to the community for contributions to raise the balance. The Joint Negro Appeal proposed to end this multitude of fund-raising drives by raising, in one campaign, the funds needed by its member agencies beyond what the Community Fund supplied. In addition, J.N.A. hoped to educate the Negro community to the importance of giving to support community institutions and agencies.

The Chicago Urban League's board was never too enthusiastic about Joint Negro Appeal. Two board members claimed that Sidney Williams took the agency into J.N.A. without authorization and without the board knowing fully what J.N.A. was all about.[58] Nevertheless, the League board reaffirmed its support of the principle of J.N.A. in March, 1955 and named its representatives to

[56] Robert Edison, Budget Analyst, to members of the Specialized Services Reviewing Committee, Dec. 6, 1955 (in the files of the Welfare Council).
[57] Minutes of the Board of Directors, Jan. 11, 1956; Feb. 8, 1956; May 9, 1956; Jan. 16, 1957.
[58] Interviews, Chicago, June 19, 1961; June 28, 1961.

participate in the 1955 campaign.[59] In July there was optimism that some of the funds needed for reorganization would be forthcoming from the J.N.A. campaign. Disillusionment had begun to set in by September, however. Dr. Calloway reported that Community Fund officials were "somewhat taken back" when they learned that the League had received nothing from the J.N.A.[60] From this time, critics of J.N.A. on the League's board became quite vocal. They pointed to the incongruity of the League's participating in a project which they termed a move toward self-segregation. This group felt that the League's budget was too large to be raised in this way and that, unlike the other participating agencies, the Urban League was city-wide in scope. Partisans of J.N.A. were able to forestall a hasty withdrawal, but their further efforts were unavailing when 1955 ended with no money having been received.[61] Early in 1956, it became apparent to the majority of the League's board that in order to rebuild the agency and provide for needed expansion the Chicago Urban League would have to raise its own budget. Finally, in April, 1956 the agency severed its relations with J.N.A.[62]

During the years 1956 to 1959, the League was probably the fastest growing private agency in Chicago, and by 1958 it had become the largest Urban League branch in the nation. Fundamental to this growth was cooperation from the Community Fund. Although the Community Fund had to be reminded that the reorganized League was "their baby," the Fund became quite liberal in its support. Over this period, allocations to the League were increased approximately 50 per cent each year, except in 1959. In successive stages, the Fund's contributions increased from $45,000 in 1956 to over $90,000 in 1958 and 1959. The League's budgets had kept pace with these increases and had reached approximately $225,000 by 1959.[63]

This rapid growth placed a great fund-raising burden on the board of directors, as well as on the executive director and the staff. Although there was an improved climate of acceptance after the reorganization, no machinery existed for raising the unprecedented

---

[59] Minutes of the Board of Directors, Mar. 2, 1955.
[60] *Ibid.*, Sept. 14, 1955.
[61] *Ibid.*, Sept. 14, 1955; Dec. 14, 1955.
[62] *Ibid.*, Apr. 16, 1956.
[63] Memorandum from Edwin C. Berry to Linn Brandenburg, Chicago Community Fund, Feb. 9, 1957 (copy in League files); Minutes of the Board of Directors, Jan. 19, 1960; Chicago Urban League *Newsletter*, Apr.-May, 1958.

amounts sought, and it was not certain that friendships made during reorganization could be translated into dollars and cents.

The board's efforts to organize itself for fund raising began early in 1957 when James C. Worthy accepted the chairmanship of the finance committee. Worthy would be the mainstay of the League's fund raising for the next several years. Under his leadership, the board's finance committee was expanded in 1958 into a financial council designed to establish a "systematic and comprehensive fund-raising program." One major goal was to get increased support from businessmen and their firms. The search for new business supporters began with the establishment of the advisory committee during reorganization and became a continuing effort. It was facilitated greatly by the election to the board of directors of more business executives and men with business contacts. In April, 1956 William Caples of Inland Steel and E. H. Reed of International Harvester offered to approach an informal organization of "representatives of the larger businesses in the city" about supporting the League's financial campaign.[64] In 1957 "top business leaders" were invited to a luncheon where they were briefed on the race relations problems facing Chicago and the role of the Urban League. The idea of holding such luncheons caught on and eventually some of the participants organized the League's business advisory council. Equally as important as these group contacts were personal contacts made by individual board members. These activities showed results; for business support increased each year. One board member was led to predict that one day the League would receive its entire support from business.[65]

The organizers of League fund raising, however, aimed at broad city-wide support from numerous groups. The campaign organization usually entailed breakdowns into divisions — such as labor, foundations, membership, religious, benefits, and special gifts. These divisions were modified and refined from campaign to campaign, but the objective was the same — broad appeal. There was special effort to win support in the Negro community. These efforts also bore results in the form of more money from membership contributions and support of Urban League benefits.

Through the years, benefits remained an important source of income. The three Chicago Urban League auxiliaries — the Leaguers,

[64] Minutes of the Board of Directors, April 16, 1956.
[65] *Ibid.*, Nov. 20, 1957.

the Urbanaides, and the Women's Division — sponsored affairs each year. The Urbanaides' affairs were usually quite elaborate and netted the agency between $5,000 and $10,000 each year. Other clubs, individuals, and groups also sponsored League benefits. Alpha Kappa Alpha Sorority divided the proceeds from its annual affair between the Chicago Urban League and the National Association for the Advancement of Colored People. Sammy Davis, Jr. gave a great lift to year-end fund raising in 1957 by staging a one-man benefit at the Chicago Civic Opera.[66] In 1959 *Playboy* Magazine offered the Urban League the opportunity to sponsor the first night of a three-night jazz festival, and the $25,000 realized from this festival saved the 1959 budget from near disaster. The agency closed the year with a deficit of just over $1,000.[67]

From time to time, the funds raised from these other sources were supplemented by grants from foundations. Usually these were special purpose grants, either not renewable or for a limited number of years. The Chicago Community Trust, however, made both special grants and annual contributions. Other foundation contributors during this period included the Field Foundation, the Division Fund, and the Fund for the Republic. In the same category with these grants was a special gift from the Chicago Association of Commerce and Industry to support the League's Youth Guidance Project.

Since Urban League programing depends largely upon the size and competence of the professional staff, the course of program development followed the fortunes of fund raising. The close relationship between program and budget often meant that new activities were undertaken only after considering their effect on fund raising. Moreover, once committed to a total program of a given scope, it was very difficult to cut back. By far the largest percentage of the budgets went for salary, and the only way to make any sizable reduction was to cut staff. Even if no program expansion was anticipated, some budget expansion was required; salary increments alone would necessitate this. These problems were compounded by the League's rapid rate of expansion and by the budgeting practices of the Community Fund. It was usually not until April or May before final action was taken on the budget by the Community

[66] Chicago Urban League *Newsletter,* Apr.-May, 1958; Minutes of the Board of Directors, Dec. 18, 1957.
[67] *Ibid.,* June 17, 1959; Sept. 16, 1959; Jan. 19, 1960.

Fund, and it was even later in the year before the League could gauge the success of its own fund raising.

There was a degree of program ambiguity inherent in the reorganized Chicago Urban League. In spite of assertions as to the definitive nature of the policy statement, views differed on what constituted proper program content and on the limitations the policy statement placed on methods of program execution. The reorganization had been, in large measure, the work of conservatives, and many of the new board members were convinced that the "new" League would undertake a "moderate" program acceptable to business and other conservative interests. This was the image fostered by Nathaniel O. Calloway; and as president of the board of directors from 1955 to 1960, he tried to keep the agency on what he considered to be a sound course — one that would not lead to another reorganization. The purpose of the Urban League, he said

> was to help a minority (Negro) to better take advantage of his rightful opportunities as well as to see that those in authority to offer them lived up to their responsibility. That the unit to be served is the family with respect to
> *Security:* employment, adequate living facilities.
> *Community organization:* responsibility as a citizen, play space.
> *Vocational training:* to become aware of job opportunities and proper preparation for them.[68]

In accomplishing this purpose, Calloway believed that the League must move diplomatically and in a "sometimes invisible way." He felt that Urban League program and policy had become indistinguishable, and, therefore, the board of directors had an active and unique role to play in program. The Urban League board must not only make policy, but its individual members also must execute it. Influential board members should work quietly behind the scenes trying to influence men who make decisions. "For example," Calloway explained, "if we have a man on the board who is influencing the mayor, he might be much more effective in getting something accomplished than all the trips to Springfield by the executive and by groups."[69] This implied a strong leadership role for the president of the board and restrictions on the initiative left to the executive director.

On the other hand, Berry envisioned a dynamic image for the

[68] *Ibid.,* Oct. 4, 1955.
[69] Interview with the author, 1961.

agency. In some respects, he did not agree with the Calloway program philosophy, even though Calloway's pronouncements were based on accepted Urban League principles. Berry asserted that the times called for a program that will "work at all times to give the agency high community visibility; this old canard about the Urban League working 'Quietly and without fanfare' is rubbish. Certainly, there are many things we do that require confidentiality but that doesn't mean that the League never does anything that is interesting, useful or newsworthy. The quiet line is more useful for a private-eye or a crook, than an agency which is attempting to alter a culture."[70] The new executive director, however, had to work within the limits set by the reorganizers. He realized that he needed the confidence and support of his board; so he was meticulous in respecting the board's policy-making function. In the beginning, his own pronouncements and program activities were kept within the limits set by rather narrow board decisions. Calloway's practice of trying to arrive at policies that reflected a consensus point of view of his heterogeneous board, although it promoted the rebuilding process, often led to delay and equivocation. Consequently, as Berry became oriented to his position, he sometimes used his technique of "testing the line" on board policies.

A major test of the board's policy-making facility came in 1957 when the executive director asked advice concerning his action on three bills before the Illinois General Assembly. All three measures covered matters of concern to Chicago Negroes. One would have raised the residence requirement for public assistance. Another was designed to remedy certain abuses practiced by some credit houses, but the most important was a bill to make merit employment or fair employment practices a matter of law in Illinois. Berry merely asked clearance to give "expert testimony" on these bills. In response, the board established a special committee to "review — in consultation with experts — the three specific bills and submit its recommendations at a meeting of the full board."[71]

The five-member committee, with Attorney William R. Ming, Jr. as chairman, reflected the diverse opinions held by board members. By unanimous vote, the committee recommended against action on the credit bill, since it dealt with "intricate and complicated matters beyond League competence at this time." Action by the League

[70] Berry, *Urban Sprawl,* p. 8.
[71] Minutes of the Board of Directors, Mar. 20, 1957.

was recommended, however, on the measures dealing with equal job opportunity and raising the residence requirements for public assistance. In recommending opposition to the latter bill, the committee split two to two, and the deciding vote was cast by the chairman. The vote favoring support of merit employment was two for, one against, and one abstaining.[72]

A special board meeting was called to consider this report. Herman W. Seinwerth of Swift and Company was a leading opponent of any League involvement in legislative matters. He pointed out that the "League Board is composed of people with widely varying interests. Obviously they are all active in serving the League because they are sold on its objectives, but there is considerable difference of opinion among the members as to the best way in which to achieve these objectives." Seinwerth had no objection to the agency furnishing "facts and figures when requested," but he was opposed to taking a position either for or against any legislative measures. Furthermore, he continued, the new statement of policy gave no indication that legislation was to be a "main focus."[73] Seinwerth expressed the opinion of a considerable segment of League supporters among business groups, where opposition to fair employment legislation was strong. Other board members contended that as a social agency the League could not evade legislative matters touching on questions of social concern. Calloway tried to calm opponents by interpreting the functions of the legislative subcommittee in an innocuous way. Its job, he said, was simply to "screen and examine legislative matters relevant to program of the League, and make recommendations for board consideration." Final action was left with the board. Berry countered this contention by calling attention to the difference between technique and policy. He said that board resolutions should represent policy, not methodology. Since the major point at issue was obviously fair employment practices legislation (FEP), a matter of grave concern to Negroes, Berry reminded the board that the "League must maintain a degree of rapport with all segments of the community, but a very close and positive rapport with the Negro segment of the population."[74]

---

[72] Sub-committee on Legislation Report to Chicago Urban League Board of Directors, revised copy, Apr. 3, 1957.

[73] Minutes of a Special Meeting of the Board of Directors, Apr. 4, 1957. It was ruled that this meeting was improperly called and, therefore, could only discuss the legislative question.

[74] *Ibid.*

When the legislative proposal came before the board again, the proponents had the upper hand. The committee's recommendation of no action on the credit measure was accepted, but after comments by Senator Marshall Korshak, the board called for further study and another report. No opposition was recorded to the recommendation that the League work for the defeat of the residence requirement bill. On the FEP bill, the main issue, the committee resubmitted a weak resolution stating the League's position. The proposed resolution declared that the elimination of discrimination in employment was of "primary concern" to the League and that the agency had information pertinent to the question, which it was willing to "share with members of the legislature." "From this information and data," the statement continued, "it appears that voluntary efforts to achieve non-discrimination in job opportunity have not substantially reduced the problem. Therefore, *we now reluctantly have come to feel that this is a matter for legislative concern and action.* The form of this specific bill is beyond the competence of the Urban League."[75] (Italics mine.)

James Worthy wanted to know how the Negro community would react to this resolution. Berry replied that he did not feel that it was forthright enough. Worthy, who reportedly had spoken against FEP measures earlier, called for a stronger statement. From the standpoint of fund raising, Worthy argued, a strong stand would alienate some in the business community but would strengthen the League in the Negro community. A weak stand would alienate both groups. He felt, therefore, that a strong resolution would be "entirely justifiable to all segments." William Caples backed this position. Since this was a question of right against wrong, Caples maintained, there was no choice but to support the FEP bill and risk losing the support of some business groups.[76] Worthy offered, as a substitute for the committee's proposal, a resolution proclaiming that the League stood "unequivocally for equality of economic opportunity." Consequently, it encouraged and supported "all responsible efforts designed to accomplish this goal, including legislative enactments." The resolution endorsed the bill then before the legislature, but it disclaimed faith in legislation as the principal way to

[75] Sub-committee on Legislation Report to Chicago Urban League Board of Directors, Apr. 3, 1957.

[76] Minutes of the Board of Directors, Apr. 17, 1957. For a somewhat disparaging interpretation of this action see James Q. Wilson, *Negro Politics: The Search for Leadership* (Glencoe, Ill.: The Free Press, 1960), p. 140.

"accomplish the goal of equal job opportunity." The answer was education, not legislation. The final paragraph, probably addressed primarily to the business community, commended "the excellent educational efforts, directed toward similar ends, of many individual employers, employer associations, labor organizations, and civic groups."[77]

The adoption of this resolution, as mild as it was in tone, marked the beginning of a departure from the philosophy of sterile research propounded during the reorganization. In 1959 when the FEP bill began its biennial journey through the Illinois General Assembly to its senate graveyard, the League's board was ready to recognize the efficacy of legislation as a method of education.[78] Furthermore, with the adoption of the 1957 resolution, the board began to recognize, though haltingly, that conclusions usually derive from research. And facts do not always speak for themselves. If League research was to be meaningful, the agency had to set forth its conclusions boldly, act on them, and stand ready to face the consequences. At the same time, however, the agency had to be ever mindful of its financial vulnerability.

There was seldom need for such decisions, however, in relation to formal program activities, since these, by and large, followed the principles of the statement of policy. Formal programs emphasized the traditional methods of research, community organization, and public relations. In its first community organization project, the League's community services department brought various block groups and community organizations together into the Central South Side Community Council. This project was undertaken in cooperation with the Welfare Council of Metropolitan Chicago to foster greater community involvement in problems such as housing, hospital needs, and delinquency.[79] Throughout the period, the research department, along with the other programing departments, wrote formal reports on racial violence in Chicago and on discrimination in housing, hospitals, and employment. The public relations department tried to keep these matters before the public through the mass media of communications, from speakers' platforms, and in League publications.

Berry's first major program proposal, the League's Youth Guidance Project, was also quite consistent with the reorganization phi-

---

[77] *Ibid.*

[78] Minutes of the Board of Directors, Feb. 18, 1959.

[79] *Ibid.*, Dec. 19, 1956.

losophy. In 1956 and 1957 leaders in business and industry were concerned that a shortage of skilled manpower might retard Chicago's economic growth. Population trends showed that the rapidly increasing Negro population promised the greatest manpower potential. The League saw in this situation an opportunity to serve the Negro community and business interests, while, at the same time, winning influential friends and supporters. Beginning in late 1956, the League took every opportunity to publicize its analysis of the city's dilemma. With an increasing Negro population and a decreasing white population, the League argued, it was inevitable that more Negro workers would be available to Chicago industry, whether they were wanted or not. But the drop-out rates of all-Negro high schools were quite high, and many who remained in school were not being adequately prepared to take advantage of the demands for skilled workers.[80]

Moreover, Negroes needed special motivation to help them break the pattern of accepting the status quo. Since many jobs had been closed to them, Negro youth developed a "psychological attitude" which "discouraged high level job preparation." Many Negro parents, themselves the victims of limited educational and economic opportunities, could not foster higher levels of aspiration in their children. Guidance counselors in the *de facto* segregated schools were also inadequate to the task, since many of them were "prisoners of racial stereotypes." Under such circumstances, most Negro youth remained unaware of the opportunities available to them in Chicago. The League concluded that: "These various factors combine to seriously restrict proper utilization of Chicago's labor force and represent a distinct handicap, not only to its Negro citizenry, but to the further growth and expansion of Chicago business and industry."[81] By working through community organizations and in cooperation with business groups, the press, and school officials, the League proposed to launch a massive campaign of community education. It hoped to break the pattern of acceptance by focusing attention on the various aspects of the problem.

As was expected, this project appealed to industrial groups. The Community Fund indicated its approval by authorizing a special

---

[80] Chicago Urban League, *Two Year Report on the Youth Guidance Project 1958-1959* (Chicago: Chicago Urban League, 1960), p. 1.

[81] Chicago Urban League, Employment and Guidance Department, Fact Sheet on Youth Guidance Project, Feb. 12, 1958 (mimeo. copy in League files).

fund-raising campaign in 1956. Ernest H. Reed and other board members worked to organize a representative advisory committee and to get the cooperation of the Chicago Association of Commerce and Industry. By October, 1957 these efforts had met with sufficient success that the project could be formally launched. The Association of Commerce and Industry established a liaison committee for the project and contributed $10,000 annually toward its support. The remainder of the $17,500 annual budget came from the Chicago Community Trust and the Division Fund.[82]

The climactic event of the period 1956 to 1959 symbolized the success of the reorganization and rebuilding of the Chicago Urban League. During this period, the agency's budgets increased at an unprecedented rate, and its fund-raising efforts were much improved. The board became "well-balanced, dedicated and hard working," and recruiting board members was no longer a major problem. By instituting the "most favorable" professional salary scale in the Urban League movement, the Chicago branch was able to attract a well-qualified staff.[83] In 1958 the staff had grown from three in 1956 to twenty-six, and Berry could boast that the agency had "experienced not one single resignation on professional staff level and extremely little secretarial turnover."[84] In recognition of these accomplishments, Theodore W. Kheel and Lester B. Granger, president and executive director respectively of the National Urban League, came to Chicago in November, 1959 to present Nathaniel O. Calloway and Hugo B. Law the Two Friends Award, the National Urban League's highest honor.[85] This event, in retrospect, seemed the height of irony. Within three years Calloway would be trying to destroy their creation, and Law would be working to preserve the product of their joint labors.

---

[82] See Chicago Urban League, *Two Year Report on the Youth Guidance Project,* p. 2; Minutes of the Board of Directors, Oct. 16, 1957; Mar. 19, 1958; Apr. 16, 1958; Aug. 20, 1958; Oct. 15, 1958. For a rather critical staff evaluation, see Memorandum from Employment and Guidance Director and Staff to Employment and Guidance Committee and Project Sub-committee, June 24, 1959 (mimeo. copy in League files).

[83] Edwin C. Berry, "Personnel and Program Standards in the Urban League," Sept. 5, 1956 (remarks made during the 1956 Annual Conference of the National Urban League, Cincinnati, Ohio).

[84] Edwin C. Berry, "An Address to Chicago Urban League Annual Meeting Luncheon," Nov. 24, 1958.

[85] Report of the Executive Director to the Board of Directors, Sept. 16, 1959; National Urban League, *The Urban League Story 1910-1960: Golden 50th Anniversary Yearbook* (New York: National Urban League, 1961), p. 29.

9

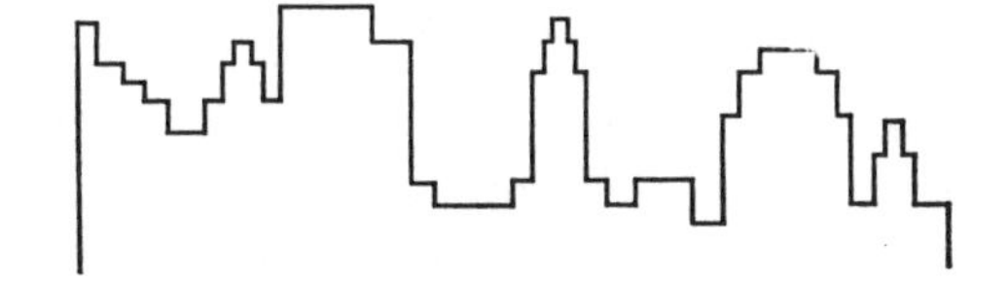

SINCE 1960: THE REVOLUTION OF EXPECTATION

During its nearly fifty-year history, the Urban League in Chicago, a legacy of World War I and the Negro migration, has had to adjust to wars, postwar reconstructions, depressions, and to the social disorganization produced by racial violence; but none of these adjustments compared in depth and significance with that required during the hectic 1960's.

"The Urban League movement," Whitney M. Young, executive director of the National Urban League, wrote in 1962, "if it is to continue to be of service . . . cannot close its eyes to the new and real revolution of expectation which has become internalized in practically every Negro citizen, and which has created an entirely different climate and mood." He continued, in a letter to a Chicago Community Fund official: "For us to ignore this fact of life and not relate to it, while at the same time attempt to maintain the uniqueness and basic integrity of our program, would not only invite contempt and disrespect, but — more tragic for Chicago and our other communities — would result in the loss of leadership to fanatic and irresponsible groups waiting to seize any opportunity to exploit racial problems and convert now-tense situations into violent holocausts."[1]

Young's declaration epitomized the dilemma facing the Chicago Urban League when the "Negro Revolution" reached Chicago.

[1] Whitney M. Young and Henry Steeger, New York, to Arthur Kruse, July 24, 1962. Unless another source is indicated, all letters, memoranda, and other manuscript materials cited are from the files of the Chicago Urban League.

How could the agency maintain the confidence and respect of the Negro community by relating positively to the new movements astir in the city and adjust its programs and policies to make them relevant to the rapidly changing times without alienating important supporters and endangering its existence? The Chicago League, with the improvements made in its operations between 1955 and 1960, was in better condition than some other local Urban Leagues to make the needed adjustments. Even so, any modifications had to be made with due regard to the constraints imposed by the agency's perennial concerns — fund raising, programing, administration, and policy-making — and by its relations with the Community Fund, the Welfare Council, and other groups and organizations in the city. Considering the internal and external difficulties involved, perhaps the crowning achievement of the Chicago Urban League in the 1960's was its adjustment to the "Negro Revolution." In the beginning, however, efforts at policy and program changes and attempts to loosen the restraints within which it worked produced reciprocal convulsions.

Even so, revisions in programs and methods were neither initiated nor instituted in spectacular ways. Fortunately for the League, such an approach was not needed to gain the confidence of the Negro community; for it probably would have resulted in the loss of many white supporters. The fact that the agency was able to retain the confidence and respect of the Negro community resulted from one of the paradoxes of the reorganization and rebuilding period. Actually, the Chicago League was largely conservative in orientation from 1955 to 1960; but Edwin C. Berry, as executive director, managed to project a militant image for the agency, even while keeping his speeches and other pronouncements within the limits of rather conservative policies set by the board of directors.

Often it was not what Berry said but the reaction to it that produced and sustained the reputation for militancy. In 1957, for instance, speaking to fellow officials at the National Urban League's conference in Detroit, Berry characterized Chicago as the most segregated large city in the United States. This speech drew an immediate rebuttal from Mayor Richard Daley and a critical editorial from the *Chicago Tribune*. The editor of the *Chicago Daily Defender,* however, expressed the general reaction of the Negro community when he asserted: "Mr. Berry did not exaggerate a bit when he criticized Chicago. In fact, he was too restrained, too mild in his description of the evil forces at work in this metropolis."[2] Several weeks later, Berry told the board of directors that requests for staff members "to speak, consult and counsel with all types of community groups have more than doubled since the *Tribune* editorial over any comparable period during the existence of the reorganized Chicago Urban League."[3] The repetition of such incidents, along with actual accomplishments, facilitated the retention of Negro support.

In interpreting and justifying increasingly aggressive activities to somewhat conservative white supporters, there were two effective procedures available. On the one hand, it could be pointed out that the League could not accomplish anything without Negro support. This argument was included in the board of directors' reply to the criticisms following the Detroit speech. A statement released by board president Nathaniel O. Calloway declared that the Negro citizens of Chicago "look to the Urban League to reveal the truth, without fear or favor." Furthermore, "those who would like to see the Chicago Urban League become docile and subservient should realize that such an Urban League would be worthless, even to themselves."[4] The second technique for justifying more militant actions was to place them within the context of accepted Urban League procedures. The two techniques were supplementary and mutually reinforcing, and both were used during the speech controversy. Berry's speech, the League maintained, was an outgrowth of the agency's research and educational functions. Calloway's statement declared: "It is the Urban League's job to place the facts about Chicago's interracial situation before the people of Chicago. Therefore, we welcome the present discussion and consider it highly helpful as an educational force."[5]

Although the process of adjustment accelerated in tempo during the 1960's, it was still gradual and rather subtle. As long as a favorable image could be maintained among the agency's diverse constituency, Urban League leaders preferred that publicity center on programs and accomplishments, rather than on internal adjustments. Moreover, the more permissive climate in race relations which accompanied the "Negro Revolution" made many aggressive Urban League actions seem relatively moderate.

Then too, adjustment involved much more than questions of mili-

[2] *Chicago Daily Defender,* Sept. 10, 1957.
[3] Minutes of the Board of Directors, Oct. 16, 1957.
[4] Statement by Nathaniel O. Calloway, 3rd draft, Sept. 25, 1957.
[5] *Ibid.*

tancy and moderation. The growing intensity of the struggle for Negro equality poignantly highlighted the complexity and interrelatedness of the multiple barriers facing Negroes in Chicago and other cities throughout the country. Negro leaders came to realize that the breaching of one barrier in the vicious circle of segregation and discrimination might have little effect on the Negro's general plight. It was long recognized that housing was a key issue, but open occupancy, without improvement in other areas, would not benefit those most in need of better housing. Without jobs Negroes living in slums could not escape, even if given the opportunity. Conversely, improved economic conditions would not necessarily bring better housing. The ability to take advantage of employment opportunities required levels of education and training not being reached by children in the largely segregated schools in Negro ghettoes. Moreover, complacency and resignation, born of family disorganization and poverty, stood as barriers to taking advantage of even the educational opportunities available.

Under such conditions, piecemeal attacks on less sensitive points and a few grudging concessions would not satisfy the Negro's cry for "freedom now." The tremendous rise in Negro expectation and the demands made on Negro leadership to bring fulfillment of these expectations became sources of bewilderment for many whites and of great challenge to Negro leaders. Samuel Lubell, in attempting to assess the broadening scope of Negro protest, gave expression to white bewilderment. Lubell stated:

> Currently the more militant Negro leadership seems bent on transforming the whole country into one national arena of this struggle. By stirring tensions at enough points of society, these militants appear determined to involve each of us ever more deeply in their grievances, to leave us no escape from their clamors for "freedom now," no place to hide from taking sides. . . .[6]

The most common expression of this bewilderment, however, was the often-repeated question: "What do the Negroes really want?"

The challenge to Negro leaders was twofold. In the first place, they had to continue to redouble their efforts to open the gates of opportunity. On the other hand, they had come to realize that opportunity alone was not enough. Negroes had to be able to take advantage of opportunities made available to them. Edwin C. Berry

[6] Samuel Lubell, *White and Black: Test of a Nation* (New York: Harper and Row, Publishers, 1964), pp. 1-2.

lamented in 1963 that "if full freedom came today—equality of opportunity—Negroes would not have one more job, one more good house, one whit more education than they had the day before it came."[7] Berry and other Urban League leaders, along with those of other organizations, realized that in large measure this called for work beyond boycotts, picket lines, and demonstrations. These were important, but the next step was for Negroes to prepare themselves through education, training, and stable families to enter the mainstream of American life. But if the first step was difficult, the second was even more so. As Martin Luther King, Jr. pointed out: "The average Negro is born into want and deprivation. His struggle to escape his circumstances is hindered by color discrimination. He is deprived of normal education and normal social and economic opportunities. When he seeks opportunity, he is told in effect, to lift himself by his own bootstraps, advice which does not take into account the fact that he is barefoot."[8]

The Urban League also realized that the masses of Negroes have no bootstraps. Soon after becoming executive director of the National Urban League, Whitney M. Young, Jr. was calling for a program of "action research" by the Urban League movement to focus attention on and properly interpret social problems in Negro communities. In addition, local League affiliates were urged to intensify their work on family disorganization, the major cause of social problems.[9] Young knew, however, that in the final analysis the Urban League and the Negro community were not equal to this task. His comprehensive program called for an "unprecedented domestic 'Marshall Plan' approach to these problems." Young declared:

> The American Negro has been out of the mainstream for more than three centuries and a special effort must be made to bring him into the central action of our society. The effects of more than three centuries of oppression cannot be obliterated by doing business as usual. In today's complex, technological society, a sound mind, a strong back, and a will to succeed are no longer sufficient to break the bonds of deprivation as was the case with minority groups in the past.[10]

But the domestic "Marshall Plan" was a long range solution. In

---

[7] Minutes of the Board of Directors, Sept. 17, 1963.

[8] Martin Luther King, Jr., *Why We Can't Wait* (New York: Harper and Row, Publishers, 1963), p. 11.

[9] Louis E. Lomax, *The Negro Revolt* (New York: Harper and Row, Publishers, 1962), pp. 209-218.

[10] Whitney M. Young Jr., *To Be Equal* (New York: McGraw-Hill Book Co., 1964), pp. 26-27.

the meantime the Urban League had to "seek the solution within the framework of Negro society itself" and through cooperative effort with others committed to Urban League objectives.[11] These were the challenges facing the Chicago Urban League, as well as other local branches, in the 1960's.

The greater efficiency and flexibility in administrative organization instituted after 1956 facilitated adjustments to the increased demands made on the Chicago League. The old programing departments — industrial relations, public education (public relations), and community organization — were reorganized and renamed. Only the research department retained its old title. The employment and guidance, community education, and community services departments had broader responsibilities and were more flexible in approach than their antecedents. Although each department concentrated primarily on programs within its own area, unified projects and shifts in emphasis took place without severe disruption of routine functions.

Up to 1962 the Youth Guidance Project remained the principal concern of the employment and guidance department. This project — begun in 1957 — was important for a number of reasons. Since the Association of Commerce and Industry, the Community Trust, and the Division Fund supported it with special grants, the project was not a financial burden. Many regular program features were incorporated into the guidance program and thus freed financial resources for use in other areas. Moreover, the problems connected with preparing Negro youth to take advantage of employment opportunities were significant and required solution. Another far from negligible benefit to the League was the lines of communication the program opened with the Association of Commerce and with Chicago business and industrial leaders.

The project met with general approbation from business groups and received financial support through 1961. The agency presented a two-year project report to the education committee of the Association of Commerce in March, 1960. The report was well received, and the committee recommended that the Association's board of directors renew its $10,000 grant. Although the grant was renewed, the Association's board instructed its education committee to review the policy of making such recurring contributions. An influential member of the Urban League's board also felt that it was time to

[11] *Ibid.*, p. 225.

incorporate the project into the League's regular operating budget.[12] The agency was forced to do this after 1961. In spite of continued expressions of satisfaction with the accomplishments made and a recommendation from its education committee to renew the grant for 1962, the Association's board withdrew its support.[13]

In the meantime, the employment and guidance department was working with the other League departments to get fair employment (FEP) legislation through the Illinois General Assembly. After fourteen years of failure, success finally came in 1961. The Urban League employed its full complement of tactics to help achieve this victory in the war against discrimination in employment. Over the years, there had been many individuals and groups working separately and conjointly for an FEP law in Illinois, and they all contributed in varying degrees to the final result. Nevertheless, Urban League activities were such in 1961 that Berry could boast that "the Urban League made the difference."

The publicized aspects of the League's work, and most of its covert activities, adhered closely to traditional methods. In December, 1960 the Urban League board unanimously reaffirmed the agency's unequivocal stand in favor of fair employment practices and pledged a continuation of "research, educational, organizational, and cooperative activities" leading to the passage and acceptance of an FEP law.[14] Now the departments could launch programs within the limits prescribed by this resolution. Research furnished the "facts and figures" for testimony before legislative committees and for use in mobilizing community groups. The community services department had the task of working with and through organizations of all types throughout the state to marshall public support.[15] Berry described this work as follows: "We did all the regular things involved in community organization — we visited groups and leaders — we provided them with educational materials and know-how in planning and programming — we exploited mass media always playing up the contribution of others. We studied the pressure points — we made sure that the constellation of supporting agencies and groups

[12] Minutes of the Board of Directors, April 5, 1960. See also *Chicago Tribune,* May 12, 1960.

[13] Minutes of the Board of Directors, Oct. 25, 1960; Feb. 20, 1962.

[14] Resolution Regarding Equal Job Opportunity, approved by Board of Directors, Chicago Urban League, Dec. 13, 1960.

[15] Executive Director's Report to the Chicago Urban League Board of Directors, Jan. 16, 1962.

gave expression of approval to the legislative supporters of F.E.P. . . . and that they worked with those in the Senate who had to be convinced if we were to win."[16]

The culmination of what Berry termed the "public and flamboyant" part of the League's program was a leadership conference sponsored by the employment and guidance department. Some one thousand representatives of four hundred different organizations met at Dunbar High School on February 25, 1961. They listened to speakers explain the need for and the purpose of FEP legislation, describe the provisions of the bill to be introduced in the legislature, and exhort them as to what they and their organizations could do to promote passage of the bill. The representatives also spent an hour in workshop sessions discussing specific ways to help in the campaign.[17] Commenting editorially on the conference, the editor of the *Daily Defender* declared that it had succeeded in "inoculating the people against the pernicious fallacy of indecision and inaction." Furthermore, the Chicago Urban League had demonstrated "with conviction that the people of this community are ready for constructive and effective action."[18]

Once people had been motivated to act, some organization needed to coordinate their activities and bring pressure to bear where it would count — on members of the General Assembly. The Urban League could not, however, perform this function. By policy and because of the danger of losing its tax-exempt status, the League was prohibited from lobbying on legislative matters. This did not, however, prevent the League and its individual officials and board members from cooperating with organizations that did lobby. Such an organization, the Illinois Committee for Fair Employment Practices, had existed for some time. Professor James Q. Wilson found, however, that it had been hampered in the 1940's and most of the 1950's by disunity among Negro organizations, lack of financial support from Negroes, and some rivalry "between the state NAACP conference and white groups as to which should organize the FEPC campaign."[19]

---

[16] *Ibid.*

[17] Chicago Urban League, Leadership Conference for Fair Employment Practices, Feb. 25, 1961 (mimeo. program); *Chicago Daily Defender,* Feb. 27, 1961.

[18] *Ibid.,* Feb. 28, 1961.

[19] James Q. Wilson, *Negro Politics: The Search for Leadership* (Glencoe, Ill.: The Free Press, 1960), pp. 161-163.

After 1959 the Chicago Urban League was in a better position to help infuse new life into the Illinois Committee, and the NAACP had also become stronger and more stable by this time.[20] During the 1961 campaign, the Urban League worked actively with the Illinois Committee. Richard J. Nelson, manager of the civic affairs division of Inland Steel Corporation, served as its chairman; League president Joseph H. Evans was secretary; and League vice president Hugo B. Law was chairman of the public relations committee.[21] The Committee did a good job of mobilizing support for the bill.

In the final analysis, however, the fate of the measure depended on whether or not enough Republican votes could be obtained to get it through the senate. In the fifty-eight-member senate — consisting of thirty-one Republicans and twenty-seven Democrats — thirty votes were needed to pass the bill. The Illinois Committee felt that twenty-five, or possibly twenty-six, Democrats could be counted on to vote for passage. Only one Republican, however, had voted for FEP in 1959. Of seven new Republican senators, the positions of six were uncertain, but three of the six had indicated that they might be persuaded to vote favorably. The big job, then, was to secure at least four additional votes — most of which would have to be Republican — while holding those already favorably disposed toward FEP.[22]

The Urban League did not rely on the "public and flamboyant" aspects of the program to sway these votes. As Berry said: "Something else was going on quietly and behind the facade of articulation and public demonstration." Members of the League's board worked to bring personal and organizational influence to bear on Republican senators.

The agency claimed major credit for two rather significant developments resulting from this tactic. By mid-April the Chicago Association of Commerce and Industry had passed a resolution endorsing FEP legislation in principle, and the Association's staff was instructed to frame recommendations for amending the bill then before the senate. Urban League board member Frank H. Cassell of Inland Steel was credited with spearheading the procedure which led to the Association's unprecedented resolution. He

[20] *Ibid.*, p. 163.
[21] Minutes of the Board of Directors, Feb. 21, 1961.
[22] Illinois Committee for Fair Employment Practices, The FEPC Story in Illinois with Voting Records, Feb. 25, 1961 (copy in program for Chicago Urban League Leadership Conference for Fair Employment Practices).

was backed by other League board members and other sympathetic Association members from various Chicago firms. James C. Worthy felt that the Association's action stemmed largely from the favorable atmosphere and changed attitudes produced by the cooperation between the Association and the Urban League in sponsoring the Youth Guidance Project.[23]

Urban League officials also felt that they had been instrumental in helping to transform FEP into a bipartisan issue. For years FEP in Illinois had been considered a Democratic measure. Consequently, it always passed the house, usually controlled by Democrats, and was always killed in the Republican-controlled senate. In 1961, however, there were indications that some Republicans were beginning to accept FEP, at least in principle. Symbolic of this changing opinion was a "surprise appearance" before the senate by Charles Percy — the dynamic young chairman of the board of Bell and Howell whom President Eisenhower had appointed in 1959 to head the Republican Committee on Program and Progress — to testify in favor of FEP legislation. League board members had conferred with Percy and other Republican leaders, and they claimed credit for helping persuade him to testify.[24]

After the bill had been enacted into law, signed by the Governor, and a commission appointed to administer it, the League's executive director summed up the Urban League's view of its contribution to the successful campaign. Berry exclaimed:

> It was a great victory — a bipartisan victory, with the Urban League working with and on all sides of the battle without agency identification with either political party — without lobbying, but always recognizing, stimulating and complimenting the contributions of all individuals and groups willing to help.[25]

Yet, the struggle for an effective legal remedy for discrimination in employment was not over. In 1964 and 1965 the efforts by FEP supporters to strengthen the law were countered by a Republican campaign to emasculate the statute and to intimidate members of the FEP Commission. An Urban League staff member cautioned the board of directors in May, 1965 that the agency could not

---

[23] See Executive Director's Report, Jan. 16, 1962; Minutes of the Board of Directors, Apr. 18, 1961; May 16, 1961.

[24] *Ibid.,* Apr. 18, 1961.

[25] Executive Director's Report, Jan. 16, 1962.

relax its vigilance because it was necessary to continue to "sell and re-sell the concept of FEP."[26]

Nevertheless, the FEP law, coming during a period of changing national sentiment, eventually had a great impact on the League's work in employment and guidance. After 1956 the Chicago League abandoned its attempt to operate a mass placement office and concentrated its efforts on trying to break patterns of discrimination. Dramatic accomplishments were few in the 1950's. By 1963, however, the impact of the civil rights movement, of Executive Orders by Presidents John F. Kennedy and Lyndon Johnson, and of the Illinois FEP statute began to open opportunities to Negroes with the requisite skills and training. In fact, requests for well-trained Negroes came faster than qualified people could be found. "The young, well-trained Negro," Berry wrote in 1964, "now has a chance to get into the mainstream of American economic life." His employment and guidance staff, however, was having trouble meeting the demands made on them. "They are under pressure to provide the 'instant Negro.' The employer names the job specification for which he wants a Negro and we are supposed to produce one to fill the spot with the same magic as producing a genii out of a bottle."[27] With so many businesses searching for talented "token Negroes" to show federal officials that their firms did not discriminate, Negro comedian Dick Gregory wondered if the well-known automobile rental company might not soon open a "Hertz-Rent-a-Negro" agency.

The humor of the situation was rather sardonic; for Negroes still comprised the largest percentage of the unemployed and still overloaded the welfare rolls. Yet, it was encouraging to see more talented Negroes finally getting jobs commensurate with their training and abilities. But what about the unskilled, the inadequately trained, and the Negro with only average talents? While the Urban League was helping push the talented through the opening gates of

[26] Minutes of the Board of Directors, May 11, 1965. The Republican campaign against FEP — based on a finding of discrimination by the Commission against the Motorola Corporation — was widely reported in the Chicago press in 1964 and 1965. The *Chicago Tribune* was the chief organ of the opponents of FEP. Reactions of the Urban League staff and board of directors can be found in the Minutes of the Board of Directors for Dec. 8, 1964; Mar. 9, 1965, Apr. 13, 1965, and May 11, 1965.

[27] Edwin C. Berry, "The Menace of Unemployment: Jobs, Poverty and Race," *Negro Digest,* XIII (Sept., 1964), 7-8.

opportunity, it also needed to be concerned about those who could not even reach the threshold.

In late 1962, the League began an experimental job-training program to aid unskilled welfare recipients. This was part of a broader program of job development, which was described as having the objectives of "bringing workers and jobs together, opening up new employment opportunities for skilled workers, for the youth in the community, and returning older and displaced workers to the work force."[28] The special job training project began as a cooperative venture with the Yellow Cab Company and the Cook County Department of Public Aid. A short training course was established to train welfare recipients as taxicab drivers. Those who completed the course were employed by the Yellow Cab Company. These men became self-supporting and, thus, were removed from the welfare rolls.[29] In March, 1963 the employment and guidance department reported that 156 men had completed the course and were averaging $100 a week in salary. By this time, the Cook County Department of Public Aid had taken over the training program.[30]

A similar project was begun with the Shell Oil Company to train gas station attendants. The Shell Oil project graduated its first class of thirty men in May. This brought the total number who had finished both projects to 230, and by June, 1964 the Yellow Cab Company and Shell Oil Company had hired 1,270 men off the relief rolls.[31]

The first major call for Urban League assistance in implementing a fair employment program came from Chicago banks. In August, 1963 James Baxter — a First National Bank of Chicago vice president, who attended the Urban League business luncheon series — arranged for Berry and two staff members to meet with the bank's personnel officials. These bank officers said that they wanted to open all jobs "from the beginning to management trainees" and asked the League to find qualified people to fill the openings.[32] Shortly after the conference at the First National Bank, five large commercial banks asked the League to screen applicants for them. The employment and guidance department gave top priority to

[28] Minutes of the Board of Directors, Nov. 20, 1962.
[29] *Ibid.*
[30] Executive Director's Quarterly Report to the Chicago Urban League Board of Directors, Mar. 19, 1963.
[31] Minutes of the Board of Directors, May 21, 1963; June 16, 1964.
[32] *Ibid.*, Aug. 20, 1963.

screening applicants for these surprising breakthroughs. Within a few weeks, the staff interviewed approximately 800 applicants and placed about twenty-four in bank jobs on varying levels.[33] During 1963 other firms called for assistance in implementing equal job opportunities programs, and the Association of Commerce and Industry began to encourage its members to institute such programs. In 1965 the Association formed a merit employment committee to "obtain from employers a voluntary reaffirmation of their merit employment policy and a public recognition of the need for such a program as representing good business as well as good citizenship."[34]

Several of the firms seeking Negro employees realized that the League could not supply "instant Negroes." The president of the Harris Trust Company, for example, asked the Urban League staff to assist with the firm's "pre-training program" for bank employees. Harris Trust planned to place promising young people in this training program, pay them a small stipend while in training, and assure them a job upon successful completion of the course.[35] Western Electric Company, which had already instituted a comprehensive equal opportunities program, also began a training project to relieve the general shortage of typists.[36]

As another means of bringing employers and Negroes with special skills together, the National Urban League established a Skills Bank.[37] A $100,000 grant from the Rockefeller Brothers Foundation made the project possible. The Chicago branch followed the National's example and started its own Talent and Skills Bank in 1963. According to the executive director, the Chicago bank would facilitate the League's job of "seeking promising young Negroes" and "locating under-employed and under-utilized Negroes with special skills and potentialities." It was hoped that the National League would share its grant with the Chicago League.[38] The Chicago project became one of five regional Skill Banks, and the National Urban League contributed $15,000 annually toward its support.[39] By mid-1964 the Chicago Urban League staff had interviewed 5,930

[33] *Ibid.,* Sept. 17, 1963.
[34] *Chicago Tribune,* July 26, 1965.
[35] Minutes of the Board of Directors, Sept. 17, 1963.
[36] *Ibid.,* Apr. 21, 1964.
[37] Young, *To Be Equal,* p. 85.
[38] Minutes of the Board of Directors, Sept. 17, 1963.
[39] *Ibid.,* Nov. 19, 1963.

applicants, screened and cleared 681 for placement, and placed 502 on jobs.[40]

In the general field of community services, the principal areas of concern were housing, racial violence, and the schools. It had been recognized for some time that discrimination in housing was a key barrier to integration in other areas. Moreover, much of Chicago's racial violence over the years had its roots in housing segregation. The primary importance of this problem was poignantly summarized in the introduction to a Chicago Urban League research report. After outlining the economic hardships suffered by Negroes and whites as accretions to the ghetto took place, the broader implications for Negroes, the city, and the nation were treated. The report stated: "Segregation in education, employment, social life, all are direct results of residential segregation. . . . The whole society is harmed by this process — harmed by the divisiveness of a segregated society, harmed by having to bear the burdens of Negro unemployment, harmed by the under-utilization of a large proportion of our manpower and brainpower, harmed by the image our segregated system gives the world, harmed by the unreality of living in a divided world."[41]

Given the significance of housing, it would seem that discrimination in this area would have been a major target of Negro protest. Housing, however, became a subordinate issue to employment and schools in the 1960's. There were probably several reasons for this. In the first place, white resistance remained strongest against efforts to integrate neighborhoods. Real-estate interests and other influential groups with vested interest in a dual housing market threw their considerable weight against integration. Another factor was the divided sentiment that existed within the Negro community. One scholar reported Negro politicians, for example, reluctant to embrace open occupancy. The dispersal of the Negro population would destroy their source of political strength.[42] In addition, integrated housing, as opposed to better housing, had come to be considered as largely a middle-class goal. The Chicago Commission on Human Relations concluded from a 1963 survey of states with fair housing laws that "the demand to own, rent, lease, or co-op by

---

[40] *Ibid.,* June 16, 1964.

[41] Chicago Urban League Research Report, "Housing and Race in Chicago: A Preliminary Analysis of 1960 Census Data," July, 1963, p. 1.

[42] Wilson, *Negro Politics,* pp. 202-205.

Negroes outside established neighborhoods comes chiefly from middle-income families."[43]

This does not mean that discrimination in housing was not an important area of protest. The Chicago Urban League, however, devoted a comparatively minor proportion of its resources to this problem. In many respects, the agency's fair housing program was a replica in miniature of its fair employment activities. The board of directors made a formal program possible by adopting a housing policy statement in early 1960. The statement reaffirmed the League's position that it was the right of "all persons to have the opportunity to secure housing wherever their economic capabilities and desires lead them." Staff members were encouraged to institute programs of "research, education and legislation" to help achieve the goal of equality in housing opportunity. Communication with representatives of the housing industry was also urged as a means of influencing changes in direction and policies.[44] Nevertheless, some board members seemed somewhat reticent for the agency to become too closely identified with this issue. In discussing a proposed League-sponsored housing conference, one board member was reported as suggesting that "the League should stimulate other organizations to join in on plans. He felt this should be a community-wide concern — as much the concern of whites as Negroes. He felt further that the League should try to involve the middle group of people. This will convince them that this is not strictly an Urban League or NAACP meeting, but is one of community-wide nature."[45]

The board also had trouble agreeing on a policy on "block-busting." This was the practice whereby some real-estate men moved a Negro family onto an all-white block and then, by using scare tactics, bought homes at below their value from whites to resell them at inflated prices to Negroes. Although Negroes resented the economic exploitation involved, this was an important means of acquiring more housing by expanding the ghetto. The suggested League policy statement would have put the agency on record as "categorically opposed" to the practice, while recognizing that it sprang from dis-

---

[43] Chicago Commission on Human Relations, *A Report to the Mayor and the City Council of Chicago on the Present Status and Effectiveness of Existing Fair Housing Practices Legislation in the United States as of April 1, 1963* (Chicago: City of Chicago, 1963), p. 4.

[44] Minutes of the Board of Directors, Jan. 19, 1960.

[45] *Ibid.,* Feb. 9, 1960.

crimination and prejudice. A Negro member of the board objected to the statement on the grounds that it "seemed to indicate that the League was opposed to Negroes moving into new blocks." In the end, the board approved the policy in principle and sent it back to the community services advisory committee for extensive revision.[46]

Even so, the League's housing activities were rather varied. During each legislative session, a staff member testified in favor of fair housing legislation. Urban League testimony, citing statistics, usually emphasized the causes of segregation and its baneful social and economic consequences.[47] Beginning in 1960 the League worked through the United Citizens' Committee for Freedom of Residence (FOR) to get an open occupancy bill through the legislature. By 1965 the fair housing campaign was gaining momentum, and the League was an active participant. It was hoped that this would be the year that an open occupancy bill would be enacted into law. In spite of the more intensive campaign, culminating in a demonstration on the steps of the capitol in Springfield, the General Assembly failed to pass a fair housing law. In fact, up to mid-1965 little significant progress had been made in combating segregated housing in Chicago.

Between 1960 and the summer of 1965, League efforts to reduce racial violence were supplementary to the work of many other public and private agencies. The Urban League's program concentrated mainly on working for effective police action and on arousing the public to an awareness of the potential danger. The League's Council of Religious Leaders was active in both of these areas. Composed of seventy ministers, priests, and rabbis in 1960, membership in the Council almost doubled by 1965. Council members exhorted the members of their congregations to work to relieve tensions; and where violence broke out or threatened to break out, they went in to work with the people of the areas involved and to act as observers of police practices. These activities heralded the increasing participation of religious leaders, as individuals and as members of organized groups, in the campaign for improved race relations in the city.

[46] *Ibid.*, Jan. 17, 1961.

[47] See, for example, Chicago Urban League, "Testimony of the Chicago Urban League to the House Executive Committee 72nd General Assembly, State of Illinois in Behalf of HB 171, the Fair Housing Act of 1961," March 15, 1961 (mimeo.), and Chicago Urban League, "Testimony . . . Before the Senate Committee on Licensing and Miscellany on House Bill 257," May, 1965 (mimeo.).

The Urban League also helped to break through the newspaper curtain thrown around incidents of racial violence. The Chicago press adopted a policy of not publicizing racial incidents after the 1919 race riot. It was felt that the absence of publicity would keep small disturbances from spreading and from inciting more generalized rioting. Radio and television embraced this policy and helped to maintain the "barrier of silence." Ordinarily, this seemed to be a sound policy, but as tensions increased, League officials felt that public opinion should be brought to bear as a deterrent to perpetrators of mob violence. With the mass media silent, however, the general public, League officials maintained, was probably unaware of the prevalence of racial incidents and how great the potential was for large-scale conflict.

The Chicago Commission on Human Relations was concerned about the increasing number of violent incidents during the summer of 1961. A Commission representative reported to the League's Council of Religious Leaders that by July there had been 260 incidents reported to the Commission, compared with 211 for all of 1960.[48] At the end of the year, the Commission's annual report tried to minimize the danger by attributing the large number of complaints it received to, among other factors, "greater public awareness of the work of the Commission, increased confidence in the police department, and a nation-wide spirit of militance among Negroes."[49]

As a means of alerting the public to the danger, Hugo B. Law and Edwin C. Berry proposed that the League sponsor a newspaper advertisement. In July, 1961 Berry asked the Urban League board to endorse the statement — called a "Chicago Declaration of Democracy" — and approve League participation in the project. The success of the plan depended upon the League's ability to involve the major religious organizations and to solicit "various leaders in all levels of the community" as signators.[50] Representatives of several religious groups endorsed and supported the project. These included officers or staff members from the Church Federation of Greater Chicago, the Union of American Hebrew Congregations, the Catholic Interracial Council, the Chicago Board of Rabbis, and

---

[48] Minutes of the Board of Directors, July 18, 1961.
[49] Chicago Commission on Human Relations, *Highlights of 1961: Annual Report* (Chicago: Commission on Human Relations, 1962), p. 3.
[50] Minutes of the Board of Directors, July 18, 1961.

the Department of Christian Social Relations of the Episcopal Diocese of Chicago.

The big job was to obtain the needed signatures and contributions to pay for the advertisement. Several League board members assisted in this effort. They worked on the premise that if they first secured the signatures of "top business men" others would be relatively easy to obtain. Three board members concentrated on contacting white business leaders. Not many names were secured, but "they were particularly glad of the quality of the names they secured." Actually, the number was limited by the number of people contacted; for only two "turn-downs" were reported. Others, "without persuasion, attached their signatures to the declaration," and when the statement appeared, it was signed by 404 "prominent Chicagoans."[51] In assessing the effects of the project, Berry reported: "The drama of the ad attracted so much attention and was written on so widely, and interracial violence was so sharply reduced that the agreement of silence regarding news on violence was broken and I believe shall not be reinstituted in Chicago."[52]

During the school year 1961-62, school problems began to overshadow other race relations issues. The Chicago Urban League was instrumental in bringing this issue to the fore by helping to foment unrest in the Negro community over the quality of education offered in the schools. As a result, however, it again drew criticism from the Community Fund and motivated a former board member to launch a crusade seeking the return of the agency to the conservative principles of the reorganization period.

The school question was a compound of rather complex problems. Robert J. Havighurst summarized the situation facing northern cities in the introduction to his survey of Chicago schools. Professor Havighurst wrote:

> About 1960 there arose a public concern over the school program. Changes in the socioeconomic composition of the city, as well as new developments in methods of teaching and problems of de facto segregation, contributed to this often controversial discussion. This happened in all the northern industrial cities which had received substantial numbers of Negro workers from the South after the war. At the same time there were searching questions about the school program for all pupils, due to the atmosphere of criticism which political, economic, and scientific events of the 1950 decade produced. The big cities were all having "growing

---

[51] *Ibid.,* Aug. 15, 1961.

[52] Executive Director's Report, Jan. 16, 1962.

pains" related not to their own physical growth but rather to their deterioration combined with the growth of their suburbs.[53]

Even at the time Professor Havighurst was making his investigation, concern over the broader questions of the general quality of education offered in Chicago schools was being submerged by the controversy over segregation and integration. For decades Chicago had operated double shifts in some schools. This practice began during the depression, and afterwards the city was not able to build facilities fast enough to house its rapidly growing school population. Between 1930 and 1940, however, few Negroes were affected by the double shift arrangement; but during the next two decades, double shift schools became characteristic of Negro areas. By 1961 nearly all schools on split shifts served Negro neighborhoods.[54] Furthermore, there was little doubt that schools in Negro areas were attended almost exclusively by Negro children, and schools in white neighborhoods were attended by white children. Although some schools were considered integrated, a decreasing percentage of Chicago children attended such schools; and many so-called integrated schools were actually becoming segregated, or — to use the common euphemism — were in transition from predominately white to predominately Negro.

The fact that segregation existed, as Negro organizations were contending with increasing vigor, was shown by the Board of Education's racial headcount in October, 1963 and confirmed by the Advisory Panel on Integration of the Public Schools — the Hauser Panel — under the chairmanship of Philip M. Hauser. The Panel's report stated bluntly: "Negro children and teachers and other staff in the Chicago Public School System are, by and large, concentrated in predominantly Negro schools located in predominately Negro areas in the city."[55] The Hauser Panel denied, however, that this segregation resulted from "intent or design" on the part of the Board of Education. Rather, it was a "by-product of segregated patterns of settlement and housing," which was, in turn, a "product

[53] Robert J. Havighurst, *The Public Schools of Chicago: A Survey for the Board of Education of the City of Chicago* (Chicago: Board of Education of the City of Chicago, 1964), p. 2.

[54] U.S. Commission on Civil Rights, *Civil Rights U.S.A.: Public Schools, Cities in the North and West* (Washington: Government Printing Office, 1962), p. 223.

[55] Advisory Panel on Integration of the Public Schools, *Report to the Board of Education City of Chicago* (Chicago: Board of Education of the City of Chicago, Mar. 31, 1964), p. 3.

of forces built deep into the social, economic, and political fabric of the nation."[56] Nevertheless, the Panel proclaimed the elimination of *de facto* segregation to be both "legally and morally necessary." It also warned of the necessity for prompt action. The report stated:

> The problem is acute. The time for decisive action has come. It remains for reasonable men of good will, ignoring unreasonable positions on either side, to pursue indomitably the clear legal and moral goal and to achieve a solution to the sore problems which beset us.[57]

The Chicago Board of Education approved in principle both the findings and the recommendations of the Hauser Panel, but this action represented only a very small first step. Finally, it seemed that the Board had formally recognized that segregation existed in Chicago schools and that it had a legal and moral obligation to do something to promote integration. The Board remained reluctant to go beyond this feeble first step. As the school year 1964-65 drew to a close, the Chicago Urban League again documented the obvious in a research report. The researcher concluded:

> A year and a half after the Chicago Board of Education sought expert advice on school segregation, and a year after its Advisory Panel on Integration reported, public school segregation has increased rather than diminished. The number of segregated schools has increased. Pupil segregation has increased.
>
> From the standpoints of both school and race, Negro pupils are now more segregated than they were last school term. . . .[58]

It had taken nearly four years of protesting and legal action to push the Chicago Board of Education to the point where it would even approve in principle the findings and recommendations of the Hauser Report. The Chicago school protest movement probably received its principal stimulation in September, 1961 when a group of Negro parents filed a suit in the United States District Court for the Northern District of Illinois against the Chicago Board of Education and the general superintendent of schools. The plaintiffs in *Webb v. The Board of Education* charged that a deliberate policy of segregation was followed by school officials in violation of the Fourteenth Amendment and asked for injunctive relief for themselves and others similarly situated. Gerrymandering of school dis-

[56] *Ibid.*, p. 4.
[57] *Ibid.*, p. 43.
[58] Chicago Urban League Research Report, "Public School Segregation: City of Chicago 1963-1964 and 1964-1965," May 12, 1965, p. 3.

tricts, selecting school sites to insure the racial homogeneity of attendance areas, following the neighborhood school policy, and underutilizing space in white schools — these, the plaintiffs contended, were some of the devices used to maintain segregation. Benjamin C. Willis, general superintendent of schools, denied these charges; and, according to Professor John E. Coons, Dr. Willis, "in general, reaffirmed the policies of the board and supported his position with great factual detail." In 1962, the court dismissed the case, holding that the plaintiffs had not exhausted the remedies available to them under state laws.[59] Nevertheless, the *Webb* case furnished the civil rights movement with a bill of particulars for its campaign against school segregation, and the reintroduction of the suit led to the establishment of the Advisory Panel on Integration as part of an out-of-court settlement.[60]

For some time, the Chicago Urban League had been directing its research toward exploring the points at issue in the school conflict. Materials gathered by the research department were used, from time to time, in presenting testimony at Board of Education hearings and for public education activities. Then, in November, 1961, the executive director presented recommendations for an overall Urban League policy on school integration. The policy recommendations were preceded by a detailed analysis of the school situation as it related to Negro students by Mrs. Olivia Filerman and Harold Baron of the research department. Using maps and charts, Mrs. Filerman and Mr. Baron explained to the board the reasons for the growing concern among Negroes about educational opportunities in the public schools. As evidence of inequality, they pointed to the higher per pupil expenditures in white schools, to the fact that branches of schools had been established in such a way that they were either Negro or white, to the general superintendent's plan for reducing class size to thirty in white schools while classrooms remained overcrowded in Negro schools, and to the fact that over 70 per cent of the students on double shift were Negroes.[61]

Following the research report, the executive director requested board action, in the near future, on recommendations for school

[59] The brief outline of the *Webb* case presented in this paragraph is based on Professor Coons's analysis in U.S. Commission on Civil Rights, *Civil Rights U.S.A.*, pp. 209-211.
[60] Advisory Panel on Integration of the Public Schools, *Report to the Board of Education City of Chicago*, p. 2.
[61] Minutes of the Board of Directors, Nov. 21, 1961.

integration. These recommendations called for redistricting schools "on the periphery of black and white areas" to achieve integration and to relieve overcrowding and double shift schools, where possible. It was recommended that school personnel be assigned "to achieve integration on a faculty level" and that personnel be used on the basis of need and ability, rather than on the basis of race. A human relations program was advised in order to "offer expert guidance of school principals and teachers on the positive teaching of democratic ethics and curriculum building to achieve this goal." Finally, school officials would be asked to " 'bus' students from over-crowded school situations."[62]

The next month Mrs. Filerman again attended the board's meeting to review the materials presented the previous month and to apprise the directors of disturbing findings on classroom utilization disclosed in an Urban League research report released on December 12. She reported that the research department had shown 382 classrooms which had not been reported by Superintendent Willis. Consequently, unused rooms were "available for use by Negro students on doubleshift and in overcrowded classrooms." "These rooms," Mrs. Filerman asserted, "could be used to completely eliminate double shifts tomorrow, if the school board decided to put them to this use." Moreover, many schools with vacant classrooms were found to be within walking distance of Negro students on double shifts.[63]

Since the general superintendent's office no longer reported on vacant space, it had been difficult to get reliable information on space use. Various organizations had made estimates ranging from 25,000 to 75,000 available seats. At the beginning of the 1961-62 school year, some Negro parents tried to enroll their children at schools which reportedly had vacant seats. One mother who tried to register her child outside the district in which she lived explained her action in a letter to the editor of the *Sun-Times*. She had taken her child to the school in her home district on opening day and counted fifty children in her room. The school, built to accommodate 862 students, had an enrollment of about 1,800 children, some on double shifts. Reporting on the school where she tried to register her child, she said that it "did not have two in a seat. They had not only empty seats, but empty rooms. . . . I would rather have

[62] *Ibid.*
[63] *Ibid.*, Dec. 12, 1961.

my child go the the school in our district (which is across the street from us) but not as it is, overcrowded and on double shifts. I would gladly take her out of the district if she could receive a full-day education."[64]

The Urban League's report provided documented information for the growing number of parents and organizations evincing a determination to press for changes in the school situation. Since the League's study was the result of careful research, done by a reputable organization and based on Board of Education figures, it could not be ignored by school officials. The report provoked a year-long controversy over school space use. During this period, in Professor Coons's words, "the public was treated to a statistical display of prodigious and bewildering proportions." The general superintendent issued replies to the League's study on December 18, 1961 and on January 10, 1962. Both statements were unconvincing to school critics. Berry summed up the status of the controversy in mid-January. He reported to the League's board of directors that:

> Mr. Willis plays a "numbers game" — since September he has stated at different times that there are the following number of vacant or available classrooms: 1-14-143-198 — last, Oscar Shabat, Schools Director of Human Relations came up with the figure of 200.
>
> In various reports the Superintendent changes figures, definitions and usage — sometimes he talks of available classrooms, sometimes number of seats — sometimes total classrooms and other times regular classrooms, et al. No one has gotten this information accurately reported and in a standard way — not even his employers, the School Board.[65]

In spite of the seeming *opera bouffe* character of the seat-counting controversy, it was actually a question with serious implications. "If . . . space in fact existed in quantity," wrote Professor Coons, "then the refusal to permit transfers, the maintenance of overcrowded schools and double shifts, the extensive building program in the impacted areas, and the use of mobile units, suggest some serious issues."[66] Groups concerned about civil rights fully appreciated the seriousness of the situation. The Urban League's board approved a request made by the executive director for agency representatives

[64] *Chicago Sun-Times,* Oct. 10, 1961. Newspaper materials cited on the school controversy are from clippings collected by the Chicago Urban League's department of research. The author is indebted to Dr. Harold Baron, director of research, for his kind permission to use these clipping files.

[65] Executive Director's Report, Jan. 16, 1962.

[66] U.S. Commission on Civil Rights, *Civil Rights U.S.A.,* p. 198. This report gives an excellent analysis of the space controversy. See pp. 198-204.

to appear and testify at the Board of Education's budget hearing.[67] Along with spokesmen from the NAACP and CORE, Urban League representatives asked the Board of Education to declare a moratorium on new school construction until available facilities had all been "accounted for and properly used."[68]

The general superintendent of schools seemed determined, however, not to make the type of accounting demanded, and the Board of Education did not order him to do so.[69] Willis chose to separate the questions of overcrowding and integration and, thereby, made the neighborhood school policy synonymous with segregation, especially in the minds of civil rights leaders. Instead of releasing accurate and understandable space use figures, Willis tried to explain away the Urban League's vacant classroom findings and proceeded to redistribute white children, who were not overcrowded or on double shifts, in such a way as to achieve an average class size of thirty.[70] Negroes could interpret his actions as designed to circumvent their demands for quality integrated education by making it possible to justify spending large sums of money for classroom space in Negro neighborhoods. In this way, overcrowding could be relieved and double shifts ended without sending Negro children to white schools. The general superintendent's handling of this matter — while gaining for him the epithet "builder" — probably more than any of his other actions earned him the opprobrium of the civil rights movement and made him symbolic of segregated education in Chicago.

Willis set forth his plans for ending double shifts and relieving overcrowding late in 1961. At the same time, he defended the neighborhood school concept. Chicago's school problems, Willis said, resulted from the migration of people from rural to urban areas, causing a rapidly increasing school population. During the previous decade, school enrollment had increased by 146,000, and it had increased 22,000 in 1961. The policy had been simply to build schools where the children were; moreover, he denied knowing how many schools were all Negro. In any case, he agreed with James B. Conant's opinion, at that time, that Chicago would probably solve the problem of segregation more effectively by not inte-

[67] Minutes of the Board of Directors, Dec. 12, 1961.
[68] *Chicago's American,* Dec. 20, 1961.
[69] *Chicago Defender,* June 14, 1962.
[70] See U.S. Commission on Civil Rights, *Civil Rights U.S.A.,* pp. 199-200.

grating just for the sake of integration.[71] Dr. Willis did not think that the schools should become involved in such "welfare causes as the care, feeding, and transportation of children."[72]

The Willis plan called for securing mobile classrooms and renting space. He broached the subject of using trailers to eliminate double shifts in the November meeting of the Board of Education, and in December he asked for authorization to secure mobiles and to negotiate for classroom space in high rise apartments. As to vacant classrooms, Willis said that only fourteen empty rooms existed which were not scheduled to be used in the near future.[73] The Chicago Urban League, using its study of unused space as a basis, wrote to each member of the Board of Education requesting that action on using mobile classrooms be postponed until existing buildings were used.[74]

Implementation of the Willis program brought reactions from Negro groups. Spontaneously organized groups of parents, sometimes assisted by ministerial associations, led protests in the Englewood community.[75] Parents on the West Side launched a futile boycott and called upon the NAACP for assistance in negotiating with school officials. In less than two weeks, however, the West Side boycott ended without any notable accomplishments.[76]

The most aggressive protest came from Woodlawn which, unlike the other areas, had a dynamic community organization. In 1958 three Protestant ministers and a Catholic priest took steps which resulted in an invitation to Saul D. Alinsky of the Industrial Areas Foundation to come in and organize the community. Alinsky finally accepted the invitation and began work in 1960. With financial backing from the Schwartzhaupt Foundation and the Roman Catholic Archdiocese of Chicago, the militant Temporary Woodlawn Organization — later called The Woodlawn Organization

[71] *Chicago Defender,* Dec. 7, 1961.
[72] *Chicago Tribune,* Feb. 6, 1962.
[73] *Ibid.,* Dec. 12, 1961.
[74] *Ibid.* See also *Chicago's American,* Dec. 12, 1961.
[75] This group protested the use of mobile classrooms at Parker Elementary School. They achieved a minor victory by boycotting and forcing the closing of a warehouse which had been converted into an elementary school. See *Southtown Economist,* Feb. 25, 1962; *Chicago Sun-Times,* Feb. 2, 1963; *Chicago Defender,* Feb. 2-8, 1963; *Chicago Daily News,* Feb. 5, 1963.
[76] *Chicago Sun-Times,* June 19, 1962. See *Chicago Daily Defender,* Mar. 20, 1962; *Chicago Defender,* June 9-15, 1962; *Chicago Sun-Times,* June 8, 1962; *Chicago Tribune,* June 19, 1962.

(TWO) — was launched. Urban Renewal was the major issue motivating the formation of TWO; and, consequently, two of its first targets were the powerful University of Chicago and the city administration.[77]

At the same time, however, TWO was intimately and aggressively involved in the controversy over school conditions. Becoming adept at employing shock tactics, TWO was one of the most militant activist groups in the civil rights movement. It held a mass protest meeting in November, 1961 featuring teachers hooded in sheets to protect their identity.[78] The organization carried its fight downtown, where members picketed the Inland Steel Buildings where William Caples, president of the Board of Education, had his offices. Soon after the picketing began, Caples asked not to be reappointed to the Board when his term expired in April, 1962, but he denied that TWO picketing had anything to do with his decision.[79] When mobile classrooms were brought into Woodlawn, schools receiving them were boycotted, and signs appeared in homes throughout the district proclaiming: "No Willis Wagons."[80]

TWO also became involved in the vacant classroom dispute. Following attempts to refute the Chicago Urban League research findings, TWO sent groups of mothers, "truth squads," into white schools to investigate space use and to photograph any vacant classrooms found. Other members staged sit-in and walk-in demonstrations at overcrowded Negro schools. Measures taken by school officials to counter TWO activities only served to stimulate the growth of the organization and to increase its prestige. On "the very day the Negro mothers who had been sitting-in for weeks at the Burnside School planned to give up," wrote Georgie Geyer, "they were arrested, thus reinvigorating their cause."[81] Four "truth squad" mothers were arrested in February, 1962, and later were tried and convicted of criminal trespassing.[82] The actions of the

[77] An extensive treatment of TWO can be found in Charles E. Silberman, *Crisis in Black and White* (New York: Random House, 1964), pp. 308-355. Also useful is Georgie Anne Geyer, "Woodlawn: A Community in Revolt," *Chicago Scene,* III (June 7, 1962), 12-17.

[78] *Chicago Sun-Times,* Nov. 7, 1961.

[79] *Chicago Daily Defender,* Jan. 24, 1962; Feb. 22, 1962; *Chicago's American,* Mar. 7, 1962; *Chicago Daily News,* Mar. 7, 1962.

[80] *Chicago Sun-Times,* May 19, 1962; *Chicago Daily News,* May 18, 1962; *Chicago's American,* May 18, 1962.

[81] Geyer, *Chicago Scene,* III, 17.

[82] *Chicago Sun-Times,* Apr. 10, 1962; Apr. 20, 1962; *Chicago Defender,* May 16, 1962.

mothers were applauded in the Negro community. The editor of the *Chicago Daily Defender* declared that the judge who handed down the verdict had done "a disservice to this city and democracy by upholding a conviction which arose out of the efforts of the magnificent mothers to bring racial equality and justice into Chicago's public schools."[83]

The events of 1961 and 1962 were only the opening skirmishes of a continuing struggle, which has grown in complexity and intensity over the years. Since 1962 sit-ins and demonstrations have continued, city-wide boycotts have been staged, new litigation has been instituted, and appeals have been made to the federal government for assistance. First the activities of one then another organization have come to the fore, and a federation of civil rights organizations, the Co-ordinating Council of Community Organizations, has been created to bring some unity into the struggle.[84] Throughout these years, 1961-65, the Chicago Urban League has been able to maintain the respect and confidence of the more aggressive organizations. At the same time, it has attracted and held the support and goodwill of business and industrial interests. This was no small achievement.

---

[83] *Chicago Daily Defender,* May 22, 1962.

[84] It is beyond the purview of this chapter to provide an exhaustive treatment of the school controversy. Newspaper accounts are probably the best sources of information, at this time, on events since 1962. See, for example, the summary of developments made by Basil Talbott, Jr. in the *Chicago Sunday Sun-Times,* July 11, 1965.

10

SINCE 1960: ECHOES OF THE REORGANIZATION

Of the major organizations participating in the school protest movement, the Chicago Urban League was probably most susceptible to pressures from defenders of the status quo. These pressures, as in the past, created internal problems; but in the changed climate of opinion on race relations prevailing in the 1960's, the League could not be forced to make radical concessions to conservative demands. In some respects, the attacks on the League in the 1960's were beneficial to the agency. They forced Urban League officials to evaluate programs rather carefully and to give more precise definition to the role the agency should perform as a participant in the "Negro Revolution." In addition, the League worked to clarify its relationships with the Welfare Council and the Community Fund. The strength and vitality displayed by the Chicago Urban League in 1965 probably resulted as much from the conflicts of the 1960's as from the reorganization of the 1950's.

The chief critic of the Urban League's role in the school controversy was Dr. Nathaniel O. Calloway. In late January, 1962, Calloway clipped pictures from the *Chicago Defender* showing Edwin Berry and Wesley Cobb, deputy director of the Chicago League, among a group of pickets in front of the Willard School addition and enclosed copies in letters to officials of the Association of Commerce and Industry. Calloway said that he was "very chagrined at this picture." It evidenced to him a turning away from the principles established during the 1955 reorganization. Whatever the problem was at the school, Calloway was sure it only required mediation. He had always "hoped that the Urban League would be the organization that would act to mediate this sort of difficulty rather than being the organization that would pour fat on the fire and fan the flames." The hope was expressed that the matter would be "kept in mind" the next time the League's subscription and fund-raising programs were considered.[1]

It was over a month after the first letters from Dr. Calloway had gone out before the League's board of directors began learning the exact nature of the problem they faced. The executive director noted in his February report to the board that there had been "some criticism of the League's part in the school program." The executive knew that "someone" had written a letter to the former head of the Association of Commerce and Industry's Subscription Division implying that he and Cobb had violated Urban League policy by being on a picket line. In defense of his and Cobb's presence at the school, Berry said that they were there as observers. He continued: "It is our business to know all we can from eye-witness accounts [about] the important things that are going on. We also have observed the activities of CORE; conferred with those who have brought the school suits, and I recently ate dinner with Elijah Muhammed, all in the interest of adding to our fund of knowledge about the stress and strains pushing and pulling the Negro community."[2]

The following month more information was available; and, by this time, the matter had reached rather serious proportions. It was expected that supporters of Superintendent Benjamin Willis and his policies would attack the League for its activities in the school conflict, but Dr. Calloway's letters added "another very serious dimension to the criticism." As it turned out, there had been a series of letters sent to the National Urban League, the Chicago Community Fund, the Chicago Community Trust, and other League fund-raising sources in the white community.[3] Dr. Calloway charged that the Chicago League was violating its charter and that the executive director was instituting programs without board approval or consultation. Coming from a man who had been closely associated with

[1] Letter from Nathaniel O. Calloway to Urban League supporters, Jan. 31, 1962. The thermofax copy of this letter used by the author contained no inside address. It was on Dr. Calloway's letterhead and showed what was apparently his signature. Unless another source is indicated, all letters, memoranda, and other manuscript materials cited are from the files of the Chicago Urban League.

[2] Minutes of the Board of Directors, Feb. 20, 1962.

[3] *Ibid.,* Mar. 20, 1962.

the Chicago Urban League for a number of years, who had served as its president during the reorganization of 1955, and who was then a member of the National Urban League's board of trustees, these letters could not be taken lightly by their recipients. Chicago Urban League officials realized the seriousness of the situation. If they had not realized it before, its seriousness became apparent when the Community Fund asked that the matter be discussed at the League's mid-year budget review. Before making his report to the board of directors, the executive director had already established communications with officials of the Community Fund and the Community Trust. In addition, he had taken steps to involve the president and executive director of the National Urban League in the controversy.[4]

Dr. Calloway's behavior evidenced deep alienation from the Chicago Urban League and its leaders. But the removal of Berry seemed to be the principal objective of his attack. Given the conditions which prevailed at the time Berry was employed and the personalities of the two men, it was probably inevitable that a struggle for power would develop between Berry and Calloway. Both men were able and strong willed, and each, in his own way, had a certain dedication to the Chicago Urban League. Dr. Calloway, after leading the agency through the trying days of reorganization, developed a paternalistic attitude toward the League, and he came to expect a certain deference to his opinions. In addition, Calloway believed that the board of directors should exercise active and dynamic leadership in both policy-making and programing, and, as president, he tried to provide strong leadership in these areas. Naturally, Berry felt that the president was infringing upon the prerogatives of the executive director.

This situation became increasingly intolerable for Berry. The president was interpreting Urban League policies more conservatively at the same time that the executive director was trying to project a more militant image for the agency. Moreover, in the public mind, Berry, not Calloway, had come to symbolize the Chicago Urban League. It became evident in 1960 that the majority of the board of directors had chosen to follow the course charted by the executive director. The board, which elects its own officers, did not re-elect Dr. Calloway as president; instead, it chose Joseph H. Evans, pastor of the Church of the Good Shepherd. Although presidents have served for limited periods since 1960, up to that time

[4] *Ibid.*

there had not been any attempt to limit the president's tenure. Dr. Calloway had served for five years and probably could have been persuaded to continue in office. The setting, at this time, of the precedent for a limited tenure was something of a victory for the executive director.

Even so, Dr. Calloway was still a member of the board of directors, and he took full advantage of his right to dissent. Other members of the board, however, gave him little support in his periodic skirmishes with Berry during 1960. The first major test came in May, after Berry had appointed Wesley T. Cobb deputy director of the Chicago League. Dr. Calloway wrote President Evans expressing alarm over the way this appointment was made. Since this was an executive position, Calloway maintained that it fell "within the province of the Board," and, therefore, the appointment should not have been made by the executive director. Concerning the nature of the position, Calloway asserted: "Such an individual carries out from time to time and may indeed from one minute to another, be required to act as executive and to carry out the policies of the Board. I think the assurance should be given the Board by having such a person responsible to the Board on a contractual basis that he will do so, and not to be responsible to the other executive."[5]

When the matter came before the executive committee of the board of directors on May 2, this body sustained Berry. The executive committee ruled, after considerable discussion, "that the appointment of Ted Cobb to the position of Deputy Director was made in accordance with the policy and accepted practices of the agency." The board of directors "unanimously approved" the findings of its executive committee.[6]

This represented a rather humiliating defeat for a man who only a short time before had been helping to shape the destiny of the organization. Insult was added to injury when the secretary of the board failed to record in detail Calloway's statements in opposition to the trend toward reshaping the League's traditional image. Dr.

---

[5] N. O. Calloway to Joseph Evans, reproduced, without the date of the letter in the Minutes of the Board of Directors, May 10, 1960.

[6] Minutes of the Board of Directors, May 10, 1960. Berry conceded that he should have sought the advice of the board's personnel committee, but this committee was inactive. The executive committee asked that it be activated and, as a concession to the Calloway point of view, passed a rather meaningless motion providing that "the appointment of any personnel directly responsible to the Board for carrying out Board policy shall be approved by the Board."

Calloway protested this omission in a letter to Frank H. Cassell, secretary of the board, and sounded a note of warning against alienating those board members "who tend to be more conservative in matters of intergroup relations." "I am anxious to know how it was decided to leave this material out," Calloway asked, "since it does seem to me that such statements made even though the Board may not approve them, should be a part of the minutes. . . ." He continued:

> I only raise this question since I am still a great deal concerned about the general direction in which the League is moving. This is not said by way of criticism, but only because I saw the League before go down to nothing so that I had to take the responsibility of closing the League in order to straighten it out. But, we do not want to repeat these steps that were so disastrous to intergroup relations in Chicago.[7]

But, by this time the specter of reorganization had lost much of its power to frighten. The board of directors did not even discuss the substantive questions treated in the letter. Cassell only asked the board for guidance on procedure in taking the minutes of board meetings. He wanted to know whether the minutes should be in the form of "complete and verbatim notes" or a "record of action." The board ruled that a member's remarks be taken verbatim if he ask that they be made a part of the record and that "Dr. Calloway's statement be reproduced and added to the next Board proceedings."[8] This was a rather hollow victory for Dr. Calloway. Two months later he offered his resignation from the board, pleading the press of business and professional responsibilities and involvement in other civic affairs. The board tabled the resignation, however, and he was prevailed upon to remain on the board.[9]

At the end of his first year out of the presidency, Calloway still had not become reconciled to his new relationship to the Chicago League. In February, 1961 he revealed his lingering bitterness in a letter to Berry. "I regret a great deal that I have not been able to be of more help to the League during the past year," he said in closing, "but I think you will recognize that the present administration is one that without knowledge and without experience wants to remain without advice."[10]

---

[7] Calloway to Frank H. Cassell, June 17, 1960, quoted in Minutes of the Board of Directors, July 19, 1960.

[8] Minutes of the Board of Directors, July 19, 1960.

[9] *Ibid.*, Sept. 27, 1960.

[10] Calloway to Edwin C. Berry, Feb. 6, 1961.

Shortly afterward, Calloway tendered his resignation again and insisted that it be accepted. In addition to his other duties, he was now chairman of a committee which was revising the National Urban League's articles of affiliation with its local branches. Following the recommendation of the executive committee, the board voted unanimously to "accept with regret" Dr. Calloway's resignation and to send him a letter over the signature of the president "expressing the Board's appreciation for his services and leadership with the Chicago Urban League."[11]

Under the circumstances, it was not unusual that Dr. Calloway did not launch his attack in 1962 through the board of directors. He would have found little support there. By this time, also, the administration could not be accused of being one "without knowledge and without experience"; for Calloway's old colleague and fellow Chicago League rebuilder Hugo B. Law had been elected president in December, 1961.[12]

Law was no newcomer to the Urban League movement. He began his League activities in 1938 and became a member of the Chicago Urban League board of directors in 1943. During his eighteen years on the board, he had worked with three executive directors, participated in two reorganizations, and served as a trustee of the National Urban League. Law remained committed to the Urban League idea, and he was optimistic about the prospects for realizing some Urban League goals. But he was not a naive "do-gooder." In his first presidential statement to the Chicago League board, he recalled the doubts his Urban League experiences produced at times. "Now," he confessed,

> this experience, over the years, showed a discouragingly spotty picture. I saw successes and failures, across the country and here in Chicago. But it seemed to me, more and more that the failures were outweighing the successes and that, somehow, Urban Leagues weren't getting the full value out of this tremendous basic idea.
>
> Certainly, Chicago and the nation have needed, and now need desperately, the unique and powerful type of cooperative force which the Urban League represents. But I must confess that, too often, I just didn't find it living up to its potential. Often, my sense of being part of a failure was so strong that I can only wonder about my staying with it and spending the great amount of time that I consistently poured into it.[13]

---

[11] Minutes of the Board of Directors, Mar. 21, 1961.

[12] *Ibid.*, Dec. 12, 1961.

[13] Statement by Hugo B. Law to the Chicago Urban League Board of Directors, Jan. 16, 1962.

Law's doubts concerning the efficacy of the League were gone by the time he became president of the Chicago branch. He exulted:

> So I'm very happy to be able to say that, as far as Chicago is concerned, I think we've left the era of failure far behind. Our reorganization, and the years that have followed it, have proved that we can make the Urban League idea work, and I'm happier about the whole thing than I've ever been. I don't feel, any longer, that we are missing the boat. I'm convinced that we now have the kind of program which makes the most of the potentialities of the basic Urban League idea. We have a great staff. And we have a great Board.[14]

With this roseate picture in mind, Law began his term as president with high expectations. His administration would be largely one of consolidation. Expansion would continue, and programing would be refined and properly financed. But all of this would be done at a less hectic and frenzied pace than had been necessary from 1956 up to this time. During his first year in office, however, Law was destined to be a conservator, rather than a consolidator. In 1962 Law found himself pitted against his former colleague in rebuilding the agency in 1955-56. It was somewhat ironical that Law, the white member of the rebuilding team, would have to justify the Chicago Urban League's adaptation to the "Negro Revolution" in the face of criticisms and efforts to discredit the agency coming from Calloway, the Negro member.

On April 3, 1962, about two months after he had mailed his letters to League supporters, Dr. Calloway finally sent Urban League board members a statement of his charges against the League. These were grouped as ten points, but they were all related to Calloway's two basic criticisms — the departure of the Chicago League from traditional methods and procedures and the activities of the executive director. "The Urban League is a social work organization," Calloway informed the board members; "it is *not* a civil rights organization. The image of the League is *not* its executive."[15]

Points two through ten tried to show that the Chicago League had in fact become a civil rights organization and that the image of the executive director was the image of the League. The agency's transformation was evidenced by the "rabble rousing" tone of some of its public meetings, the fact that it had lost "prestige with the power structure of the City," and the picture published of the executive

---

[14] *Ibid.*

[15] Calloway to Members of the Chicago Urban League Board of Directors, Apr. 3, 1962.

director and his deputy in the "midst of a group of pickets." From accepted social work techniques, the agency had turned to civil rights techniques — such as legislation, strikes, picketing, sit-ins, boycotts, and passive resistance. Although he had nothing against these methods, Dr. Calloway said, as his activities with other organizations would attest, they were not Urban League methods.[16]

Berry was the villain of the piece. Calloway could no longer excuse Berry's actions, as he had done in 1961, by theorizing that he was being "misled perhaps in a sentimental fashion over people who may appear close to you or who may appear willing to help you without analyzing the situation."[17] Berry knew sound Urban League policies; for he had learned them under the tutelage of Dr. Calloway. "It was I," Calloway wrote, "who hired Mr. Berry. As part of the terms of his employment, he wrote a section of what is now the basic policy of the Chicago Urban League. Therefore, he knows it very well. It is my impression at the present time that the President of the League defends Mr. Berry, and not the policies, programs, or purposes of the Urban League."[18]

What the Chicago Urban League needed was "internal policing" to bring its operations in line with the policies established during the reorganization. The executive director should be controlled and required to "follow the policies and programs laid out for him." It was not a purpose of the agency "to maintain a platform for personal aggrandizement by social work somersaults." On the contrary, the agency should be serving as a "basis of contact with all the power structures of this City." Calloway pledged to continue his "insistence" until the agency returned to its proper functions.[19]

A special meeting of the board of directors was held on April 5 to give board members an opportunity to meet Whitney M. Young, who had recently been appointed executive director of the National Urban League. Young was in the city in order, among other things, "to get some answers to the criticisms that have been leveled against the League by Dr. Calloway." Calloway was present and made a statement summarizing his charges. He insisted, however, that he admired both Berry and Law and that nothing he said should be taken as personal attacks on these men. Calloway suggested that a special committee be appointed to discuss the points he had raised.

---

[16] *Ibid.*
[17] Calloway to Berry, Feb. 6, 1961.
[18] Calloway to Members of the Board of Directors, Apr. 3, 1962.
[19] *Ibid.*

He also suggested that the president and executive director of the National League be invited to participate in the discussion. Several board members objected to the appointment of a special committee and insisted that the entire board hear anything Dr. Calloway had to say. The board agreed to hold a special meeting for this purpose.[20]

Young was in something of a dilemma. Criticisms leveled by a trustee of the National League, who in the past had played a very significant role in the Chicago League, could not be dismissed as irresponsible. Yet, he probably could not fully accept the validity of the criticisms, since the Chicago branch was considered one of the most active and progressive affiliates in the Urban League movement. So, at this time, he merely admonished the board to be "very honest" in discussing the basic issues and to "be prepared to document to the contrary" if it felt the charges to be false. Young said that he and the national president, Henry Steeger, would attend the special meeting, if the Chicago board thought it important.[21]

The executive committee of the board of directors, to which the question of a special meeting was referred, decided to discuss the Calloway criticisms at the regular board meeting for April, rather than a week earlier in a special meeting. When notified of this change, Calloway informed Law that his "unusually busy schedule" would not permit him to attend the regular meeting, and it would be several weeks before he would be available for another meeting.[22]

Actually, there was little to be gained from a meeting with Dr. Calloway. For the Chicago board to have conceded the soundness of any of Calloway's major charges would have been an admission of improper conduct and a vote of no confidence in the executive director. Although at least one director felt that "a few mistakes of strategy and approach" had been made, there was no apparent disposition among board members toward repudiating either the League's basic program or the leadership of its executive director. The board's primary concern, then, was with justifying the agency's program to the Community Fund and other major fund-raising sources.

With a national trustee involved, it was also essential that National League officials understand the nature of the controversy and

[20] Minutes of the Board of Directors, Apr. 5, 1962.
[21] *Ibid.*
[22] *Ibid.*, Apr. 17, 1962; Law to Calloway, Apr. 9, 1962; Calloway to Law, Apr. 12, 1962.

its possible pernicious consequences for the future of the local branch. Berry and Law wanted more than understanding, however; they sought the active support of the national organization. Whitney Young returned to the city during the weekend of April 13, accompanied by Henry Steeger, the national president. They met with Calloway and were briefed on the situation by Law and Berry. Since those directly involved were all members of the Urban League family, Young and Steeger hoped that reasonable discussion would settle the internal problems without publicity and without acrimony. Consequently, they viewed themselves as mediators.[23] On the one hand, they affirmed Dr. Calloway's right to criticize, but they agreed that his "action was carried out in a highly improper way." On the other hand, however, they reserved judgment on the grounds for Calloway's criticisms, while praising the program and "excellent leadership" of the Chicago League.[24] In any case, the national officials wanted the local leaders to take the initiative in resolving the difficulty.

When the controversy came to the Chicago board on April 17, there were three questions for determination. Two of these concerned Dr. Calloway. The National League asked the Chicago branch to recommend what action, if any, should be taken against Calloway as a member of the national board of trustees. In addition, it was felt that the Chicago board should make a direct reply to his allegations. More basic, however, was the question of the stand the board would take before the Community Fund and the Community Trust, both of which had called upon the League to provide answers to the criticisms.

Opinions varied as to what the National League should be asked to do. Some board members felt it proper to request Calloway's expulsion from the national board. Others thought he should at least be censured for attempting to undermine "not only the Chicago League, but the entire League movement." Several board members who shared the strong feelings of those who advocated expulsion or censure opposed these rather extreme measures. They argued that this action would only serve to intensify the controversy by providing Dr. Calloway new excuses for attacking the agency. Voices of moderation prevailed, and the board decided to make no

[23] Henry Steeger to Calloway, June 26, 1962.

[24] Steeger to Law, Apr. 16, 1962; Steeger to Berry, Apr. 16, 1962; Minutes of the Board of Directors, Apr. 17, 1962.

recommendation but to transmit a record of its action to the National League.[25]

Similar moderation was exercised in the letter sent to Dr. Calloway. A suggested draft, which not only denied Calloway's three basic allegations but also contained a rather sharp personal rebuke, was circulated prior to the meeting.[26] The rebuke was deleted, and the board contented itself with a formal rejection of the contentions that it had been derelict in exercising its responsibilities, that the executive had usurped leadership prerogatives, and that the agency had "lost strength and standing" with the "power structure."[27] Several members of the board wrote personal letters either responding to each of Calloway's ten points or criticizing him for trying to hamper fund raising.[28]

The board's basic action was the adoption of a policy resolution. This resolution was not an attempt to answer the agency's critics; rather it was primarily a positive affirmation of the board's stand on the school question and on criticism of Urban League activities in general. The tone of the resolution was set in the preamble, which stated:

> From time to time, it may become necessary for the Board of Directors of any Urban League to re-establish, with complete clarity, its policies and intent with respect to matters of current interest. Such a need now seems evident in two areas of the activities of the Chicago Urban League. . . .[29]

The first part of the resolution dealt with the League and the school situation. "The League," the statement began, "within the last year, has intensified its efforts to secure and further equal educational opportunity in Chicago's public schools. These efforts are based on the League's conviction that such inequalities do exist on a scale so great as to form a major threat to the entire community's well-being — that the present philosophy, policies, and programs of the school system are, in many ways, wrongly conceived and are so inadequate as to offer little hope for the necessary correction."[30] Under these circumstances, the agency could not, "in clear con-

---

[25] *Ibid.*, Apr. 17, 1962.
[26] Draft copy of letter to Calloway, Apr. 17, 1962.
[27] Law to Calloway, Apr. 18, 1962; Minutes of the Board of Directors, Apr. 17, 1962.
[28] See Hank R. Schwab to Calloway, Apr. 6, 1962; Samuel W. Witwer to Calloway, Apr. 23, 1962.
[29] Resolution adopted by the Board of Directors of the Chicago Urban League, Apr. 17, 1962.
[30] *Ibid.*

science, avoid or shirk the fullest possible use of its facilities to act vigorously for correction of this extremely serious situation." Yet, the League did not depart from traditional Urban League methods in its school program. Fact-finding, dissemination of the facts, development of sound community organization, and communication, negotiation, and cooperation — these were Urban League methods; and these were the methods employed by the Chicago Urban League in pressing for improvement in the schools.[31]

The second part of the resolution noted that the League's involvement in the school situation had stimulated "both friendly and unfriendly questions" about the way the agency was functioning. The resolution, however, concentrated on the "unfriendly" questions. In reply to those who asked whether the board had abdicated its responsibility, the statement reiterated the board's "continuing responsibility for program activities" and expressed pride in the "organization's success in maintaining the proper functions of Board and staff." A paragraph on the need for adapting to the times was addressed to those who criticized the League's new militancy. It stated:

> The Board further declares its belief that, at this point in history, marked as it is by rapid acceleration of progress in race relations, the pace and the intensity of Urban League effort also must be accelerated — and that such accelerated and intensified efforts, are wholly appropriate to the times and are in accordance with the established policies of the Chicago Urban League and of the National Urban League.[32]

It was hoped that the board's action would close the Calloway phase of the controversy. Young and Steeger considered the matter closed and congratulated Chicago officials on their handling of the situation.[33] Young advised Law that, "in the absence of further formal complaint, expressed by legitimately responsible bodies," he regarded the "National's concern with this particular matter closed." There might be some discussion with Calloway, however, about his reaction to the Chicago board's action and his future role as a member of the national board of trustees.[34] Yet, this optimistic picture was drawn without taking into consideration Dr. Calloway's adamant adherence to his point of view.

The controversy was revived in June when Berry, in a fund-

[31] *Ibid.*
[32] *Ibid.*
[33] Young to Law, Apr. 25, 1962; Steeger to Law, Apr. 26, 1962.
[34] Young to Law, Apr. 25, 1962.

raising letter, accused League critics of attempted "economic blackmail." A local Negro newspaper published Berry's statement and gave a brief background on what it termed the "long simmering feud between local factions."[35] Calloway resumed his clipping of newspapers and letter writing; and a series of letters ensued between Calloway and Steeger and Law and Steeger, with the national president caught in the middle. Calloway accused the National League of showing bad faith by not restraining Berry from provocative action, after Calloway had stopped criticizing the Chicago branch. Calloway called for immediate action from the National League to bring the Chicago League into line, or he would take his case to the press.[36] Steeger tried to conciliate Calloway by implying that the National Urban League was still reserving its judgment on the Chicago program,[37] but Law demanded that the National get off the fence and stop giving "aid and comfort to the enemy." Furthermore, members of the Chicago board were coming to feel that the retention of Dr. Calloway on the National board was becoming more untenable.[38] Although Steeger agreed with Law that the prospects were dim for a peaceful solution to the conflict, he felt that the initiative for Calloway's removal should come from Chicago.[39] The Chicago board still considered this a problem for the national organization. "The National Board," Law contended, "is faced by a problem of very serious misconduct by one of its own members, and there should be no need for anyone else to ask for the necessary corrective action." He advised the National League board to take care of their own disciplinary problems "by using your own woodshed and switch."[40] The matter dragged on until late in July, when Calloway finally resigned from the National Urban League board.[41]

In the meantime, the Chicago League was trying to clarify its relationship to the Community Fund. On June 4 the Fund's budget committee approved a recommendation, to be presented to the Fund's board of directors, expressing "deep concern about the public controversy in which the Chicago Urban League became in-

---

[35] *Chicago Courier,* June 23, 1962.
[36] Calloway to Steeger, June 22, 1962.
[37] Steeger to Calloway, June 26, 1962.
[38] Law to Steeger, July 5, 1962.
[39] Steeger to Law, July 12, 1962.
[40] Law to Steeger, July 17, 1962; Minutes of the Board of Directors, July 17, 1962.
[41] See *Chicago Defender,* Aug. 4-10, 1962; Minutes of the Board of Directors, Aug. 21, 1962.

volved in relations with the School Board and school administration." The recommendation continued:

The Committee believes the manner in which the Chicago Urban League used its stated methods . . . could lend itself to improvement as a responsible agency.

The Committee recommends that proper communication be established by the Chicago Urban League and the Board of Education.

The Committee continues to believe that the Chicago Urban League has a vital and extremely necessary role to perform. . . . However, the Committee also believes that continued participation of the agency in the Fund imposes upon it an obligation to exercise caution in whatever it uses in relation to dealing with complex and sensitive problems such as are involved in the school situation.[42]

Many interpreted this as a call for censure; and, in essence, it was. The press reported that the League faced loss of Community Fund support and of its tax-exempt status, if it was determined that it was an "action" rather than an "education" agency. Now, rather wide dissemination was given to Dr. Calloway's charges by the daily press.[43] Except for occasional public statements, however, the League refrained from engaging in a public debate on the Community Fund problem.

Urban League leaders and board members chose to approach the situation in a confidential and conciliatory, but relatively firm, manner. The executive committee met after notice of the Fund's budget committee's action was received and agreed unanimously that the League's board should reject the recommendation. The Fund's board complied with the League's request that consideration of the recommendation be deferred and that "representatives from the respective boards be designated to meet for the purpose of exploring the full implications of the recommendation."[44] A five-member committee — consisting of James Worthy, Frank H. Cassell, William H. Robinson, Samuel W. Witwer, and Hugo B. Law — was appointed to meet with the committee from the Fund's board. Attorney George Ranney, former chairman of the Welfare Council of Metropolitan Chicago, was chairman of the Fund's committee. The other members were Mrs. Philip Block, Jr., James L. Palmer, Charles B. Weaver, and Thomas H. Beacom.[45]

---

[42] Quoted in Minutes of the Board of Directors, June 19, 1962.
[43] See *Chicago's American*, July 13, 1962; July 23, 1962; Letter to the editor from Calloway in "Voice of the People," *Chicago Tribune*, Aug. 7, 1962.
[44] Minutes of the Board of Directors, June 19, 1962.
[45] *Ibid.*, July 17, 1962.

Both the League and the Community Fund were anxious to resolve the issues in question as expeditiously as possible. For its part, the League was willing to answer the charges made against it, but it was not willing to retreat from its stand on the schools. In fact, it could not without jeopardizing its enhanced position in the Negro community. The League was also concerned about its future relations with the Fund. This involved the broad question as to the degree of influence the Fund should exert on the internal policies and programs of its member agencies. A thorough investigation was made by the Fund's committee, and the National League sent Nelson Jackson, a National League staff member, to Chicago to evaluate local operations.[46]

Soon after Jackson's visit, Young and Steeger summarized his findings in a strong letter to Arthur Kruse, executive director of the Community Fund. They reviewed the new challenges faced by the Urban League movement as a result of the "Negro Revolution" and cited the progress being made by the National Urban League and the Chicago branch in trying to make their programs relevant to the times. The attacks on the Chicago League were considered deplorable because the National had found no evidence to support them. Furthermore, valuable time had been consumed in answering the charges made, and these charges were responsible for the action being taken by the Fund. "While we make no claims that our Chicago affiliate is perfect in all its agency relationships," Young and Steeger concluded, "we do feel strongly that it is exercising effective leadership in one of America's most complex and tension-filled cities. As the Chest [Fund] itself has recognized in its annual reports and in the greatly increased contribution to the League over the last five years, the Chicago Urban League plays a key and vital role in helping the city of Chicago avoid the tragic possibilities inherent in this setting."[47]

Early in August, Kruse assured Young that the Chicago branch was still a member of the Community Fund. He assumed the League's budget for 1963 would be given the "same positive consideration" that had been given in the past.[48] On September 18 Pres-

[46] *Ibid.*, Aug. 21, 1962. A voluminous amount of material resulted from the investigations and the negotiations between the League and the Fund. The author examined these documents and has drawn conclusions from them, but he has tried to respect their confidential nature.

[47] Steeger and Young to Kruse, July 24, 1962.

[48] Kruse to Young, Aug. 7, 1962.

ident Law officially informed his board that the Fund's board unanimously rejected the recommendations of its budget committee and "declared the League to be a member in good standing of the Community Fund."[49] Following a "vote of applause" for the members of the negotiating committee, the board, with a deep sense of relief, returned to its usual duties.

The financial situation demanded immediate attention. Between February and September, 1962, fund raising suffered because of the disproportionate amount of time required in defending the agency's program. The treasurer's report in September showed that operations had been supported primarily on the contributions from the Community Fund, but these were running out. By mid-September the League had already received eleven months' advance against its 1962 allocation. The treasurer termed the organization's financial status as acute.[50] Although the Calloway controversy hampered fund raising, it was only partially responsible for the financial crisis. However, in the long run, the conflict probably helped the agency achieve greater financial stability by increasing the dedication of its workers, attracting new friends, and opening new sources of income.

Stability was the major problem. Continually confronted with the necessity for expansion, the League found that the development of financial resources did not keep pace with financial need. Throughout the 1950's, fund raising and budget making remained frenzied. Then, in 1960 the progress made toward regularizing these activities received a rather severe setback. Following the League's successful participation in the 1959 *Playboy* magazine jazz festival, the executive committee recommended an independent Urban League festival for 1960. It was projected that by securing facilities with a larger seating capacity and concentrating all efforts on the benefit the League could more than double the $25,000 net proceeds received in 1959. This would provide funds to remove all deficits from the books, would help to finance the 1960 budget, and would provide an opportunity to consolidate fund raising.

The results, however, were frustrating. Expenses greatly exceeded expectations, and box office returns were quite low. Out of gross receipts of approximately $80,000, the League realized less than $10,000.[51] The agency had to draw funds against its 1961 Com-

[49] Minutes of the Board of Directors, Sept. 18, 1962.
[50] *Ibid.*
[51] *Ibid.*, Jan. 19, 1960; Feb. 9, 1960; June 14, 1960; Sept. 27, 1960; Oct. 25, 1960; Chicago Urban League *Newsletter*, July-Aug., 1960.

munity Fund allocation in December, 1960 to help cover expenses.[52] The budget asking for 1961 was kept at the same level as for 1960 — with a minor increase of $11,174 to cover salary increments and other adjustments.[53] Even so, the Fund gave tentative approval of the $269,787 budget for 1961 with the understanding that if League fund raising had not improved by May, 1961 the budget would be revised downward.[54]

Conditions improved somewhat in 1961. Although the agency fell a little short of its goal, it set a new fund-raising record, with receipts totaling $131,400 from Urban League efforts and $135,000 from the Fund.[55] Prospects seemed good for recouping, in 1962, some of the ground lost in 1960. The budget estimate of $333,675 for 1962 reflected this optimism, as well as the pressing need for improved programing and additional staff personnel. With the nearly eight-month disruption of activities, when the year 1962 ended the League had spent $21,786 more than it received in contributions.[56]

The years 1963 to 1965 brought a great change in the fortunes of the Chicago Urban League. From a revised budget of just under $330,000 in 1963, the budgets increased to over $450,000 in 1964 and to nearly $580,000 in 1965.[57] The improved financial situation resulted from a number of factors. Buttressed by a well-planned series of low-overhead benefits, fund raising was greatly improved in 1963. This improved the agency's financial stability and made possible a resumption of expansion in 1964. Then, in 1964, Urban League programing attracted more and larger contributions from businesses and foundations. The revitalized National Urban League also provided significant financial assistance. Through the intercession of Whitney Young, the Chicago branch received a $35,000 grant from the Taconic Foundation.[58] Direct subventions were provided by the National League for several Chicago projects — including the Talent Bank, a voter registration campaign, and a leadership devel-

---

[52] Minutes of the Board of Directors, Dec. 13, 1960.
[53] *Ibid.,* Nov. 22, 1960.
[54] *Ibid.,* Feb. 21, 1961.
[55] Report of the Executive Director, Jan. 16, 1962. The agency ended the year with a deficit of nearly $22,000 in its operating funds.
[56] Chicago Urban League Financial Report, Jan. 15, 1963. In addition to the operating deficit, a $27,581 deficit in the building fund was carried on the books.
[57] Continuing budget revision makes it difficult to determine exact figures.
[58] Minutes of the Board of Directors, July 21, 1964.

opment project.[59] Chicago Urban League officials could still protest in mid-1965 that their resources were inadequate for the job they faced, but, by this time, the agency seemed well on the way toward sounder and more stable financial operations.

In 1964 the League finally resolved its housing problem. Through the efforts of its new president, A. W. Williams, the agency was given an opportunity to purchase a building at 4500 South Michigan Avenue owned by the North Carolina Mutual Life Insurance Company, of which company Williams was a vice president. Hugo B. Law — now chairman of the executive committee, a newly created office — took the initiative in assembling the necessary cash to close the deal and to provide funds for moving and renovation. Board members advanced, as loans, most of the $30,000 needed. A plan was devised whereby two-year notes bearing 6 per cent interest were issued in units of $2,500 to board members and "key friends of the League."[60] The agency moved into its new quarters before the end of July, and two months later the necessary funds were available to close the deal.[61]

---

[59] *Ibid.,* July 21, 1964; Aug. 18, 1964; Nov. 10, 1964.
[60] *Ibid.,* May 27, 1964.
[61] *Ibid.,* July 21, 1964; Sept. 8, 1964.

Conclusions

In spite of periodic professions of faith by Chicagoans in the philosophy and purposes of the Urban League, the agency has never been one of the city's top-ranking organizations in the general field of social welfare. Throughout much of its history, the League's activities have been limited to rather narrowly defined areas. It has received inadequate financial support and has had to struggle continually to maintain the goodwill of influential groups. In short, the agency has never been able to reach its full potential. Yet, in large measure, this situation has not resulted from weaknesses inherent within the organization. Rather, it has reflected an indisposition on the part of a great American city to face one of its major problems — the withholding of economic, social, and political opportunities from the sizable nonwhite segment of its population. Chicago, like the rest of the nation, has usually chosen to ignore these problems and to pretend that they do not exist. It has taken periods of crisis temporarily to awaken the city from its lethargy and to motivate it to call upon agencies such as the League for assistance, not in resolving the fundamental problems but in restoring a delicate race relations balance. During the intervals between crises, the Urban League has had to depend upon a dedicated staff and a small interracial group of reform-minded individuals — often referred to contemptuously as "do-gooders" — to nurture its principles of interracial understanding and equality of opportunity. The surprising thing is not that the Urban League's growth has been slow but that it has been able to maintain almost continuous operation for nearly fifty years as a "voice crying in the wilderness." During this period, the

League, in its small but significant way, has been able to help in directing the course of inevitable changes in race relations. Even though progress has been slow, halting, and uneven, concepts of racial adjustment have undergone revision. Of necessity, the League has reflected the dominant climate of opinion during the different periods of its history.

Between 1915 and 1919, Chicago had to become reconciled to the fact that Negroes were becoming a significant minority in the city's population. The mass exodus of Negroes from the South in search of economic advancement and greater political and social opportunities intensified the race question in Chicago. Although many employers aided this migration and welcomed the new labor supply, most Chicagoans seemed unwilling to think of the newcomers as a permanent addition to the city's population. Even some employers thought of them as a temporary substitute for immigrant labor, which would again be available after World War I. Nevertheless, if Chicagoans looked upon the migration as a temporary phenomenon and expected southern Negroes to return home, the Negro migrants did not. They had come to Chicago to stay, and many of their fellows in the South were awaiting an opportunity to join them in the "promised land." It was not until the riot of 1919 that grudging recognition was given to the fact that Negroes should have a larger voice in the economic, social, and political affairs of the city. The solution found was, in essence, to provide white support for the establishment of a Negro subcommunity with its own institutions and way of life. The economic structure of this Negro city within a city, however, depended upon the employment of the Negro masses in the general economy.

The depression disrupted this scheme of racial adjustment. The superstructure of Negro business institutions could not stand without the foundation of earnings by the masses in jobs outside the Negro community. This economic crisis exploded the myth of a Negro subeconomy. Gradually Negroes began to realize that advancement could come only through their entrance into the mainstream of Chicago economic life. During the depression, the concept of racial integration — in the sense of equal participation in the institutions of the city — began to develop. White citizens, however, have been slow in accepting this concept. World War II brought some progress in economic integration, but social integration has been slower and has met with stubborn resistance. The major social objective sought has been free access to the housing market, but the only significant breakthrough in this area has been in getting a degree of adherence to the principle of open occupancy in public housing.

Since the end of the depression, the problem in Chicago race relations has been to close the gap between Negro aspirations and the receptiveness of the white community. Neither of these factors has been static, but Negro aspirations have risen faster than the degree of white acceptance. The two can meet only at that point where the Negro is granted equal and unfettered opportunity — that is, where caste no longer becomes a determinant of social, economic, and political status. Through the years, the Chicago Urban League has tried to serve as a stimulant to Negro aspirations, as a prod to white conscience, and as a bridge across the chasm separating the views of the two groups. The League's efforts to carry out these difficult functions are probably best exemplified in the careers of its executive directors.

T. Arnold Hill, the first executive, helped to earn the League a place on the Chicago scene. In 1916, the organization needed an "accommodating" leader, one who could win white friends for the Negro, and Hill met the required specifications. He was tactful and diplomatic and had been embued with Urban League ideals by the founders of the movement. Aside from his efforts in recruiting supporters, however, his job was relatively clear-cut. There were jobs for Negroes on the bottom rung of industry, and Hill and the League were expected to screen the labor supply and provide their supporters among employers the best men for the jobs offered. In the meantime, they were trying to win more supporters among employers and, thereby, more jobs for Negroes. In addition, the League helped in the adjustment of these workers — teaching them proper work habits and modes of acceptable social behavior. Although Negroes had idealized conceptions of northern conditions, their level of aspiration was not very high. Principally they were looking for work, any kind of work, and shelter in the Negro community. On the other side, the problem was to get white acceptance of the Negro's right to live in Chicago. Up to 1921, Hill had the support of employers in fostering such acceptance, and during the riot of 1919, Negroes had served notice that they intended to remain in the city. After 1921, Hill could not span the gap between white and Negro opinions. Employers no longer needed Negro workers in large numbers and withdrew or reduced their financial support of the League. In addition, Negroes rejected Hill as a political leader. From 1921 to 1925, the principal basis for League appeal to the white community was for charity to relieve Negro suffering during periodic recessions.

Coming to Chicago as executive in 1925, A. L. Foster tried to adjust to the situation as he found it. He asked the white community to support him and the League in working to improve the general race relations situation, but this approach attracted only limited support. In the Negro community he expounded the prevailing doctrine of racial advancement through Negro business. Then, when the Negro community began to reject "accommodating" or "compromise" type leadership and began to clamor for aggressive action, Foster had to adjust to this change. He knew that conservative white supporters of the League expected the agency to help in maintaining the status quo — to provide what they called "sane" leadership. Without the confidence of Negroes, however, the League would have degenerated into a self-seeking dispenser of white charity. Foster, therefore, attempted to appease both Negro and white opinions. World War II closed the final curtain on the Chicago Negro's acceptance of "compromise" leadership, except in politics. The major problem confronting the League as the war ended was to end its dualism and still maintain the confidence of both the white and Negro communities.

This phenomenal task fell to Sidney Williams. Williams was an exponent of aggressive Negro protest and probably would have made a significant imprint on an all-Negro organization or one dedicated to overt action. But his career in the Chicago Urban League only brought him frustration. He could not reconcile social work methods with his militant philosophy. Although many white people were beginning to acknowledge, in theory, the Negro's right to first-class citizenship, they were sensitive about the methods used in reaching this objective. Williams succeeded in ending the League's dualism, but he did it in a way that antagonized the agency's white supporters. Instead of an organization dedicated to education, persuasion, and cooperation, Williams used the League for militant protest activities. In large measure, however, it was not his goals which were objectionable to many supporters, but the methods he employed in trying to attain them. In any case, Williams help to prepare the way for his successor.

Since 1956, the Chicago Urban League, under Edwin C. Berry,

has been more successful in combining aggressiveness with social work procedures. In spite of his aggressiveness, Berry has been able to appeal to and to gain the support of widely disparate groups. But the changing climate of opinion and the work of his predecessors have facilitated his work. The growth of activist groups in Chicago and in other sections of the country still make the League seem quite moderate in comparison. Furthermore, the "new" Urban League has been built on the heritage of the "old" Urban League. Each of the former executives "sold" the Urban League idea to different interest groups. Many of these groups may have had imperfect ideas of what an Urban League was supposed to be, but they believed in an Urban League. In addition, each executive, in response to changing conditions, raised the level on which the League attacked the problems confronting Negroes. A list of the problems faced in 1956 contained the same categories as one would have in 1916, but the nature of these problems had changed. In 1916, Hill worked with these problems in their most elemental form. Negroes were trying to gain a foothold in the labor force. They were seeking any form of shelter available and the right to consideration in the use of public and some private facilities. After 1934 and particularly after 1940, the situation became more complex. While most Negroes were still struggling on the elemental level, others were seeking better jobs, better housing, and equality of treatment in the use of public and private facilities. By 1956, the Negro's higher level of aspiration, the development of more articulate Negro leadership, and the more sympathetic hearing being given by white leaders had enabled the League to abandon working on individual problems and to concentrate on facilitating the entrance of Negroes into the mainstream of Chicago's economic, social, and political life. The "new" Urban League has made significant contributions to the efforts being made to realize this goal; but without the "old" Urban League, there could have been no "new" Urban League.

Bibliography

I. PRIMARY SOURCES

A. Manuscripts

Chicago Urban League. Files.
———. Minutes of the Board of Directors. 1949-65.
———. Minutes of the Executive Committee. 1949-56.
Gould, Howard D. Personal Files.
Lawson, Victor F. MSS. Newberry Library. Chicago, Illinois.
Levinson, Salmon O. MSS. University of Chicago Library.
Rosenwald, Julius. MSS. University of Chicago Library.
State of Illinois. Office of the Secretary of State. Chicago Urban League Certificate of Corporation. June 13, 1917.
Welfare Council of Metropolitan Chicago. Chicago Urban League Service Reports. 1934-56.
———. Files on the Chicago Urban League.

B. Government Publications

U.S. Commission on Civil Rights. *Civil Rights U.S.A.: Public Schools, Cities in the North and West.* Washington: Government Printing Office, 1962.
U.S. Department of Commerce. Bureau of the Census. *Negro Population 1790-1915.* Washington: Government Printing Office, 1918.
U.S. Department of Labor. Division of Negro Economics. *The Negro at Work During the World War and During Reconstruction,* by George Edmund Haynes. Washington: Government Printing Office, 1921.
———. *Negro Migration in 1916-17.* Washington: Government Printing Office, 1919.

C. Books, Reports, and Pamphlets

Baker, Ray Stannard. *Following the Color Line: An Account of Negro Citizenship in the American Democracy.* New York: Doubleday, Page and Company, 1908.

Berry, Edwin C. *Urban Sprawl: Its Impact on Urban League Programming.* Chicago: Chicago Urban League, Public Relations Department, 1960.

Bowen, Louise de Koven. *Speeches, Addresses, and Letters of Louise de Koven Bowen, Reflecting Social Movements in Chicago,* comp. Mary E. Humphrey. 2 vols. Ann Arbor, Michigan: Edwards Brothers, Inc., 1937.

Chicago Association of Commerce and Industry. *Contributor's Handbook: A Classified List of Local Civic, Health and Welfare Organizations.* 1914-57.

Chicago Urban League. *Annual Reports.* 1917-47.

———. *Statement of Policies and Areas of Service.* Undated pamphlet.

———. *Two Year Report on the Youth Guidance Project 1958-1959.* Chicago: Chicago Urban League, 1960.

Commons, John R. *Races and Immigrants in America.* New York: The Macmillan Company, 1913.

Croly, Herbert. *Progressive Democracy.* New York: The Macmillan Company, 1914.

Du Bois, William E. B. *The Philadelphia Negro: A Social Study.* Philadelphia: University of Pennsylvania, 1899.

Frazier, E. Franklin. *The Negro Family in Chicago.* Chicago: University of Chicago Press, 1932.

Hampton Negro Conference. *Report.* Vol. II. Hampton, Virginia: Hampton Institute Press, 1898.

Haynes, George Edmund. *The Negro at Work in New York City: A Study in Economic Progress.* New York: Columbia University, 1912.

Kellor, Frances A. *Out of Work: A Study of Employment Agencies, Their Treatment of the Unemployed, and Their Influence upon Homes and Business.* New York: G. P. Putnam's Sons, 1904.

Municipal Voters' League of Chicago. *Twenty-seventh Annual Preliminary Report.* 1923.

National Housing Policy Conference. *A Report to the Nation.* St. Louis, 1951.

National Urban League. *Bulletin.* 1913-20.

———. *Fiftieth Anniversary Yearbook,* ed. William R. Simms. New York: National Urban League, 1961.

———. *Fortieth Anniversary Yearbook.* New York: National Urban League, 1950.

———. *How Unemployment Affects Negroes.* New York: National Urban League, March, 1931.

———. *A Quarter Century of Progress in the Field of Race Relations, 1910-1935: Twenty-fifth Anniversary Souvenir Booklet.* New York: National Urban League, 1935.

New York Charities Directory. New York: Charity Organization Society, 1907-11.

Ovington, Mary White. *Half a Man: The Status of the Negro in New York.* New York: Longmans, Green, and Co., 1911.

———. *The Walls Came Tumbling Down.* New York: Harcourt, Brace and Company, 1947.

Scott, Emmett J. *Negro Migration During the War.* "Carnegie Endowment for International Peace: Preliminary Economic Studies of the War." No. 16. New York: Oxford University Press, 1920.
Villard, Oswald Garrison. *Fighting Years: Memoirs of a Liberal Editor.* New York: Harcourt, Brace and Company, 1939.
Weyl, Walter E. *The New Democracy.* Rev. ed. New York: The Macmillan Company, 1914.
Young, Whitney M., Jr. *To Be Equal.* New York: McGraw-Hill Book Co., 1964.

D. Articles and Periodicals

Baker, Ray Stannard. "What Is a Lynching?" *McClure's Magazine,* XXIV (January, 1905), 299-314. XXIV (February, 1905), 422-430.
Berry, Edwin C. "The Menace of Unemployment: Jobs, Poverty and Race," *Negro Digest,* XIII (September, 1964), 4-11.
Bridges, Horace J. "The First Urban League Family," in Chicago Urban League. *Two Decades of Service.* Chicago: Chicago Urban League, 1936.
Chicago Urban League *Newsletter.*
Evans, William L. "The Negro in Chicago Industries," *Opportunity: A Journal of Negro Life,* I (February, 1923), 15-16.
Fisk University News. Vols. I-V.
Foster, Albon L. "Twenty Years of Interracial Goodwill Through Social Service," in Chicago Urban League. *Two Decades of Service.* Chicago: Chicago Urban League, 1936.
Haynes, George Edmund. "Interracial Social Work Begins," in National Urban League. *Fortieth Anniversary Yearbook.* New York: National Urban League, 1950.
Hill, T. Arnold. "The Negro in Industry, 1926," *Opportunity: A Journal of Negro Life,* V (February, 1927), 51-52, 63.
———. "Recent Developments in the Problem of Negro Labor," in National Conference of Social Work. *Proceedings* (Chicago: University of Chicago Press, 1921), pp. 321-325.
———. "Why Southern Negroes Don't Go South," *The Survey,* XLIII (November 29, 1919), 183-185.
Jones, Eugene Kinckle. "The National Urban League," *Opportunity: A Journal of Negro Life,* III (January, 1925), 12-15.
———. "Progress: The Eighteenth Annual Report of the Activities of the National Urban League," *Opportunity: A Journal of Negro Life,* VII (April, 1929), 114-121.
Kellor, Frances A. "Assisted Emigration from the South: The Women," *Charities,* XV (October 7, 1905), 13-14.
———. "Southern Colored Girls in the North," *Charities,* XIII (March 11, 1905), 584-585.
Miller, Kelly. "The Economic Handicap of the Negro in the North," *The Annals of the American Academy of Political and Social Science,* XXVII (May, 1906), 543-550.

"National Urban League Adopts Strong Platform," *Life and Labor,* IX (November, 1919), 294-295.

Opportunity: A Journal of Negro Life. Vols. I-XXVII.

Ovington, Mary White. "Fresh Air Work Among Colored Children in New York," *Charities,* XVII (October 13, 1906), 115-117.

———. "The Negro Home in New York," *Charities,* XV (October 7, 1905), 25-30.

———. "The Negro in the Trades Unions in New York," *The Annals of the American Academy of Political and Social Science,* XXVII (May, 1906), 551-558.

Pillsbury, Albert E. "Negro Disfranchisement as It Affects the White Man," in National Negro Conference. *Proceedings . . . 1909* (New York, 1909), pp. 180-196.

Reid, Ira DeA. "Industrial Problems in Cities — New York City," *Opportunity: A Journal of Negro Life,* IV (February, 1926), 68-69.

Russell, Charles Edward. "Address," in National Negro Conference. *Proceedings . . . 1909* (New York, 1909), pp. 220-221.

Sayre, Helen B. "Negro Women in Industry," *Opportunity: A Journal of Negro Life,* II (August, 1924), 242-244.

Schurz, Carl. "Can the South Solve the Negro Problem?" *McClure's Magazine,* XXII (January, 1904), 259-275.

"Secretariat," *Opportunity: A Journal of Negro Life,* VI (March, 1928), 84-89.

Speed, John Gilmer. "The Negro in New York: A Study of the Social and Industrial Conditions of the Colored People in the Metropolis," *Harper's Weekly,* XLIV (December 22, 1900), 1249-50.

"Sustaining the Urban League Movement," *Opportunity: A Journal of Negro Life,* IV (June, 1926), 173-174.

"The Urban League Campaign," *Opportunity: A Journal of Negro Life,* IV (July, 1926), 207-208.

Walling, William English. "The Negro and the South," in National Negro Conference. *Proceedings . . . 1909* (New York, 1909), pp. 98-109.

———. "The Race War in the North," *The Independent,* LXV (September 3, 1908), 529-534.

"The White Man's Problem," *The Arena,* XXIII (January, 1900), 1-30.

Wood, L. Hollingsworth. "The Urban League Movement," *Journal of Negro History,* IX (April, 1924), 117-126.

E. Newspapers

Chicago Broad Ax
Chicago Courier
Chicago Daily Defender
Chicago Daily News
Chicago Defender
Chicago Sun-Times
Chicago Tribune
Chicago's American
Clipping files, Chicago Urban League Department of Research

F. Other Sources

Calloway, Nathaniel O. "Administration of an Urban League: From a Board Member's View Point." Speech delivered before the Annual Conference of the National Urban League, Cincinnati, Ohio, September 5, 1956.
Chicago Urban League. "Leadership Conference for Fair Employment Practices." February 25, 1961. (Mimeographed.)
Chicago Urban League Research Report, "Housing and Race in Chicago: A Preliminary Analysis of 1960 Census Data," July, 1963.
———. "Public School Segregation: City of Chicago 1963-1964 and 1964-1965," May 12, 1965.
Berry, Edwin C. "An Address to Chicago Urban League Annual Meeting Luncheon." November 24, 1958.
———. "Personnel and Program Standards in the Urban League." Remarks made before the Annual Conference of the National Urban League, Cincinnati, Ohio, September 5, 1956.

G. List of Persons Interviewed: Chicago, Illinois

Howard S. Bazel
Nathaniel O. Calloway
Earl B. Dickerson
Odessa Cave Evans
Olivia Filerman
Albon L. Foster
Irene McCoy Gaines
Howard D. Gould
William E. Hill
Alexander L. Jackson
Leonard Jewell, Sr.
Frayser T. Lane
Hugo B. Law
Vera Shane Thompson

II. SECONDARY SOURCES

A. Books, Reports, and Pamphlets

Abrams, Charles. *Forbidden Neighbors: A Study of Prejudice in Housing.* New York: Harper and Brothers, 1955.
Advisory Panel on Integration of the Public Schools. *Report to the Board of Education City of Chicago.* Chicago: Board of Education of the City of Chicago, 1964.
Baker, Paul E. *Negro-White Adjustment: An Investigation and Analysis of Methods in the Interracial Movement in the United States: The History, Philosophy, Program, and Techniques of Ten National Interracial Agencies, Methods Discovered Through a Study of Cases, Situa-*

tions, and Projects in Race Relations. Pittsfield, Mass.: Sun Printing Co., 1934.

Buckler, Helen. *Doctor Dan: Pioneer in American Surgery.* Boston: Little, Brown and Company, 1954.

Cayton, Horace R., and George S. Mitchell. *Black Workers and the New Unions.* Chapel Hill: University of North Carolina Press, 1939.

Chicago Commission on Human Relations. *Highlights of 1961: Annual Report.* Chicago: Commission on Human Relations, 1962.

———. *The People of Chicago: Five Year Report, 1947-1951.* Chicago, 1952.

———. *A Report to the Mayor and the City Council of Chicago on the Present Status and Effectiveness of Existing Fair Housing Practices Legislation in the United States as of April 1, 1963.* Chicago: City of Chicago, 1963.

———. *The Trumbull Park Homes Disturbances; A Chronological Report August 4, 1953 to June 30, 1955.* Chicago, 1955.

Chicago Commission on Race Relations. *The Negro in Chicago: A Study of Race Relations and a Race Riot.* Chicago: University of Chicago Press, 1922.

Chicago Department of City Planning. *Rehousing Residents Displaced from Public Housing Clearance Sites in Chicago, 1957-1958.* Chicago, 1960.

Drake, St. Clair. *Churches and Voluntary Associations in the Chicago Negro Community.* Report of a W.P.A. Project. Chicago, 1940. (Mimeographed.)

Drake, St. Clair, and Horace R. Cayton. *Black Metropolis: A Study of Negro Life in a Northern City.* New York: Harcourt, Brace and Company, 1945.

Filler, Louis. *Crusaders for American Liberalism.* New ed. Yellow Springs, Ohio: The Antioch Press, 1950.

Franklin, John Hope. *From Slavery to Freedom: A History of American Negroes.* New York: Alfred A. Knopf, Inc., 1947.

Havighurst, Robert J. *The Public Schools of Chicago: A Survey for the Board of Education of the City of Chicago.* Chicago: Board of Education of the City of Chicago, 1964.

Hofstadter, Richard. *The Age of Reform: From Bryan to F. D. R.* New York: Vintage Books, 1960.

King, Martin Luther, Jr. *Why We Can't Wait.* New York: Harper and Row, Publishers, 1963.

Lasswell, Harold D., and Dorothy Blumenstock. *World Revolutionary Propaganda: A Chicago Study.* New York: Alfred A. Knopf, Inc., 1939.

Lewis, Lloyd, and Henry Justin Smith. *Chicago: The History of Its Reputation.* New York: Harcourt, Brace and Company, 1929.

Lomax, Louis E. *The Negro Revolt.* New York: Harper and Row, Publishers, 1962.

Long, Herman H., and Charles S. Johnson. *People vs. Property: Race Restrictive Covenants in Housing.* Nashville, Tenn.: Fisk University Press, 1947.

Lubell, Samuel. *White and Black: Test of a Nation.* New York: Harper and Row, Publishers, 1964.

Mayor's Commission on Human Relations. *Human Relations in Chicago: Report for Year 1946.* Chicago, 1946.

———. *Race Relations in Chicago: Report for 1945.* Chicago, 1945.

Mayor's Committee on Race Relations. *Race Relations in Chicago.* Chicago, 1944.

Meier, August. *Negro Thought in America, 1880-1915: Racial Ideologies in the Age of Booker T. Washington.* Ann Arbor: The University of Michigan Press, 1963.

Myrdal, Gunnar. *An American Dilemma: The Negro Problem and Modern Democracy.* New York: Harper and Brothers Publishers, 1944.

National Urban League. *Racial Conflict; A Home Front Danger: Lessons of the Detroit Riot.* New York: National Urban League, 1943.

Sandburg, Carl. *The Chicago Race Riots, July, 1919.* With an Introductory Note by Walter Lippmann. New York: Harcourt, Brace and Howe, 1919.

Silberman, Charles E. *Crisis in Black and White.* New York: Random House, 1964.

Spero, Sterling D., and Abram L. Harris. *The Black Worker: The Negro and the Labor Movement.* New York: Columbia University Press, 1931.

Sutherland, Edwin H., and Harvey J. Locke. *Twenty Thousand Homeless Men: A Study of Unemployed Men in the Chicago Shelters.* Chicago: J. B. Lippincott Company, 1936.

Weaver, Robert C. *Negro Labor: A National Problem.* New York: Harcourt, Brace and Company, 1946.

Werner, M. R. *Julius Rosenwald: The Life of a Practical Humanitarian.* New York: Harper and Brothers Publishers, 1939.

Who's Who in Colored America, 1928-29: A Biographical Dictionary of Notable Living Persons of African Descent in America, ed. Joseph J. Boris. 2nd ed. New York: Who's Who in Colored America Corp., 1929.

Wilson, James Q. *Negro Politics: The Search for Leadership.* Glencoe, Ill.: The Free Press, 1960.

B. Articles

Bennett, Lerone, Jr. "North's Hottest Fight for Integration," *Ebony,* XVII (March, 1962), 31-38.

Brandenburg, Linn. "Central Joint Financing of Private Health and Welfare Services in Chicago," *Social Service Yearbook, 1944* (Chicago Council of Social Agencies, 1945), pp. 1-17.

Elson, Alex. "Social Legislation," *Social Service Yearbook, 1938* (Chicago Council of Social Agencies, 1938), pp. 102-105.

"Employment and Vocational Services," *Social Service Yearbook, 1943* (Chicago Council of Social Agencies, 1943), pp. 27-36.

Geyer, Georgie Anne. "Woodlawn: A Community in Revolt," *Chicago Scene,* III (June 7, 1962), 12-17.

Glick, Frank Z. "The Illinois Emergency Relief Commission," *The Social Service Review,* VII (March, 1933), 23-48.

Goldsmith, Samuel A. "Financing Social Work in Chicago," *Social Service Yearbook, 1935* (Chicago Council of Social Agencies, 1936), pp. 99-111.

Haynes, George Edmund. "The Negro at Work: A Development of the War and a Problem of Reconstruction," *American Review of Reviews,* LIX (April, 1919), 389-393.

Hughes, Elizabeth A. "Housing," *Social Service Yearbook, 1937* (Chicago Council of Social Agencies, 1938), pp. 80-84.

Lee, B. F., Jr. "Negro Organizations," *The Annals of the American Academy of Political and Social Science,* XLIX (September, 1913), 129-137.

Rich, Adena M. "Protective Services," *Social Service Yearbook, 1938* (Chicago Council of Social Agencies, 1938), pp. 92-95.

Smith, Mary Roberts. "The Negro Woman as an Industrial Factor," *Life and Labor,* VIII (January, 1918), 7-8.

Washington, Forrester B. "Reconstruction and the Colored Woman," *Life and Labor,* IX (January, 1919), 3-7.

Weaver, Robert C. "Racial Tensions in Chicago," *Social Service Yearbook, 1943* (Chicago Council of Social Agencies, 1944), pp. 1-8.

Williams, Fannie Barrier. "Social Bonds in the 'Black Belt' of Chicago: Negro Organizations and the New Spirit Pervading Them," *Charities,* XV (October 7, 1905), 40-44.

Woodbury, Coleman. "Housing," *Social Service Yearbook, 1936* (Chicago Council of Social Agencies, 1937), pp. 88-91.

C. Unpublished Studies

Counse, Dorothy, Louise Gilbert, and Agnes Van Driel. "The Chicago Urban League." Unpublished study in the files of the Welfare Council of Metropolitan Chicago, June 18, 1936.

Jackson, Nelson C. "An Evaluation of the Chicago Urban League." Unpublished study, May, 1955.

Jones, Eunice Joyner. "A Study of the Urban League Movement in the United States." Unpublished Master's thesis, New York University, 1939.

Lawrence, Charles Radford. "Negro Organizations in Crisis: Depression, New Deal, World War II." Unpublished Ph.D. dissertation, Columbia University, 1952. (Microfilmed.)

McMillen, Wayne. "A Survey of the Administrative and Personnel Practices of the Chicago Urban League." Unpublished study, July, 1946.

Stokes, Arthur Paul. "The National Urban League: A Study in Race Relations." Unpublished Master's thesis, Ohio State University, 1937.

Thomas, Lottie Mornye. "An Historical Evaluation of the Place the Chicago Urban League Holds in the Community." Unpublished Master's thesis, School of Social Work, Atlanta University, 1943.

Index

About the Author

Arvarh Strickland is Professor Emeritus of History at the University of Missouri–Columbia. He is the author or editor of numerous books, including *Selling Black History for Carter G. Woodson: A Diary, 1930–1933, by Lorenzo J. Greene* (University of Missouri Press) and *The African American Experience: A Historiographical and Bibliographical Guide.*